CALIFORNIA EDITION

HOUGHTON MIFFLIN

Math Steps

HOUGHTON MIFFLIN

Boston • Atlanta • Dallas • Denver • Geneva, Illinois • Palo Alto • Princeton

Grateful acknowledgment is given for the contributions of

Student Book

Rosemary Theresa Barry
Karen R. Boyle
Barbara Brozman
Gary S. Bush
John E. Cassidy
Dorothy Kirk

Sharon Ann Kovalcik
Bernice Kubek
Donna Marie Kvasnok
Ann Cherney Markunas
Joanne Marie Mascha
Kathleen Mary Ogrin

Judith Ostrowski
Jeanette Mishic Polomsky
Patricia Stenger
Annabelle L. Higgins Svete

Teacher Book
Contributing Writers

Dr. Judy Curran Buck
Assistant Professor of Mathematics
Plymouth State College
Plymouth, New Hampshire

Dr. Richard Evans
Professor of Mathematics
Plymouth State College
Plymouth, New Hampshire

Dr. Mary K. Porter
Professor of Mathematics
St. Mary's College
Notre Dame, Indiana

Dr. Anne M. Raymond
Assistant Professor of Mathematics
Keene State College
Keene, New Hampshire

Stuart P. Robertson, Jr.
Education Consultant
Pelham, New Hampshire

Dr. David Rock
Associate Professor,
 Mathematics Education
University of Mississippi
Oxford, Mississippi

Michelle Lynn Rock
Elementary Teacher
Oxford School District
Oxford, Mississippi

Dr. Jean M. Shaw
Professor of Elementary Education
University of Mississippi
Oxford, Mississippi

ISBN: 0-395-98009-7

12 13 14 15-B-05 04 03 02 01 00

Contents

Unit 1 Place Value, Money, and Time 1

Unit 2 Addition 35

Unit 3 Subtraction 63

Unit 4 Multiplication to 5 87

Unit 5 Multiplication and Division to 5 113

Unit 6 Geometry, Data, and Probability 141

Unit 7 Fractions 171

Unit 8 Multiplication and Division to 9 195

Unit 9 Multiplying and Dividing by 1-Digit Numbers 221

Unit 10 Measurement 249

Unit 11 Decimals 277

Tables of Measures 299

Glossary 300

UNIT 1 • TABLE OF CONTENTS

Place Value, Money, and Time

CALIFORNIA STANDARDS	**Lesson**	**Page**
NS 1.1, 1.3, 1.5	**1** Place Value to Thousands	3–4
NS 1.1, 1.3, 1.5	**2** Place Value to Hundred Thousands	5–6
NS 1.2; A/F 1.1	**3** Algebra • Compare and Order	7–8
A/F 1.1	**4** Algebra • Place Value: Money	9–10
MR 1.1, 3.3; A/F 2.2	**5** Algebra • Problem Solving Strategy: Find a Pattern	11–12
A/F 1.1	**6** Algebra • Counting Money	13–14
A/F 1.1	**7** Algebra • Money Values	15–18
	8 Counting Change	19–20
MR 2.3; A/F 2.2	**9** Algebra • Problem Solving Application: Use a Chart or Table	21–22
	10 Ordinal Numbers and the Calendar	23–24
	11 Time to the Five Minutes	25–26
	12 Time to the Minute	27–28
	13 A.M. and P.M.	29–30
	• Unit 1 Review	31–32
	• Cumulative Review ★ Test Prep	33–34

Dear Family,

During the next few weeks, our math class will be learning about place value. They will explore numbers to hundred thousands and extend the idea of place value to money.

You can expect to see homework that provides practice with comparing and ordering numbers. The following ideas may be helpful if assistance is needed.

Comparing and Ordering Numbers

To compare **4,569, 4,280,** and **4,100,** write the numbers one above the other in table form.

1. Compare the thousands digits. Since all the digits are 4, we need to look at the hundreds digits.

Thousands	Hundreds	Tens	Ones
4	5	6	9
4	2	8	0
4	1	0	0

2. Compare the hundreds digits.
   Since 2 is greater than 1, **4,280 > 4,100.**
   Since 5 is greater than 2, **4,280 < 4,569.**

The numbers in order from least to greatest are: **4,100   4,280   4,569**

During this unit students will need to continue using place value with whole numbers and money. Home is the ideal place for your child to practice telling time and using money.

Sincerely,

Place Value to Thousands

Understanding **place value** can help you read and write numbers. The number **3,219** is shown using place-value blocks.

A cube of one thousand (**1,000**) represents ten hundreds.

Here are four ways to write about the number **3,219**:

Table Form

Thousands	Hundreds	Tens	Ones
3	**2**	**1**	**9**
The value of **3** is **3** thousands or **3,000**.	The value of the **2** is **2** hundreds or **200**.	The value of the **1** is **1** ten or **10**.	The value of the **9** is **9** ones or **9**.

Expanded Form

3,000 + 200 + 10 + 9

Standard Form

3,219

The comma makes it easier to read.

Word Form

three thousand, two hundred nineteen

Read the number.

1. 1,892   4,358   6,079

Fill in the blanks.

Th	H	T	O

2. 1,364 = ___   or ___ + ___ + ___ + ___

3. 6,590 = ___   or ___ + ___ + ___ + ___

4. 9,216 = ___   or ___ + ___ + ___ + ___

5. 8,702 = ___   or ___ + ___ + ___ + ___

Write the value of the underlined digit.

6. 2,4<u>7</u>9 _____   <u>4</u>,135 _____   7,6<u>4</u>5 _____   5,<u>9</u>20 _____

7. 6,<u>3</u>01 _____   1,78<u>2</u> _____   <u>3</u>,094 _____   2,<u>7</u>56 _____

Complete the sentences.

8. In **7,621,** _____ is in the thousands place; _____ is in the tens place.

9. In **4,039,** _____ is in the ones place; _____ is in the hundreds place.

10. In **2,987,** _____ is in the thousands place; _____ is in the ones place.

11. In **9,214,** _____ is in the hundreds place; _____ is in the tens place.

12. In **3,640,** _____ is in the thousands place; _____ is in the hundreds place.

13. In **6,856,** _____ is in the tens place; _____ is in the ones place.

Problem Solving Reasoning	**Solve.**

14. Jo and Shayla counted pennies they saved. Jo counted **2,384** pennies. Shayla counted two thousand, four hundred one pennies. Who saved the most pennies? _____

15. Soo Sung shows the number nine thousand, two hundred five with place-value blocks. How many tens blocks did she use?

_____

16. The school auditorium can seat one thousand, three hundred twenty people during an assembly. Will there be enough seats if **1,302** people come to an assembly? _____

17. The Mississippi River is two thousand, three hundred forty-eight miles long. Write that number in standard form.

_____

Test Prep ★ Mixed Review

18 Samuel saw 4 dogs and 4 cats at the pet contest. How many animals did Samuel see in all?

A 8
B 9
C 10
D 11

19 Sumi needs to sell 17 raffle tickets. She has sold 9 tickets so far. How many more tickets does Sumi need to sell?

F 6
G 8
H 17
J 26

You can use place-value tables to show greater numbers.

Thousands				Ones		
Hundred Thousands	Ten Thousands	One Thousands		Hundreds	Tens	Ones
5	3	9	,	2	4	7

Standard Form
539,247

Expanded Form
500,000 + 30,000 + 9,000 + 200 + 40 + 7

Word Form:
five hundred thirty-nine thousand, two hundred forty-seven

To read **539,247** first say the part of the number to the left of the comma. Then say the part to the right.

In the number **539,247**

the value of **5** is **500,000** (five hundred thousand).
the value of **3** is **30,000** (thirty thousand).
the value of **9** is **9,000** (nine thousand).
the value of **2** is **200** (two hundred).
the value of **4** is **40** (forty).
the value of **7** is **7** (seven).

Write the number in standard form.

1. **30,000 + 6,000 + 100 + 20 + 1** _____

2. **50,000 + 3,000 + 700 + 8** _____

3. seventy-four thousand, nine hundred sixty-three _____

4. six hundred ninety-five thousand, one hundred four _____

Use the number 860,175 to complete the statement.

5. The value of **7** is _____ tens.

6. The value of **8** is _____ hundred thousands.

7. The value of **1** is _____ _____.

8. The value of **6** is _____ _____.

9. The value of **5** is _____ _____.

Write the value of the underlined digit.

10. 74,9<u>6</u>3 _____   1<u>5</u>0,674 _____

11. <u>3</u>,257 _____   27,0<u>3</u>6 _____

12. 54,8<u>4</u>0 _____   6,90<u>5</u> _____

13. 1,<u>8</u>26 _____   4<u>2</u>,750 _____

14. 6<u>7</u>5,104 _____   <u>3</u>0,816 _____

Write _true_ or _false._

15. 12,820 = twelve thousand, eight hundred twenty _____

16. 24,999 = 20,000 + 4,000 + 900 + 90 + 9 _____

17. 5,661 = 56 thousand 6 tens 1 one _____

18. 32,362 = thirty thousand, three hundred sixty-two _____

19. 219,675 = 200,000 + 10,000 + 9,000 + 600 + 70 + 5 _____

Problem Solving
Reasoning

Solve.

20. In the Center City election, one hundred nineteen thousand, nine hundred twenty-two people voted. Write the number in standard form.

_____

21. Mt. Whitney is the highest point in California. It is **14,494** feet high. Write the number in words.

_____

_____

22. The population of Uma's town is **45,761** people. Write the number in word form.

_____

_____

23. A new football stadium holds seventy-three thousand, five hundred people. Write the number in standard form.

_____

Test Prep ★ Mixed Review

24 Kim collected thirty-five pine cones from the woods. Which shows this number?

A 35   C 350

B 305   D 3,500

25 May has 45 marbles. Sam has 52 marbles. Claire has 39 marbles and Bob has 28. Who has the most marbles?

F May   H Claire

G Sam   J Bob

Compare and Order

You can compare numbers using symbols.
To compare numbers begin at the left.

> The symbol < means **is less than,** > means **is greater than.**

Compare hundreds.

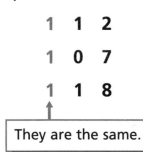

1 1 2
1 0 7
1 1 8

> They are the same.

Compare tens.

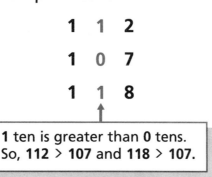

1 1 2
1 0 7
1 1 8

> **1** ten is greater than **0** tens. So, **112 > 107** and **118 > 107.**

Compare ones.

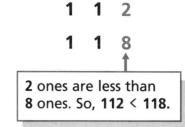

1 1 2
1 1 8

> **2** ones are less than **8** ones. So, **112 < 118.**

The numbers in order from **least to greatest:**   107   112   118

The numbers in order from **greatest to least:**   118   112   107

Write <, >, or =.

1.	23 ◯ 32	68,743 ◯ 68,743	288 ◯ 289
2.	1,156 ◯ 997	21,478 ◯ 30,681	10,070 ◯ 10,700
3.	16,899 ◯ 16,899	8,590 ◯ 8,596	1,066 ◯ 106
4.	41,346 ◯ 42,873	2,456 ◯ 2,340	34,908 ◯ 3,498
5.	143,568 ◯ 143,568	99,007 ◯ 109,030	564,338 ◯ 564,339

Write the missing numbers to complete the number sequence.

6.	_____	50	51	_____	53	_____
7.	3,000	6,000	_____	12,000	_____	_____
8.	74,132	_____	74,130	_____	74,128	_____
9.	_____	1,147	1,148	_____	_____	1,151
10.	12,000	13,000	_____	_____	_____	17,000
11.	_____	132,500	_____	132,700	_____	132,900

Write <, >, or =.

12. $10{,}000 + 60 + 5$ ◯ $1{,}650$ 3 hundreds 5 tens ◯ 305

13. $60{,}002$ ◯ six thousand $13{,}670$ ◯ $13{,}000 + 600 + 70$

14. $153{,}098$ ◯ $153{,}198$ five thousand, six ◯ $5{,}060$

Write the numbers in order from least to greatest.

15. 201, 98, 149, 45, 235 _____ _____ _____ _____ _____

16. 34,000, 23,000, 85,000, 57,000 _____ _____ _____ _____

Write the numbers in order from greatest to least.

17. 44,098, 24,216, 103,567, 19,854

_____ _____ _____ _____

Problem Solving Reasoning Solve.

18. Jacob is in charge of the concert tickets. He places the tickets in order from least to greatest. How will he place these tickets?

13,756   13,569   13,432   13,567

_____

19. Li has these number cards.

How can she place the cards to make the greatest number and the least number possible?

_____ _____

 Quick Check

Name the value of the underlined digit.

1. 5<u>6</u>3_____

2. <u>4</u>,097_____

3. 3,<u>8</u>20_____

4. 1<u>2</u>6,054_____

5. 83,05<u>4</u>_____

6. <u>2</u>45,707_____

Write the numbers from greatest to least.

7. 4,079, 3,856, 4,211 _____

8. 9,999, 36,402, 1,989 _____

Work Space.

Name _____

Place Value: Money

1 dollar	1 dime	1 penny
100 cents	**10** cents	**1** cent
100¢	**10¢**	**1¢**

You can write money values using a dollar sign ($) and a decimal point(.)

The value of a dollar is   The value of a dime is   The value of a penny is

$1.00   **$.10**   **$.01**

Write the value.

1.

400¢ + 30¢ + 6¢ = 436¢
$4.00 + $.30 + $.60 = $4.36

_____

2.

 $ ___ . ___

3.

 $ ___ . ___

4.  $ ___ . ___

Complete the table.
Then use $ and . to write each value.

	Dollars	Dimes	Pennies	
5. Five dollars and six cents				_____
6. One dollar and eighteen cents				_____
7. Two dollars and thirty-four cents				_____
8. Twenty-one cents				_____

Count. Fill in the blanks.

9. $ .98, $ .99, _____, _____, _____, _____

10. $2.25, $2.30, $2.35, _____, _____, _____

11. $ .02, $ .04, $ .06, _____, _____, _____

Problem Solving
Reasoning **Solve.**

12. Martha found **300** pennies in one jar, **60** pennies in a second jar, and **7** pennies in a third. Use a $ and . to write the total amount she found.

_____

13. Emil wants to buy a tuna sandwich that costs **$4.75**. He has **4** dollars, **5** dimes, and **6** pennies. Does he have enough money? How do you know?

_____

Test Prep ★ Mixed Review

14 **Which shape continues the pattern?**

?

A ▲

B ○

C ●

D △

15 **Which is the missing word in this pattern?**

first, second, _____, fourth

F fifth

G three

H five

J third

Finding a pattern can help you solve problems.

433 A B **437** A B **441** A B **445** A B **449** A B

Bucky Lane

434 A B **438** A B **442** A B **446** A B **450** A B

> **Problem**
>
> Anna's friend Jill lives at **442A** Bucky Lane. Anna is going to Jill's house. She has this map. How can the map help her find the two-family house?

---

① Understand   As you look at Jill's address, ask yourself questions.

- What does the number mean?

  It identifies each house on Bucky Lane.

- What does the letter mean?

  It identifies a unit in each house. Unit A and Unit B.

---

② Decide   Look at the map. Do you see any patterns?

Even numbered houses, ending in 0, 2, 4, 6, 8, are on the right. Odd numbered houses, ending in 1, 3, 5, 7, 9, are on the left.

House numbers increase by 4.

The units in the houses are arranged AB AB AB.

---

③ Solve   Use the pattern to find Jill's house.

- On which side of the street is Jill's house?   _____

- How many houses do you pass to get to Jill's house?   _____

- What is the number of the house just before Jill's house?   _____

---

④ Look back   Check your answer.

- Explain how the patterns on the map helped you find Jill's house.

_____

Use **find a pattern** or any other strategy.

The walkway to Jill's house is made of rectangular bricks and square bricks. This is a drawing of part of the walkway.

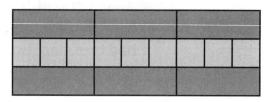

1. Describe a pattern that you see in the walkway.

   Think: How do the bricks create a pattern?

   Answer: _____

   _____

2. The walkway is **10** rectangular bricks long on one side. How many square bricks are in the entire walkway?

   _____

Study the place-value blocks.

3. Draw what the next set of blocks will look like.

4. Describe the pattern in the numbers.

   _____

Extend Your Thinking

5. Would the pattern with the place-value blocks continue? Why or why not?

   _____

   _____

6. Create your own pattern problem with place-value blocks or objects.

It is as much as **5** nickels,

or **1** dime and **3** nickels,

A **quarter** is
worth **25¢**.

or **2** dimes and **1** nickel.

It is as much as **2** quarters

or **5** dimes.

A **half dollar** is
worth **50¢**.

Complete. Write the name of the coin and its value.

1.

2 quarters = **1** _____

or _____ ¢.

2.

5 nickels = **1** _____

or _____ ¢.

3.

5 dimes = **1** _____

or _____ ¢.

4.

2 dimes and **1** nickel =

1 _____ or _____ ¢.

Complete.

5. A nickel = _____ pennies.   A half dollar = _____ quarters.

6. A dime = _____ pennies.   A half dollar = _____ dimes.

7. A dime = _____ nickels   A dollar = _____ pennies.

8. A quarter = _____ pennies.   A dollar = _____ nickels.

How much are the coins worth? Add the values as you count the coins.

9.

_____ _____ _____ _____ _____   _____ _____ _____ _____ _____ _____

| Problem Solving |
| Reasoning |

Solve.

10. Ed has a half dollar. Ted has **3** dimes and **4** nickels. Ned has **1** dime, **5** nickels, and **15** pennies. They say they have the same amount of money. Do they?

_____

11. Suppose you have **25¢**. You do not have a quarter. Name the coins you might have. Then find four more ways to show **25¢**.

_____

_____

Test Prep ★ Mixed Review

12. When Emilio left for school, this is what the clock showed:

What time did Emilio leave?

A 7:00

B 7:30

C 12:00

D 12:30

13. Which of these shows the next number on the number line?

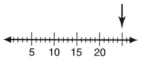

F 21

G 22

H 25

J 30

STANDARD

Suppose you have **2** quarters, **1** dime, and **3** pennies.
How much money do you have?

Count: **25¢, 50¢, 60¢, 63¢**   You have **63¢** or **$.63.**

Use the words to fill in the blanks.

penny	nickel	dime	quarter	half dollar	dollar

1.

A _____   A _____   A _____

is worth _____ ¢.   is worth _____ ¢.   is worth _____ ¢.

2.

A _____   A _____   A _____

is worth _____ ¢.   is worth _____ ¢.   is worth _____ ¢.

Use $ and . to write the amounts.

3.

thirty cents   _____

eight cents   _____

twelve cents   _____

sixteen cents   _____

fifty–five cents   _____

ninety–eight cents   _____

forty–nine cents   _____

eighty cents   _____

twenty–five cents   _____

Use ¢ to write the amounts.

4.

seventy–five cents   _____

sixty-nine cents   _____

twenty cents   _____

eleven cents   _____

nine cents   _____

thirteen cents   _____

ninety–two cents   _____

forty–three cents   _____

eighteen cents   _____

Write each amount of money.

5.

_____

6.

_____

7.

_____

8.

_____

9.

_____

10.

_____

Solve.

11. I have **25¢**. I have only 3 coins. Draw the coins I have.

12. I have **16¢**. I have only **4** coins. Draw the coins I have.

Match.

13.

14.

15.

16.

Complete.

17. A half dollar is worth _____ ¢ more than a quarter.

18. A dime is worth _____ ¢ less than a half dollar.

19. A quarter is worth _____ dimes and _____ nickel.

20. A dollar is worth _____ quarters.

21. A dollar is worth _____ half dollars.

Loop the name in each box that has the greatest value.

22.

quarter	dollar	dime	nickel
dime	nickel	nickel	dollar
half dollar	dime	penny	half dollar

Use $ and . to write these amounts.

23. 3 dollars and **4** dimes _____

24. 9 dollars and **2** quarters _____

25. 1 dollar and **6** nickels _____

26. 8 dollars and **1** half dollar _____

27. 6 dollars and **7** dimes _____

| Problem Solving |
| Reasoning |

Solve.

28. José sells name signs. He charges **3** dollars for wood, **10** cents for each letter, and **25** cents for paint. If you buy a sign with your first name, how much would you have to pay? Show your work.

_____

29. Greta bought a book for **$5.99**. She paid the shopkeeper with the exact amount of money. What bills and coins could she have used?

_____

✓ Quick Check

Use a $ and . to write each value.

1. two dollars and thirty-eight cents _____

2. nine dollars and five cents _____

3. sixty-five cents _____

Work Space.

Complete.

4. **1** nickel is worth _____ pennies

5. **1** quarter is worth _____ nickels

Write how much.

6.  _____

7.  _____

Name _____

Jeanette bought a book cover for **29¢**.

She gave Mr. Stone a dollar bill.

Here is how Mr. Stone counted out Jeanette's change:

29¢	30¢	40¢	50¢	$1.00

Jeanette's change was **71¢**.

Complete.

1. Earl bought a pencil for **10¢**. He gave Mr. Stone a quarter. Mr. Stone gave Earl a nickel and a dime. Did Mr. Stone give the correct change? _____

Does the cost of the pencil plus the amount of change equal the amount that Earl gave Mr. Stone? _____

2. Ruby bought a notebook for **49¢**. She handed Mr. Stone a dollar bill. Mr. Stone gave her change with the fewest coins possible.

What coins did he give her? _____

How did he count the change? _____

3. Larry needed a ruler that cost **15¢**. He had a half dollar to give Mr. Stone.

What coins did he give him? _____

How did he count the change? _____

4. Each child has **2** dimes, or **20¢**, to spend. Draw the fewest coins each child could get in change after spending each amount.

Spend: 12¢ _____

15¢ _____

5. Each child has a quarter, or **25¢**, to spend. Draw the fewest coins each child could get in change after spending each amount.

Spend: 20¢ _____

5¢ _____

Problem Solving
Reasoning

Solve.

6. Mr. Hu owns a video store. He gives only quarters for change. Which price do you think he charges for a video?

$8.98 $8.29 $8.25 $8.79

_____

7. Erica buys popcorn. She gets **$.67** back in change. If she got the fewest coins possible, what coins did she get? Draw them.

Test Prep ★ Mixed Review

8 What number goes in the box and makes this number sentence true?

$3 + 5 = \boxed{} + 3$

A 2

B 3

C 5

D 8

9 Mohamed had a dime and a nickel in his pocket. What was the total value of the coins?

F 2

G 5¢

H 10¢

J 15¢

Sometimes you need to use data from the chart to solve problems.

In this lesson you will need to use the information from the charts to find quantities or costs.

Number of Stools	Number of Legs
1	3
2	6
3	9
4	12
5	15
6	18

Number of Tables	Number of Legs
1	4
2	8
3	12
4	16
5	20
6	24

Tips to Remember:

1. Understand	2. Decide	3. Solve	4. Look back

- Read each problem carefully. Circle the important words and numbers.
- Ask yourself: What information do I need from the chart?
- Try to break the problem into parts.

Solve. Use a chart.

1. Mr. Chiang asks Dale to make **2** tables and **4** stools. How many legs will Dale need for this job?

Think: Do you need information from one of the charts or both charts?

_____

Answer: _____

2. At the end of the month Dale had **10** legs left over. He wanted to make a table and some stools for himself. How many stools could he make?

Think: Do you need to add or subtract to solve this problem?

_____

Answer: _____

Number of Stools	Price
1	$10
2	$15
3	$20
4	$25
5	$30
6	$35

Number of Tables	Price
1	$20
2	$30
3	$40
4	$50
5	$60
6	$70

5. What is the price of **2** tables and **3** stools?

6. How much more is the price of **3** tables than **3** stools?

7. Mr. Chin's order cost **$55**. What furniture could Dale be making for Mr. Chin?

8. The Harts wanted to spend **$50** on gifts from Dale's Carpentry Shop. What items could the Harts buy that cost exactly **$50**?

Extend Your Thinking

9. Look back at the Stool Leg and Table Leg charts. Explain a pattern you see in one of the charts.

10. Look back at Dale's Price charts. What could be the reason that the price of the second table or chair isn't twice the cost of the first table or chair?

When we talk about the months of the year or the days of the week, we often use **ordinal numbers.**

Ordinal Numbers		Months of the Year	Days in the Month
first	1st	January	31
second	2nd	February	28
third	3rd	March	31
fourth	4th	April	30
fifth	5th	May	31
sixth	6th	June	30
seventh	7th	July	31
eighth	8th	August	31
ninth	9th	September	30
tenth	10th	October	31
eleventh	11th	November	30
twelfth	12th	December	31

Ordinal numbers show the order or position of something.

May

Sun	Mon	Tues	Wed	Thurs	Fri	Sat
	1	2	3	4	5	6
7	8	9	10	11	12	13
14	15	16	17	18	19	20
21	22	23	24	25	26	27
28	29	30	31			

Here are some other ordinal numbers:

eighteenth	18th	twenty-fifth	25th	fortieth	40th
twentieth	20th	thirtieth	30th	forty-ninth	49th

Use the information above to complete the questions.

Give the date in May for the:

1. first Wednesday _____   fourth Tuesday _____

2. second Wednesday _____   third Saturday _____

Which day of the week is

3. the **20th?**_____   the **2nd?**_____   the **3rd?** _____

4. the **28th?**_____   the **5th?** _____   the **15th?**_____

5. Name the eleventh month. Which month has fewer days than the month you named?

_____

6. Use ordinal number words. Which months have **30** days?

_____

_____

Read carefully. Give the month that is

7. 2 months before June _____ 4 months after May _____

8. the **6th** month after May _____ 3 months before July _____

9. the **8th** month after
January _____ 2 months before
December _____

Complete.

10. _____ is the first day of the *school* week.

11. _____ is the last day of the week.

12. _____ comes **3** days after Monday.

13. _____ comes **2** days before Friday.

14. Wednesday is the _____ day of the week.

15. Friday is the _____ day of the week.

16. The first day of the week is _____.

Days of the week	
1st	Sunday
2nd	Monday
3rd	Tuesday
4th	Wednesday
5th	Thursday
6th	Friday
7th	Saturday

**Problem Solving
Reasoning** **Solve.**

17. What is your favorite holiday?
Tell in which month of the year
the holiday falls. Use both the
ordinal number and the ordinal
number word.

18. I am a day of the week. I come
4 days after Tuesday. I am not a
school day. Write my name and
the ordinal number word that
tells my order in the week.

Test Prep ★ Mixed Review

19 Which number is in the same
family of facts as

6 + 8 = 14

A $14 - 8 = 6$

B $6 \times 8 = 48$

C $14 + 8 = 22$

D $8 - 66 = 2$

20 Mark saw 3 birds on the pond, 2
birds on the grass, and 7 birds in a
tree. How many birds did Mark
see in all?

F 5

G 9

H 10

J 12

Name _____

Time to the Five Minutes

It takes **5** minutes for the minute hand to move from one number to the next number.

20 minutes after **9**, or **9:20**

Time in the second half of each hour is often given in minutes remaining until the next hour.

10 minutes to **3**, or **2:50**

How many minutes past the hour is it?

1.

_____ minutes after _____

or

_____

_____ minutes after _____

or

_____

_____minutes after _____

or

_____

How many minutes to the hour is it?

2.

_____ minutes to _____

or

_____

_____ minutes to _____

or

_____

_____minutes to _____

or

_____

Show the time on each clock.

3.

    1:35   **20 minutes to 3**   **8:50**   **20 minutes after 11**

Problem Solving Reasoning   Solve.

4. Concetta was to meet Marco at **7:55** in front of the school. Concetta arrived at **10** minutes before **8**. Was she early or late? Tell how you know.

_____

5. On the clock the hour hand is between the **9** and the **10**. The minute hand is on the **7**. Beth says it is **9:35**. Seth says it is almost ten minutes to **7**. Who is correct?

_____

 Quick Check

Draw the fewest coins.

1. You buy a toy for 65¢. You give the clerk **$1.00**.

Draw how much change you get.

65¢

Work Space.

Write an ordinal number word to complete.

2. January is the first month of the year.
February is the _____ month.

3. Monday is the second day in the week.
Wednesday is the _____ day.

Give the time.

4.    **5.**    **6.**

      :   :   :
    _____   _____   _____

The small marks between the numbers help you tell time to the minute.

28 minutes after **7**   **11** minutes to **9**

7:28   8:49

Match the times with the clocks.

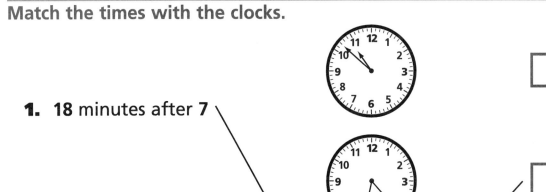

1. **18** minutes after **7**

2. **14** minutes to **4**

3. **23** minutes after **6**

4. **8** minutes to **11**

5. **2** minutes after **12**

6. **4** minutes to **6**

6:23

7:18

10:52

3:46

12:02

5:56

Show the time. Draw the hands on each clock.

7.

    5:30   4:55   7:26   2:13

8.

    6:06   10:35   11:13   3:23

Complete.

Time Now

| 12:00 |

9. What was the time a half-hour ago? _____

| 8:41 |

10. What will the time be **9** minutes from now? _____

| 1:30 |

11. What was the time **10** minutes ago? _____

Problem Solving Reasoning   **Solve.**

12. Anna went to bed at **3** minutes before **9**. What time did her digital clock show? _____

13. Mrs. Jackson leaves for work at **8:43**. Mr. Jenkins leaves at half past **8**. Who leaves later?

_____

Test Prep ★ Mixed Review

14 Karim has 45 baseball cards. His sister has 32 baseball cards. How many do they have in all?

  A 13

  B 27

  C 63

  D 77

15 Maria has 57 marbles. Sue has 21 marbles. How many more marbles does Maria have?

  F 36

  G 38

  H 76

  J 78

A.M. and P.M.

MIDNIGHT ◄——— A.M. TIME ———► NOON ◄——— P.M. TIME ———►

| 12 1 2 3 4 5 6 7 8 9 10 11 | | 12 1 2 3 4 5 6 7 8 9 10 11 |

The time from **12** o'clock midnight until **12** o'clock noon is A.M. time.

The time from **12** o'clock noon until **12** o'clock midnight is P.M. time

---

The clocks on this page tell about Jane's day. Write the correct time to finish each sentence. Write A.M. or P.M. to show whether it is before noon or afternoon.

1.

Jane gets up at

_____

She eats breakfast at

_____

She goes to school at

_____

2.

She eats lunch at

_____

She leaves school at

_____

She plays at

_____

3.

She studies at

_____

She has dinner at

_____

She goes to bed at

_____

7:00 A.M.
Jim leaves for school **5 hours before** lunch, he leaves at **7:00** A.M.

lunchtime

3:00 P.M.
He gets home from school **3 hours after** lunch, he gets home at **3:00** P.M.

Fill in the blanks.

4. Ten o'clock is **2 hours** earlier than _____ o'clock.

5. 7:00 A.M. is **3 hours** _____ than **4:00 A.M.**

6. 1:00 P.M. is _____ hours later than **11:00 A.M.**

7. _____ is **5 hours** earlier than noon.

Problem Solving
Reasoning

Solve.

9. Rosa began babysitting at **9:15 P.M.** She finished at **1:25.** Was the time **1:25** A.M. or **1:25** P.M. Why?

_____

10. The baseball game began at **11:00** A.M. They played for one and a half hours. What time did the game end?

_____

✓ **Quick Check**

Give the time.

Work Space.

1.

2.

3.

_____ _____ _____

Is it A.M. or P.M.?

4. 7:15 Wake up for school. _____

5. 3:00 Home from school. _____

6. 6:30 Eat dinner. _____

7. You begin a bike ride at **12:45** P.M. and finish at **1:30** P.M. How long did you ride? _____

30   Unit 1 Lesson 13

Name _____

How many blocks?
Give the standard form.

1.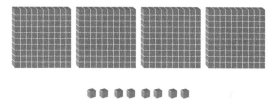

_____

2.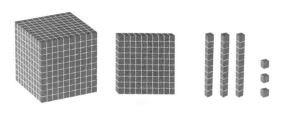

Complete.

		Th	H	T	O		
3.	432 =		4	3	2	or	_____ + _____ + _____
4.	25 =					or	20 + 5
5.	_____ =	1	9	7	6	or	1,000 + 900 + 70 + 6
6.	2,348 =	2	3	4	8	or	_____ + _____ + _____ + ___

How much money? Use $ and . to give the amount.

7.

_____

8.

_____

Continue the number sequence.

9. 98, 99, _____, _____, _____, _____

10. 210, 220, _____, _____, _____, _____

11. 4,200, 4,300, _____, _____, _____, _____

Use <, >, or =.

12. 26 ◯ 23

450 ◯ 540

1,584 ◯ 2,585

13. 83 ◯ 88

350 ◯ 351

11,864 ◯ 11,684

14. 41,110 ◯ 41,110

4,503 ◯ 4,539

711,240 ◯ 711,420

Write these times two ways.

15.

_____

or _____

16.

_____

or _____

17.

_____

or _____

Complete the sentences.

18. _____ is the 4th day of the week.

19. Thursday is the _____ day after Tuesday.

20. Which days begin with the same letter.
Use ordinal numbers.

_____ and _____.

_____ and _____.

Days of the Week	
1st	Sunday
2nd	Monday
3rd	Tuesday
4th	Wednesday
5th	Thursday
6th	Friday
7th	Saturday

Solve.

21. Jo sends her father a letter on these days of the month: 1st, 6th, 11th, 16th, 21st, and so on. What pattern do you see?

_____

22. Ali eats dinner at 6:15 P.M. In 12 hours what time will it be? Is it A.M. or P.M.?

_____

1

Class	Number of Cans Recycled
Mr. Kaufman	985
Mrs. Ruiz	1,024
Mrs. Lucio	1,305
Mr. Chan	897
Mrs. Booth	1,266

Whose class collected the most cans for recycling?

A. Mrs. Booth

B. Mrs. Ruiz

C. Mr. Kaufman

D. Mrs. Lucio

2 **Which lists the color of cars in order from those bought most to those bought least?**

Color	Number of Cars Bought
red	719
blue	688
white	723
black	708

F. black, red, blue, white

G. white, red, black, blue

H. black, white, red, blue

J. white, black, red, blue

3 **There are 300 more people in the walk-a-thon this year than last year. If 1,426 people were in the walk-a-thon last year how many people are there this year?**

A. 1,429

B. 1,456

C. 1,726

D. 4,426

4 **The builders used four thousand, two hundred seventy-six bricks to build a wall. Which shows this number?**

F. 4,276

G. 42,076

H. 40,276

J. 420,760

5 **Which number means 10,000 + 400 + 5?**

A. 145

B. 10,405

C. 10,450

D. 14,500

6 **Which number means 6,000 + 700 + 30?**

F. 600,703

G. 67,300

H. 6,730

J. 6,073

7 The cross-country train trip went 2,845 miles last summer. What is the value of 8 in 2,845?

A. 8 tens

B. 8 hundreds

C. 8 thousands

D. NH

8 Marty used an almanac to learn that 73,091 people live in his state. What is the value of 3 in 73,091?

F. 3 ones

G. 3 thousands

H. 3 tens

J. 3 hundreds

9 Mrs. Lopez travels all over the world for her job. Which lists the months in order from those she traveled least to those she traveled the most?

Month	Miles Traveled
April	8,977
May	11,022
June	10,845
July	10,472

A. April, July, June, May

B. May, June, July, April

C. June, July, May, April

D. April, May, June, July

10 Which of these shows where the arrow is pointing on the number line?

F. 130

G. 180

H. 1,300

J. NH

UNIT 2 • TABLE OF CONTENTS

Addition

CALIFORNIA STANDARDS	Lesson	Page
NS 2.1; A/F 1.2	**1** Algebra • **3-Digit Addition**	37–38
NS 2.1	**2** **Regrouping Ones**	39–40
NS 2.1	**3** **Regrouping Tens**	41–42
NS 2.1	**4** **Regrouping More Than Once**	43–44
MR 2.3	**5** Problem Solving Application: **Use a Graph**	45–46
	6 **Three Addends**	47–48
NS 1.4	**7** **Rounding Numbers**	49–50
NS 1.4	**8** **Round to the Nearest Thousand**	51–52
NS 1.4, 2.8; MR 2.6	**9** **Estimating Sums**	53–54
NS 2.1, 3.3	**10** **Addition with Money**	55–56
NS 2.1, 3.3	**11** **4-Digit Addition**	57–58
NS 3.3; MR 3.2	**12** Problem Solving Strategy: **Conjecture and Verify**	59–60
	• **Unit 2 Review**	61
	• **Cumulative Review ★ Test Prep**	62

Dear Family,

In the math lessons planned for the coming weeks, the class will be learning to add numbers up to four digits with regrouping. They will learn to round numbers and estimate sums.

You can expect to see homework that provides practice in rounding and adding numbers. This sample explains the process of rounding.

Rounding of Numbers

Rule: If the digit we need to look at is less than **5** we round down.
　　　If the digit is **5** or greater we round up.

To estimate **43 + 59,** we round the numbers to the nearest ten. We look at the ones digit. The estimated sum is **40 + 60 = 100.** The actual sum is **102.**

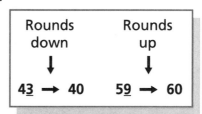

To estimate **134 + 565,** we round to the nearest hundred. We look at the tens digit. The estimated sum is **100 + 600 = 700.** The actual sum is **699.**

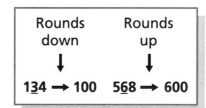

To estimate **6,843 + 4,123,** we round to the nearest thousand. We look at the hundreds digit. The estimated sum is **11,000.** The actual sum is **10,966.**

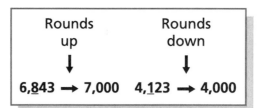

More examples: **346** rounded to the nearest ten is **350.**
　　　　　　　　4,893 rounded to the nearest ten is **4,890.**
　　　　　　　　3,548 rounded to the nearest hundred is **3,500.**

During this unit, students need to continue practicing addition skills.

Sincerely,

We can add **3**-digit numbers just as we added **2**-digit numbers:

> 1. Add the ones.
> 2. Add the tens.
> 3. Add the hundreds.

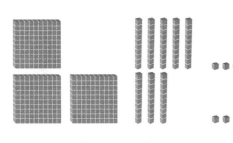

hundreds   tens   ones

385 blocks in all

Table Form

Hundreds	Tens	Ones
1	5	3
+ 2	3	2
3	8	5

Short Form

```
  1 5 3
+ 2 3 2
  3 8 5
```

Add.

1.

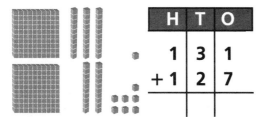

H	T	O
1	3	1
+1	2	7

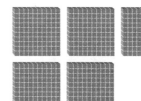

H	T	O
3	4	5
+2	0	1

2.

H	T	O
3	6	9
+2	3	0

H	T	O
7	3	8
+2	2	1

H	T	O
6	4	1
+1	5	2

H	T	O
8	5	0
+1	0	7

3.

```
  680        432        729         31        807        126
+213       +547       +110        +54       +192       +362
```

4.

```
  793         40        743        403         76        216
+103        +19       +112       +263        +20       +632
```

5.

```
  554        462        813         34        306        813
+113       +303       +166        +43       +681       +132
```

Use the telephone keys to find a sum for these words.

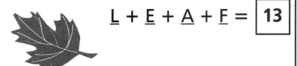

$$\underset{5}{JKL} + \underset{3}{DEF} + \underset{2}{ABC} + \underset{3}{DEF}$$

$$\underline{L} + \underline{E} + \underline{A} + \underline{F} = \boxed{13}$$

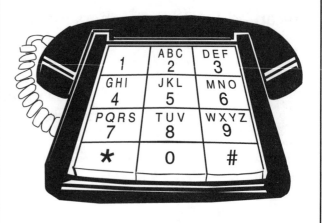

	ABC	DEF
1	2	3
GHI	JKL	MNO
4	5	6
PQRS	TUV	WXYZ
7	8	9
*	0	#

6. ___ + ___ + ___ = ☐

7. ___ + ___ + ___ = ☐

8. What is the sum for your first name? _____

Solve.

9. The sum of two numbers is **787**. One of the numbers is **521**. Is the other number **266** or **265**? How do you know?

_____

10. A free muffin is given to students who join the math club. If **236** banana and **312** apple muffins were given away, how many students joined?

_____

Test Prep ★ Mixed Review

11 **Which of these shows where the arrow is pointing on the number line?**

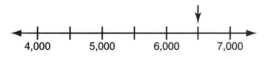

```
4,000   5,000   6,000   7,000
```

A 6,001

B 6,100

C 6,500

D 7,000

12 **Which lists the number of cans in order from the most to the least?**

Cans Collected	
Grade 1	1,624
Grade 2	986
Grade 3	1,381

F 1,624, 986, 1,381

G 986, 1,381, 1,624

H 1,624, 1,381, 986

J 986, 1,624, 1,381

Regrouping Ones

Here is the way to regroup ones when you add.

> 1. Add the ones. Regroup.
> 2. Add the tens.
> 3. Add the hundreds.

Example.

H	T	O
4	2	8
+ 1	6	6

1. Add the ones. Regroup.

H	T	O
	1	
4	2	8
+ 1	6	6
		4

14 ones = 1 ten 4 ones

2. Add the tens.

H	T	O
	1	
4	2	8
+ 1	6	6
	9	4

3. Add the hundreds.

H	T	O
	1	
4	2	8
+ 1	6	6
5	9	4

We can also add without the table.

Table Form

H	T	O
	1	
4	6	7
+ 1	2	4
5	9	1

H	T	O
	1	
3	5	4
+ 3	3	8
6	9	2

Short Form

$$\overset{1}{4}67$$
$$+124$$
$$591$$

$$\overset{1}{3}54$$
$$+338$$
$$692$$

Add. Remember–start with the ones.

1.

H	T	O
2	5	9
+ 2	1	8

H	T	O
5	7	1
+ 2	1	9

H	T	O
3	5	7
+ 1	2	6

H	T	O
6	3	7
+ 2	5	6

2.

H	T	O
7	1	9
+ 2	4	2

H	T	O
6	8	5
+ 3	0	9

H	T	O
5	7	8
+ 2	1	6

H	T	O
4	6	3
+ 1	1	8

Add.

3.

519	639	758	354	408
+229	+232	+106	+337	+209

4.

665	518	346	234	139
+119	+364	+515	+228	+455

5.

448	224	449	729	887
+249	+219	+339	+169	+107

6.

452	842	323	648	256
+139	+109	+259	+237	+306

Problem Solving Reasoning Solve.

7. Sue plays a game with Tyrone. She has **246** more points than Tyrone. He has **427** points. How many points does Sue have?

8. Do you need to regroup when you add **318** and **445**? Do the problem and then explain why or why not?

Test Prep ★ Mixed Review

9 The newspaper reported that **235,497** people live in Center City. This is **10,000** more people than 5 years ago. How many people lived in Center City 5 years ago?

A 335,497

B 245,497

C 225,497

D 135,497

10 During a read-a-thon Fisher School students read 137,894 pages, East School students read 141,058 pages, and Old Post students read 138,709 pages. Which lists the schools in order from the most pages read to the least pages?

F Fisher, East, Old Post

G Old Post, Fisher, East

H Fisher, Old Post, East

J East, Old Post, Fisher

Sometimes you regroup tens to hundreds.

> 1. Add the ones.
> 2. Add the tens. Regroup.
> 3. Add the hundreds.

Example.

H	T	O
1	6	4
+3	8	2

1. Add the ones.

H	T	O
1	6	4
+3	8	2
		6

2. Add the tens. Regroup.

H	T	O
¹		
1	6	4
+3	8	2
	4	6

14 tens = 1 hundred 4 tens

3. Add the hundreds.

H	T	O
¹		
1	6	4
+3	8	2
5	4	6

Here are some other examples.

Table Form

H	T	O
¹		
4	6	2
+3	8	1
8	4	3

H	T	O
¹		
2	3	4
+1	8	2
4	1	6

Short Form

$$\begin{array}{r} ^1 \\ 462 \\ +381 \\ \hline 843 \end{array}$$

$$\begin{array}{r} ^1 \\ 234 \\ +182 \\ \hline 416 \end{array}$$

Add. Start with the ones.

1.

H	T	O
3	1	3
+1	9	2

H	T	O
2	9	2
+	3	2

H	T	O
4	8	5
+1	4	1

H	T	O
2	6	8
+3	4	1

H	T	O
5	8	2
+1	3	1

2.

H	T	O
6	9	1
+1	2	2

H	T	O
3	3	3
+1	9	4

H	T	O
1	7	6
+2	3	1

H	T	O
3	9	2
+1	3	4

H	T	O
5	5	5
+1	7	2

Add.

3.

$$\begin{array}{r}354\\+283\end{array}$$
$$\begin{array}{r}672\\+275\end{array}$$
$$\begin{array}{r}692\\+191\end{array}$$
$$\begin{array}{r}243\\+192\end{array}$$
$$\begin{array}{r}262\\+392\end{array}$$

4.

$$\begin{array}{r}472\\+261\end{array}$$
$$\begin{array}{r}550\\+354\end{array}$$
$$\begin{array}{r}492\\+294\end{array}$$
$$\begin{array}{r}153\\+292\end{array}$$
$$\begin{array}{r}292\\+420\end{array}$$

5.

$$\begin{array}{r}314\\+291\end{array}$$
$$\begin{array}{r}472\\+240\end{array}$$
$$\begin{array}{r}161\\+274\end{array}$$
$$\begin{array}{r}463\\+161\end{array}$$
$$\begin{array}{r}284\\+341\end{array}$$

6.

$$\begin{array}{r}143\\+291\end{array}$$
$$\begin{array}{r}432\\+212\end{array}$$
$$\begin{array}{r}394\\+182\end{array}$$
$$\begin{array}{r}432\\+193\end{array}$$
$$\begin{array}{r}431\\+162\end{array}$$

| Problem Solving |
| Reasoning |

Solve.

7. Yoko and Dan collect baseball cards. Dan has **348** cards. Yoko has **271** more cards than Dan. How many cards does she have?

8. Omar adds **482** and **293**. How many place-value blocks does Omar need to show the number of tens in the sum?

✔ **Quick Check**

Add.

Work Space.

1.
$$\begin{array}{r}482\\+315\end{array}$$

2.
$$\begin{array}{r}205\\+73\end{array}$$

3.
$$\begin{array}{r}146\\+742\end{array}$$

4.
$$\begin{array}{r}409\\+176\end{array}$$

5.
$$\begin{array}{r}356\\+235\end{array}$$

6.
$$\begin{array}{r}748\\+35\end{array}$$

7.
$$\begin{array}{r}293\\+41\end{array}$$

8.
$$\begin{array}{r}125\\+683\end{array}$$

9.
$$\begin{array}{r}470\\+569\end{array}$$

Regrouping More Than Once

Sometimes you need to regroup twice.

1. Add the ones. Regroup.

H	T	O
	1	
2	8	3
+ 1	9	9
		2

12 ones = **1** ten **2** ones

2. Add the tens. Regroup.

H	T	O
1	1	
2	8	3
+ 1	9	9
	8	2

18 tens = **1** hundred **8** tens

3. Add the hundreds.

H	T	O
1	1	
2	8	3
+ 1	9	9
4	8	2

Here are some other examples.

Table Form

H	T	O
1	1	
4	3	7
+ 3	9	6
8	3	3

H	T	O
1	1	
2	7	5
+ 4	7	8
7	5	3

Short Form

```
  1 1
  4 3 7
+ 3 9 6
  8 3 3
```

```
  1 1
  2 7 5
+ 4 7 8
  7 5 3
```

Add. Remember to regroup.

1.

H	T	O
4	2	6
+ 3	9	8

H	T	O
2	5	2
+ 1	8	9

H	T	O
3	9	4
+ 3	3	8

H	T	O
6	6	5
+ 1	5	9

H	T	O
2	7	1
+ 4	8	9

2.
```
  283      159      449      372      478
+ 187    + 186    + 371    + 599    + 383
```

3.
```
  188      399      464      193      399
+ 295    + 272    + 266    + 269    + 592
```

4.
```
  153      286      375      254      382
+ 368    + 466    + 497    + 279    + 549
```

Add.

5.

198	297	193	374	659
+435	+396	+229	+376	+192

6.

266	579	184	247	359
+498	+342	+579	+383	+176

7.

486	187	599	248	458
+248	+154	+189	+492	+168

Write <, >, or =.

8. 143 + 300 ◯ 250 + 100   430 + 270 ◯ 509 + 171

9. 215 + 425 ◯ 320 + 320   742 + 200 ◯ 800 + 138

Problem Solving Reasoning **Solve.**

10. Mrs. Garcia writes **346 + 587** on the board. How many times will she need to regroup to find the sum? How do you know?

_____

11. Suppose you want to show your friend how to regroup more than once in addition. Write the addition exercise you would use.

_____

Test Prep ★ Mixed Review

12 Keisha's class recycled 345 pounds of newspaper. Bill's class recycled 414 pounds of newspaper. How much did the two classes collect in all?

A 759
B 761
C 768
D 769

13 There were 268 boys and 325 girls marching in the parade. How many children marched in the parade?

F 483
G 493
H 583
J 593

Name _____

A sports store kept a record of the baseball bats they sold in one week. This bar graph shows the bats they sold.

In this lesson you will use the data from graphs to solve problems.

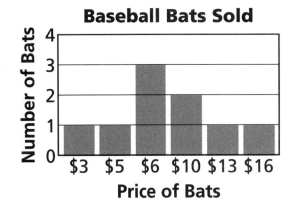

Baseball Bats Sold

Number of Bats / Price of Bats

Tips to Remember:

| 1. Understand | 2. Decide | 3. Solve | 4. Look back |

• Ask: Have I solved a problem like this before?
• Compare the graphs with the words and numbers in the problem. Find the facts you need.
• If needed, write a number sentence. Ask yourself: What numbers should I use? What operations should I use?

Study the graph. Then solve the problems.

1. How many different prices for bats are shown in the graph?

   Think: Where on the graph are prices for bats given?

   _____

   Answer: _____

2. How many baseball bats that cost **$10** or more were sold?

   Think: What bars show bats that cost **$10** or more? What number sentence can I write to show the total?

   _____

   Answer: _____

3. How many baseball bats were sold in all?

   _____

4. How much money would you spend if you bought a bat at each price?

   _____

Backpacks Sold

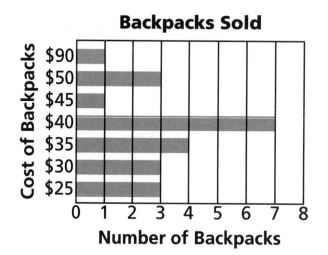

5. What was the price of the backpack that was sold the most?

_____

6. What is the difference between the greatest and least price?

_____

7. How many backpacks that cost less than **$40** were sold? How do you know?

_____

_____

8. A father bought a **$25** backpack for each of his two children. He bought a **$40** backpack for himself. How much money did he spend?

_____

9. Last year the Hidalgo Family spent **$100** on backpacks. This year they bought all the **$30** backpacks shown on the graph. Which year did they spend more money on backpacks?

_____

10. How many of the backpacks that were sold cost less than **$50**?

_____

Extend Your Thinking

11. Backpacks are so popular, their prices are increasing. If each backpack in the graph increased in price by **$5**, would the graph look different? Explain.

_____

_____

12. Why do you think only one **$90** backpack was sold?

_____

_____

_____

Adding with three numbers is like adding with two numbers.

T	O
¹	
1	5
2	3
+3	6
7	4

Regroup the ones.
14 ones = **1** ten **4** ones

H	T	O
	¹	
1	8	6
2	3	0
+5	5	2
9	6	8

Regroup the tens.
16 tens = **1** hundred **6** tens

We can add three numbers without the table.

Examples.

```
  403          38         1 1          1 1
  253          70          45          234
+ 143        + 61         386          167
  799         169        + 253        + 173
                          684          574
```

Add. Remember to regroup if needed.

1.

H	T	O
2	4	3
	7	4
+2	5	3

H	T	O
	3	5
4	5	2
+4	1	1

H	T	O
9	2	
9	1	
+1	1	1

H	T	O
7	5	9
	8	5
+	4	1

H	T	O
	8	2
3	0	6
+	9	4

Add.

2.
```
  335         524         21          456         24
   46          12         41           54         97
+282        +  89        +13         +168        +57
```

3.
```
  228          43         156         315         225
   30          44         142         342          80
+141         +46        +192        +222        +183
```

Add.

4.

246	465	725	25	434
251	12	33	84	131
+202	+ 86	+199	+86	+234

5.

556	374	56	258	56
110	104	41	156	24
+280	+220	+81	+350	+481

6.

557	249	556	248	542
87	52	284	230	119
+131	+ 42	+ 23	+256	+ 83

Write <, >, or =.

7. $400 + 155 + 250$ ◯ 815 $\qquad$ 642 ◯ $150 + 150 + 200$

8. 527 ◯ $120 + 220 + 240$ $\qquad$ $110 + 400 + 250$ ◯ 688

Problem Solving Reasoning Solve.

9. Kim needs to sell **400** baskets of potatoes each week. Monday she sold **87** baskets. Wednesday she sold **170**. Saturday she sold **98** baskets. Did Kim sell enough potatoes?

10. Write a **3**-digit number, a **2**-digit number, and a **1**-digit number. Be sure the numbers have the least value possible. Do not use zeros. What is the sum of the numbers?

Test Prep ★ Mixed Review

11 Which number comes next in the pattern?

1, 3, 5, 7, _____

A 6 $\qquad$ C 9

B 8 $\qquad$ D 12

12 Which number means $20,000 + 4,000 + 700 + 6$?

F 204,706 $\qquad$ H 24,706

G 24,760 $\qquad$ J 2,476

This number line shows how to count by tens to **100**.

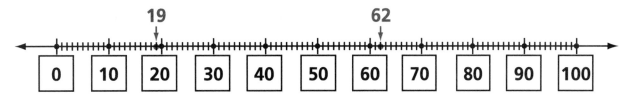

Look at the dots for **19** and **62**. You can see that

19 is between | 10 | and | 20 | , but it is closer to | 20 |

62 is between | 60 | and | 70 | , but it is closer to | 60 |

To **round** a number to the **nearest ten**, look at the ones digit.

| If the ones digit is less than **5** round down. | If the ones digit is **5** or more round up. |

34 is between **30** and **40**.
34 *rounds down* to **30**.

34 → 30

56 is between **50** and **60**.
56 *rounds up* to **60**.

56 → 60

Put a box around the correct answer.

1. 9 is closer to   **0**   **10**   87 is closer to   **80**   **90**

2. 59 is closer to   **50**   **60**   43 is closer to   **40**   **50**

3. 13 is closer to   **10**   **20**   64 is closer to   **60**   **70**

4. 96 is closer to   **90**   **100**   48 is closer to   **40**   **50**

Round each number to the nearest ten.

5. 31 → _____   35 → _____   74 → _____

6. 92 → _____   87 → _____   48 → _____

7. 14 → _____   68 → _____   5 → _____

Here is a number line for tens and hundreds:

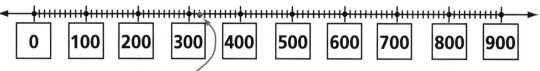

320 is closer to 300 than to 400

To round a number to the **nearest hundred,** look at the tens digit.

| If the tens digit is less than **5** round down. | If the tens digit is **5** or more round up. |

139 *rounds down* to **100.**

139 → 100

450 *rounds up* to **500.**

450 → 500

Round each number to the nearest hundred.

8. 781 → _____   125 → _____   515 → _____

9. 426 → _____   550 → _____   708 → _____

Problem Solving Reasoning Solve.

10. May saw about **30** birds at the zoo. What is the least number of birds she may have seen? What is the greatest number?

_____

11. Luis writes a number. When he rounds the number to the nearest ten, he gets **40.** Name six numbers he may have written.

_____

✓ Quick Check

Add.

Work Space.

1.   2 7 6
     + 4 5 9

2.   4 1
        2 6
     + 3 5

3.   5 7 3
        6 1 0
     + 2 8 9

Round to the place value of the underlined digit.

4. 4̲3 ____   **5.** 1̲57 ____   **6.** 6̲33 ____

7. 2̲6 ____   **8.** 6̲5 ____   **9.** 3̲81 ____

Here is a number line for hundreds and thousands.

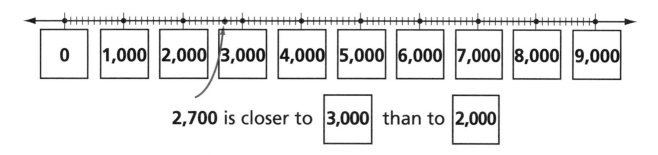

| 0 | 1,000 | 2,000 | 3,000 | 4,000 | 5,000 | 6,000 | 7,000 | 8,000 | 9,000 |

2,700 is closer to 3,000 than to 2,000

To round a number to the **nearest thousand,**
look at the hundreds digit.

| If the hundreds digit is less than **5 round down.** | If the hundreds digit is **5 or more round up.** |

1,300 is between **1,000** and **2,000**.
1,300 *rounds down* to **1,000**.

1,300 → 1,000

3,670 is between **3,000** and **4,000**.
3,670 *rounds up* to **4,000**.

3,670 → 4,000

Put a box around the correct answer.

1. **4,100** is closer to   **4,000**   **5,000**   **3,400** is closer to   **3,000**   **4,000**

2. **7,501** is closer to   **7,000**   **8,000**   **1,346** is closer to   **1,000**   **2,000**

3. **9,800** is closer to   **9,000**   **10,000**   **12,978** is closer to   **12,000**   **13,000**

4. **46,450** is closer to   **46,000**   **47,000**   **35,099** is closer to   **35,000**   **36,000**

Round each number to the nearest thousand.

5.   **1,800** → _____   **1,250** → _____   **9,449** → _____

6.   **5,180** → _____   **2,346** → _____   **1,001** → _____

7.   **9,104** → _____   **3,901** → _____   **6,790** → _____

8.   **74,598** → _____   **12,222** → _____   **62,543** → _____

9.   **58,441** → _____   **35,467** → _____   **86,056** → _____

Round to the nearest ten.

10. 67 → _____   163 → _____

11. 89 → _____   234 → _____

12. 1,456 → _____   7,125 → _____

13. 43,681 → _____   57,488 → _____

Round to the nearest hundred.

14. 348 → _____   452 → _____

15. 198 → _____   550 → _____

16. 1,346 → _____   6,783 → _____

17. 27,451 → _____   13,065 → _____

Round to the place value of the underlined place.

18. 8̲5 → _____   7̲68 → _____   4,9̲08 → _____

19. 83,4̲61 → _____   21̲,345 → _____   2̲,680 → _____

20. 2,0̲50 → _____   56̲7 → _____   47,51̲2 → _____

Problem Solving Reasoning Solve.

21. Hector rounds **5,249** to the nearest thousand. Rosa rounds **5,249** to the nearest hundred. Who gets the greater answer?

_____

22. A number rounded to the nearest thousand is **6,000**. It has a **5** in the thousands place. Name the digits that could be in the hundreds place.

_____

Test Prep ★ Mixed Review

23 Mrs. Samay's art class is using 140 yards of blue ribbon and 275 yards of red ribbon. How much ribbon will the class use in all?

   A 315 yards   **C** 415 yards

   B 405 yards   **D** 425 yards

24 Mr. Lyle buys two bags of seed. One bag weighs 175 pounds, the other weighs 125 pounds. What is the total amount of seed?

   F 200 pounds   **H** 300 pounds

   G 290 pounds   **J** 390 pounds

Sometimes an exact answer is not needed. Then numbers are rounded to give an estimate.

Example.   Estimate   3 9
                                   + 5 2

Estimated sum	**Actual sum**

3 9 rounds to →   4 0   3 9
+ 5 2 rounds to → + 5 0   + 5 2
                              9 0   9 1

The estimated sum is **90**.

The estimated sum is close to the actual sum, **91**.

Round to the nearest ten. Estimate each sum.

1.   9 7 →   7 2 →   1 2 →
       + 4 4 → + _____   + 1 5 → + ____   + 6 8 → + ____

Round to the nearest hundred. Estimate each sum.

2.   2 5 3 →   1 4 1 →   4 3 6 →
       + 1 4 9 → + _____   + 1 6 5 → + ____   + 1 2 7 → + ____

Use estimation to choose the correct answer.

3.   6 1   A. **89**   B. **69**   C. **75**   D. **79**
       + 1 8

4.   6 8   A. **87**   B. **41**   C. **97**   D. **107**
       + 2 9

5.   1 1 2   A. **109**   B. **199**   C. **75**   D. **89**
       + 8 7

6.   5 6   A. **79**   B. **97**   C. **78**   D. **87**
        3 3
       + 8

Estimating can help you check your answer.

Actual work:

```
  4 2
+ 3 7
-----
  7 9
```

Our estimate tells us that our actual answer should be around **80**.

If we estimate:

```
  4 2  →    4 0
+ 3 7  →  + 4 0
--------------
            8 0
```

Solve the problems. Then check by estimating.

	Actual Work	Estimate
7. Rita's gas gauge on her truck is broken. She has to put gas in every **200** miles. She drove **86** miles Monday and **55** miles on Tuesday. Does she need gas?		

Problem Solving Reasoning   Solve.

8. Pedro has some baseball cards. If you round the number of cards to the nearest ten, you get **640**. If you round the number to the nearest hundred, you get **600**. Could Pedro have **649** cards?

9. Dean is thinking of a number between **80** and **90**. If you round the number to the nearest ten, you get **80**. If you add the digits you get eleven. What number is he thinking of?

_____

☑ **Quick Check**

Round to the underlined digit.

1. 2<u>8</u>7 _____   **2.** <u>4</u>,603 _____   **3.** 5,<u>4</u>73 _____

Round to the nearest ten. Estimate the sum.

4.
```
  1 8  →
+ 3 5  →  + ____
```

5.
```
  2 4  →
+ 7 7  →  + ____
```

Round to the nearest hundred. Estimate the sum.

6.
```
  4 3 8  →
+ 2 7 9  →  + ____
```

7.
```
  1 0 9  →
+ 2 1 1  →  + ____
```

Work Space.

Addition with Money

You can use what you learned about adding
hundreds, tens, and ones to add money.

Example	1. Add the pennies. Regroup	2. Add the dimes.	3. Add the dollars.
$7 . 3 6 + . 2 9	¹ $7 . 3 6 + . 2 9 ____ 5	¹ $7 . 3 6 + . 2 9 ____ 6 5	¹ $7 . 3 6 + . 2 9 ____ $7 . 6 5

Remember to use the $ and . in the answer.

Use the menu to solve.

🍎🥪🍎 TODAY'S SPECIALS! 🍎🥪🍎

apple	35¢	tuna sandwich	$2.65
banana	40¢	hamburger	$3.55
milk	89¢	salad	$1.75
pudding	$1.25	pickle	59¢

1. Yuri bought a tuna sandwich and a pickle.
How much did he spend? _____

2. Syvonne bought a hamburger, salad, and milk.
How much did she spend? _____

3. Manuela has **$2.25.** Can she buy a salad and a milk? _____

4. Geraldo has **$4.80.** He buys a hamburger, an apple,
and milk. Does he get change? How much? _____

5. Jane and Shane have **$10** to spend for lunch. They plan to
eat the same lunch. Choose the lunch items they can eat
without spending more than **$10.** Show your work.

_____

_____

Use the menu. Circle the lunch that costs less.

6.

 or  |  or  |  or

---

Solve.

7. Aman, Ruthie, and Phyllis each have a penny bank. Aman has **262** pennies, Ruthie has **245** pennies, and Phyllis has **302** pennies. How many pennies do they have in all? _____

Use **$** and **.** to write the amount. _____

8. Liam has **$2.50** to spend for a snack. He buys as many different items as he can. How much does Liam spend?

_____

What did he buy?

_____

Problem Solving
Reasoning **Write a number sentence. Solve.**

9. Sung wants to buy a hammer for **$9,** wood for **$53,** and paint for **$29.** He plans to bring **$90** to the store. Is it enough money?

_____

10. Lucia went shopping to buy a notebook and a pen. She bought a notebook for **$3.59** and a pen for **$2.75.** How much did she spend?

_____

Test Prep ★ Mixed Review

11 Mary has **1,457** pennies. Last month she had **100** fewer pennies. How many pennies did Mary have last month?

A 457

B 1,357

C 1,447

D 1,547

12 The float in the parade used 231 red roses, 145 white roses, and 360 yellow roses. How many roses were used in the float?

F 636

G 646

H 736

J 746

The place-value table shows thousands. You can add numbers in thousands.

1. Add the ones. Regroup if needed.
2. Add the tens. Regroup if needed.
3. Add the hundreds.
4. Add the thousands.

Thousands	Hundreds	Tens	Ones
1	2	5	7	= 1,257

Here are some examples.

Table Form

Th	H	T	O
2	1	2	3
+ 1	0	5	1
3	1	7	4

Th	H	T	O
		1	1
2	3	6	8
+ 6	1	4	5
8	5	1	3

Short Form

```
  1 1
6,378
+1,052
7,430
```

```
  2 1
1,567
2,183
+ 162
3,912
```

Try these addition problems.

1.

Th	H	T	O
6	4	0	2
+ 3	3	9	1

Th	H	T	O
5	9	1	1
+ 1	0	3	9

Th	H	T	O
1	0	3	7
	4	3	2
+ 6	1	6	8

Th	H	T	O
3	5	3	8
		8	6
+ 1	1	5	2

2.

```
  1,608
+ 1,118
```

```
  6,103
+ 3,329
```

```
  8,317
+   293
```

```
  2,208
+ 1,729
```

```
  1,036
+ 8,399
```

3.

```
$12.58
+  3.92
```

```
 4,160
   123
+2,077
```

```
$14.89
   1.13
+10.50
```

```
 3,318
   158
+5,462
```

```
 2,200
 1,118
+  387
```

We can also regroup hundreds to thousands.

1. Add the ones.	2. Add the tens. Regroup.	3. Add the hundreds. Regroup.	4. Add the thousands.
4,381 +3,742 _____ 3	¹ 4,381 +3,742 _____ 23	¹ ¹ 4,381 +3,742 _____ 123	¹ ¹ 4,381 +3,742 _____ 8,123

11 hundreds = 1 thousand + 1 hundred

Add.

4.
$$\begin{array}{r} 2,933 \\ +1,462 \\ \hline \end{array} \qquad \begin{array}{r} 6,908 \\ +2,132 \\ \hline \end{array} \qquad \begin{array}{r} 2,431 \\ +5,869 \\ \hline \end{array} \qquad \begin{array}{r} 5,301 \\ +2,997 \\ \hline \end{array} \qquad \begin{array}{r} \$18.32 \\ +18.13 \\ \hline \end{array}$$

Problem Solving Reasoning Solve.

5. Which two years were computer sales the highest? How many computers were sold during those two years?

_____

6. How would the graph change if **1,500** more computers had been sold in 1997?

_____

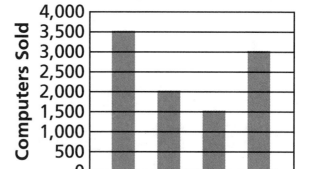

Computer Store Sales

 Quick Check

Add.   Work Space.

1. $4.75
      + 3.16

2. $6.90
      + 2.44

3. $4.15
      + 7.08

4. 1,362
      +4,054

5. 7,118
      +2,394

6. 5,623
      +1,484

To solve some problems you may need to make a guess about the answer to get started.

This "guess" is called a conjecture. You need to check or verify to see if your conjecture is correct and then try again.

Problem

Jason spent $3.95. He bought 3 items from the snack bar. What did he buy?

Snack Bar Menu	
apple	$1.10
milk	$1.35
chips	$1.40
juice	$1.30
muffin	$1.25

---

1 **Understand**   Reread the problem, ask yourself questions.

- How much money did Jason spend?

    He spent $3.95

- How many items did Jason buy?

    He bought 3 items.

- What do you need to find? _____

---

2 **Decide**   Choose a method for solving the problem.

- Try the Conjecture and Verify strategy.
- What will be your first guess?

    First guess: apple, chips and milk

---

3 **Solve**   Verify your conjecture. Try again if necessary.

First Guess: Try again.

apple   Cost: **$1.10**   _____

chips   Cost: **$1.40**   _____

milk   Cost: **$1.35**   _____

Total   **$3.85**

Answer _____

---

4 **Look back**   Check your answer.

- How did the first guess help with your next try?

_____

Use Conjecture and Verify or any other strategy you have learned.

1. Michael spent **$3.70** at the snack bar. He bought **3** items. What items did he buy?

Think: What **3** items could be bought for **$.25** less than **$3.95**?

_____

Answer: _____

2. Maria had **$5**. After she bought lunch, she had **$1** left. What items did she buy at the snack bar?

Think: What items could Maria buy that totaled **$4?**

_____

Answer: _____

3. Emily has dimes and nickels. She has **3** more dimes than nickels. She has a total of **11** coins.

a. How many dimes and nickels does Emily have?

_____

b. Can Emily buy anything from the snack bar with her money? Explain.

_____

4. How many hours a week is the pool open?

_____

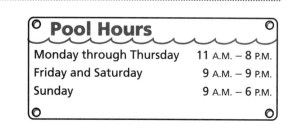

Pool Hours

Monday through Thursday	11 A.M. – 8 P.M.
Friday and Saturday	9 A.M. – 9 P.M.
Sunday	9 A.M. – 6 P.M.

5. Todd works at the pool. He works on Monday and Wednesday from **11 A.M.** until **5 P.M.**, and on Friday from **1 P.M.** until the pool closes. How many hours does Todd work? _____

Extend Your Thinking

6. Suda spent **$3.85** at the snack bar. How do you know she bought either milk or a muffin, but not both?

_____

_____

7. How can a guess that is not right help you solve a problem?

_____

_____

60 Unit 2 Lesson 12

Add. Remember to regroup.

1. $\begin{array}{r} 123 \\ +194 \\ \hline \end{array}$	**2.** $\begin{array}{r} 252 \\ +489 \\ \hline \end{array}$	**3.** $\begin{array}{r} \$1.84 \\ +2.95 \\ \hline \end{array}$	**4.** $\begin{array}{r} 148 \\ +383 \\ \hline \end{array}$
5. $\begin{array}{r} 5,199 \\ +4,555 \\ \hline \end{array}$	**6.** $\begin{array}{r} \$1.67 \\ +3.99 \\ \hline \end{array}$	**7.** $\begin{array}{r} 362 \\ +554 \\ \hline \end{array}$	**8.** $\begin{array}{r} 2,449 \\ +3,239 \\ \hline \end{array}$
9. $\begin{array}{r} \$1.81 \\ +3.32 \\ \hline \end{array}$	**10.** $\begin{array}{r} 174 \\ +378 \\ \hline \end{array}$	**11.** $\begin{array}{r} \$4.53 \\ +3.79 \\ \hline \end{array}$	**12.** $\begin{array}{r} 2,272 \\ +1,564 \\ \hline \end{array}$

Round to the place of the underlined place.

13. 6̲5 → _____

14. 1̲,168 → _____

15. 1̲34 → _____

16. 9̲14 → _____

17. 2,̲456 → _____

18. 8,1̲45 → _____

Round to the nearest ten. Estimate each sum.

19. $\begin{array}{r} 83 \rightarrow \\ +47 \rightarrow \end{array}$ + _____

20. $\begin{array}{r} 154 \rightarrow \\ +76 \rightarrow \end{array}$ + _____

21. $\begin{array}{r} 96 \rightarrow \\ +17 \rightarrow \end{array}$ + _____

Solve.

22. Keino picks a 2-digit number. He writes the number three times and finds that the sum is **297**. What is the number? What strategy did you use?

_____

23. The number of pairs of socks in Megan's drawer, rounds to **20**. What is the greatest number of pairs she could have? What is the least number?

_____

1 The car was driven 57,461 miles before it broke down. What is the value of 7 in 57,461?

A 7 thousands

B 7 hundreds

C 7 tens

D 7 ones

2 Which number means 100,000 + 50,000 + 4,000?

F 154

G 100,540

H 10,540

J 154,000

3

Town	Number of People
Aston	16,859
Carby	20,400
Hillvale	20,199
Southtown	17,654

Which town had the most number of people living in it?

A Aston

B Carby

C Hillvale

D Southtown

4 Last year Kato's farm planted 462 tomato plants. What is the number rounded to the nearest hundred?

462

F 400   **H** 470

G 460   **J** 500

5 Zora spent $4.31 on Monday and $2.76 on Tuesday. How much did Zora spend altogether on both days?

A $7.17

B $7.07

C $6.17

D $2.55

E NH

6 Gilmore's Farm Supply Store sold 2,408 pounds of grain last year and 3,423 pounds of grain this year. How many pounds of grain did it sell in all?

F 6,831

G 5,835

H 5,821

J NH

UNIT 3 • TABLE OF CONTENTS

Subtraction

CALIFORNIA STANDARDS	Lesson	Page
NS 2.1	**1** Algebra • **3-Digit Subtraction**	65–66
NS 2.1	**2** Algebra • **Regrouping Tens to Ones**	67–68
NS 2.1	**3** **Regrouping Hundreds to Tens**	69–70
NS 2.1	**4** **Regrouping Twice in Subtraction**	71–72
NS 2.1	**5** **Subtracting from Zeros**	73–74
NS 2.1, 3.3	**6** Algebra • **Subtraction with Money**	75–76
MR 2.3	**7** **Problem Solving Strategy: Act It Out**	77–78
NS 1.4, 2.8; MR 2.6	**8** **Estimating Differences**	79–80
NS 2.1, 3.3	**9** **4-Digit Subtraction**	81–82
MR 2.3, 2.6	**10** **Problem Solving Application: Use a Map**	83–84
	• **Unit 3 Review**	85
	• **Cumulative Review ★ Test Prep**	86

Dear Family,

Our math class will be spending the next few weeks learning to subtract numbers up to four digits with regrouping. Once again the students will use rounding, this time to estimate differences.

Homework will consist of practicing subtraction skills with whole numbers and money. The sample shows the subtraction method.

Subtracting with More Than One Regrouping

	First, regroup a ten and subtract ones.	Next, regroup a hundred and subtract tens.	Then, subtract the hundreds.
Example: $\begin{array}{r} 346 \\ -158 \\ \hline \end{array}$	H T O 3 16 3 4̸ 6̸ -158 8	H T O 2 13 16 3̸ 4̸ 6̸ -158 88	H T O 2 13 16 3̸ 4̸ 6̸ -158 188

The difference is **188**.

You can check the subtraction with addition.

$$\begin{array}{r} {}^{2\ \ 13\ \ 16} \\ \cancel{3}\ \cancel{4}\ \cancel{6} \\ -1\ 5\ 8 \\ \hline 1\ 8\ 8 \end{array} \qquad \begin{array}{r} {}^{1\ \ 1} \\ 1\ 8\ 8 \\ +1\ 5\ 8 \\ \hline 3\ 4\ 6 \end{array}$$

During this unit, students will need to continue practicing their basic facts for addition and subtraction.

Sincerely,

Subtracting 3-digit numbers is like subtracting 2-digit numbers.

> 1. Subtract the ones.
> 2. Subtract the tens.
> 3. Subtract the hundreds.

Start with **323** blocks.
Take away **121**.

How many are left?

202 blocks left

Table Form

H	T	O
3	2	3
− 1	2	1
2	0	2

Short Form

```
  3 2 3
− 1 2 1
  2 0 2
```

difference

Subtract.

1.
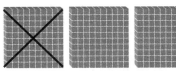
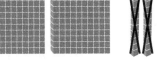

H	T	O
4	8	6
− 3	8	6

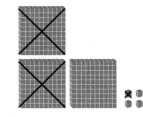

H	T	O
3	0	4
− 2	0	1

2.

```
  847        76       958       749       356       249
− 617      − 56     − 420     − 438     − 150     − 119
```

3.

```
  994       784       535        86       979       554
− 271     − 362     − 115      − 42     − 870     − 113
```

4.

```
   73       867       355       547       889       953
 − 61     − 460     − 135     − 416     − 527     − 732
```

Addition and subtraction are inverse operations.
So, you can check subtraction with addition.

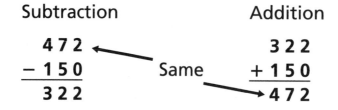

Subtraction		Addition
472		322
− 150	Same	+ 150
322		472

Subtract. Add to check the answer.

5.
356	215	924	419	966
− 141	+ 141	− 301 + ___	− 106 + ___	− 351 + ___
	356			

6.
548	257	841	599
− 106 + ___	− 131 + ___	− 620 + ___	− 389 + ___

7.
831	686	881	697
− 220 + ___	− 543 + ___	− 200 + ___	− 481 + ___

Problem Solving Reasoning Solve.

8. Mrs. Chang is planning a train trip for **20** students. The train has **275** seats, but **252** tickets are already sold. Can Mrs. Chang bring her class? How can you check the answer?

_____

9. Hockey sticks are on sale at a store. When the store opened there were **685** hockey sticks. By closing time **231** were left. How many hockey sticks were sold during the day?

_____

Test Prep ★ Mixed Review

10 This year 200 fewer cans were collected than last year. If **4,384** cans were collected last year, how many were collected this year?

    A 4,184   **C** 4,484

    B 4,284   **D** 5,384

11 Mae has 84 stamps in her stamp collection. What is that number rounded to the nearest ten?

    F 70   **H** 80

    G 75   **J** 85

Name _____

Sometimes you need to regroup when subtracting.

Example. Start with **231**.
Take away **116**.
How many blocks are left?

H	T	O
2	3	1
− 1	1	6

1. Not enough ones.
Regroup a ten.
Subtract the ones.

2. Subtract the tens.

3. Subtract the hundreds.

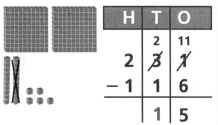

H	T	O
	2	11
2	3̶	1̶
− 1	1	6
		5

H	T	O
	2	11
2	3̶	1̶
− 1	1	6
	1	5

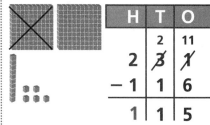

H	T	O
	2	11
2	3̶	1̶
− 1	1	6
1	1	5

The difference is **115**.

Find the difference.

1.

H	T	O
	5	14
8	6̶	4̶
− 4	2	8
	3	6

H	T	O
5	7	4
− 3	2	9

H	T	O
2	9	6
− 1	4	7

H	T	O
5	7	3
− 1	2	7

2.

H	T	O
6	9	8
− 3	2	9

H	T	O
4	6	2
− 2	3	4

H	T	O
9	3	5
− 4	2	6

H	T	O
5	9	7
− 4	5	9

3.

H	T	O
3	8	5
− 2	6	8

H	T	O
6	5	1
− 4	2	9

H	T	O
8	5	3
− 2	4	6

H	T	O
4	6	1
− 1	2	9

	Table Form		Short Form	Check

Table Form

H	T	O
	5	17
4	~~6~~	~~7~~
− 2	4	9
2	1	8

Short Form

$$\begin{array}{r} {}^{5\ 17}\\ 4\cancel{6}\cancel{7}\\ -\,2\,4\,9\\ \hline 2\,1\,8 \end{array}$$

Same

Check

$$\begin{array}{r} {}^{1}\\ 2\,1\,8\\ +\,2\,4\,9\\ \hline 4\,6\,7 \end{array}$$

Subtract. Add to check the answer.

4.

$$\begin{array}{r} {}^{6\ 11}\\ 8\cancel{7}\cancel{1}\\ -\,2\,4\,2\\ \hline \end{array} \quad \begin{array}{r} {}^{1}\\ 6\,2\,9\\ +\,2\,4\,2\\ \hline 8\,7\,1 \end{array}$$

$$\begin{array}{r} 8\,1\,6\\ -\,5\,0\,3\ +\ \underline{\quad}\\ \end{array} \quad \begin{array}{r} 8\,7\,2\\ -\,2\,3\,9\ +\ \underline{\quad}\\ \end{array} \quad \begin{array}{r} 8\,9\,6\\ -\,2\,7\,3\ +\ \underline{\quad}\\ \end{array}$$

5.

$$\begin{array}{r} 8\,4\,7\\ -\,3\,2\,9\ +\ \underline{\quad}\\ \end{array} \quad \begin{array}{r} 8\,9\,1\\ -\,4\,7\,8\ +\ \underline{\quad}\\ \end{array} \quad \begin{array}{r} 8\,9\,6\\ -\,6\,3\,8\ +\ \underline{\quad}\\ \end{array} \quad \begin{array}{r} 8\,8\,5\\ -\,5\,1\,9\ +\ \underline{\quad}\\ \end{array}$$

6.

$$\begin{array}{r} 7\,4\,8\\ -\,2\,2\,9\ +\ \underline{\quad}\\ \end{array} \quad \begin{array}{r} 6\,9\,1\\ -\,4\,7\,8\ +\ \underline{\quad}\\ \end{array} \quad \begin{array}{r} 3\,4\,7\\ -\,1\,2\,8\ +\ \underline{\quad}\\ \end{array} \quad \begin{array}{r} 5\,9\,4\\ -\,2\,3\,7\ +\ \underline{\quad}\\ \end{array}$$

Problem Solving Reasoning — Solve.

7. On Monday the Super Juice stand had **245** bottles of Banana Blast juice. If **126** bottles were sold, how many bottles of juice were left?

_____

8. Sing had **445** stickers in her book. She bought more stickers. Now she has **563**. How many stickers did she buy? How can you check your answer?

_____

Test Prep ★ Mixed Review

9 The pet store has 258 goldfish in a tank. What is that number rounded to the nearest hundred?

A 100

B 200

C 250

D 300

10 Which number is less than 15,341?

F 15,390

G 14,908

H 16,001

J 15,522

Regrouping Hundreds to Tens

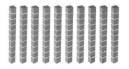

STANDARD

Remember:

1 hundred = **10** tens

Start with **419** blocks.
Take away **276**.
How many are left?

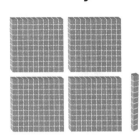

H	T	O
4	1	9
− 2	7	6

1. Subtract the ones.

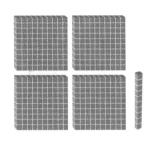

H	T	O
4	1	9
− 2	7	6
		3

2. Not enough tens, so regroup a hundred. Subtract the tens.

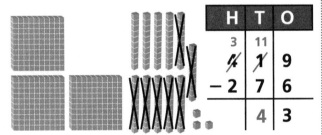

H	T	O
³4̸	¹¹1̸	9
− 2	7	6
	4	3

4 hundreds **1** ten =

3 hundred **11** tens

3. Subtract the hundreds.

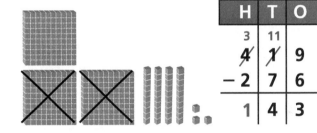

H	T	O
³4̸	¹¹1̸	9
− 2	7	6
1	4	3

The difference is **143.**

Subtract.

1.

H	T	O
⁸9̸	¹⁶6̸	4
− 1	9	2

H	T	O
7	8	8
− 2	9	4

H	T	O
3	4	8
− 1	8	2

H	T	O
5	3	8
− 1	8	7

2.

H	T	O
9	6	6
− 6	8	4

H	T	O
6	7	9
−	9	5

H	T	O
9	8	6
− 6	9	4

H	T	O
5	7	7
−	8	6

Subtract.

3.

H	T	O
⁴5̸	¹⁴4̸	7
− 1	8	3

H	T	O
8	4	2
− 1	9	1

H	T	O
5	7	2
− 2	9	1

H	T	O
4	6	2
− 1	8	2

H	T	O
6	4	2
− 2	8	1

Find the difference. Add to check the answer.

4.

$$
\begin{array}{r} {}^{3}\;{}^{17} \\ 4̸7̸3 \\ \times 182 \\ \hline 291 \end{array}
\qquad
\begin{array}{r} {}^{1}\\ 291 \\ +182 \\ \hline 473 \end{array}
\qquad
\begin{array}{r} 968 \\ -292 \\ \hline \end{array} +\rule{1.5cm}{0.4pt}
\qquad
\begin{array}{r} 284 \\ -\;91 \\ \hline \end{array} +\rule{1.5cm}{0.4pt}
\qquad
\begin{array}{r} 547 \\ -183 \\ \hline \end{array} +\rule{1.5cm}{0.4pt}
$$

5.

$$
\begin{array}{r} 942 \\ -351 \\ \hline \end{array} +\rule{1.5cm}{0.4pt}
\qquad
\begin{array}{r} 823 \\ -231 \\ \hline \end{array} +\rule{1.5cm}{0.4pt}
\qquad
\begin{array}{r} 786 \\ -372 \\ \hline \end{array} +\rule{1.5cm}{0.4pt}
\qquad
\begin{array}{r} 243 \\ -\;91 \\ \hline \end{array} +\rule{1.5cm}{0.4pt}
$$

Problem Solving Reasoning **Solve.**

6. Pablo counted **318** students in the cafeteria. If **146** were girls, how many were boys? How can you check your answer?

_____

7. Lakeside School has **439** students. In the school election only **298** students voted. How many students did not vote?

_____

 Quick Check

Subtract.

1.
$$\begin{array}{r} 789 \\ -256 \\ \hline \end{array}$$

2.
$$\begin{array}{r} 431 \\ -120 \\ \hline \end{array}$$

3.
$$\begin{array}{r} 647 \\ -533 \\ \hline \end{array}$$

4.
$$\begin{array}{r} 894 \\ -612 \\ \hline \end{array}$$

5.
$$\begin{array}{r} 572 \\ -135 \\ \hline \end{array}$$

6.
$$\begin{array}{r} 861 \\ -256 \\ \hline \end{array}$$

7.
$$\begin{array}{r} 341 \\ -219 \\ \hline \end{array}$$

8.
$$\begin{array}{r} 983 \\ -546 \\ \hline \end{array}$$

9.
$$\begin{array}{r} 638 \\ -152 \\ \hline \end{array}$$

10.
$$\begin{array}{r} 457 \\ -283 \\ \hline \end{array}$$

11.
$$\begin{array}{r} 925 \\ -641 \\ \hline \end{array}$$

12.
$$\begin{array}{r} 764 \\ -394 \\ \hline \end{array}$$

Work Space.

Regrouping Twice in Subtraction

Use what you have learned to regroup twice.

Example.

	H	T	O
	4	5	1
−	1	6	3

1. Not enough ones, so regroup a ten. Subtract the ones.

	H	T	O
		4	11
	4	5̷	1̷
−	1	6	3
			8

2. Not enough tens, so regroup a hundred. Subtract the tens.

	H	T	O
	3	14	11
	4̷	5̷	1̷
−	1	6	3
		8	8

3. Subtract the hundreds.

	H	T	O
	3	14	11
	4̷	5̷	1̷
−	1	6	3
	2	8	8

The difference is **288**.

> 1. Regroup a ten if needed. Subtract the ones.
> 2. Regroup a hundred if needed. Subtract the tens.
> 3. Subtract the hundreds.

Subtract.

1.

	H	T	O
	6	17	14
	7	8̷	4̷
−	4	9	9
	2	8	5

	H	T	O
	6	2	6
−	3	6	9

	H	T	O
	4	7	8
−	3	8	9

	H	T	O
	5	8	5
−	3	9	8

2.

	H	T	O
	3	1	5
−	1	7	8

	H	T	O
	9	7	1
−		8	3

	H	T	O
	7	6	2
−		8	6

	H	T	O
	1	3	5
−		5	7

Subtract. Add to check the answers.

3.
$$877 - 298 +$$ ____
$$452 - 287 +$$ ____
$$517 - 289 +$$ ____
$$815 - 456 +$$ ____

4.
$$538 - 139 +$$ ____
$$742 - 47 +$$ ____
$$345 - 279 +$$ ____
$$732 - 283 +$$ ____

5.
$$871 - 456 +$$ ____
$$254 - 88 +$$ ____
$$724 - 387 +$$ ____
$$543 - 87 +$$ ____

6.
$$951 - 475 +$$ ____
$$325 - 238 +$$ ____
$$846 - 469 +$$ ____
$$517 - 348 +$$ ____

Write <, >, or =.

7. 570 − 270 ◯ 300   150 ◯ 750 − 650   320 − 200 ◯ 180

Solve.

8. The difference between two numbers is greater than **350**. Could the two numbers be **862** and **496**? How do you find out?

_____

9. Bob starts with the number **785**. He subtracts a number with **6** ones, **9** tens, and **5** hundreds. How many times does he regroup? What is his answer?

_____

Test Prep ★ Mixed Review

10 There were 6,321 tickets sold for the concert. What is that number rounded to the nearest thousand?

    A 6,000   C 6,300

    B 6,200   D 7,000

11 The bakery sold 325 blueberry muffins and 167 banana muffins in one week. About how many muffins were sold altogether?

    F 650   H 500

    G 600   J 350

Subtracting from Zeros

Use what you know about regrouping to subract from zero.

Regroup a ten. Subtract.

1.

H	T	O
	7	10
6	8̸	0̸
− 3	4	3
3	3	7

H	T	O
	8	10
2	0̸	0̸
− 1	3	2
1	5	8

```
  470        580        870
- 247      - 415      - 431
```

2.
```
  990        340        560        560        470
- 264      - 116      - 329      - 118      - 235
```

3.
```
  680        790        980        470        990
- 147      - 269      - 342      - 131      - 455
```

Regroup a hundred. Subtract.

4.

H	T	O
7	10	
8̸	0̸	5
− 4	3	4
3	7	1

H	T	O
8	10	
9̸	0̸	7
− 3	4	3

```
  808        509        608
- 187      - 275      - 413
```

5.
```
  809        905        908        703        605
- 427      - 352      - 297      - 131      - 341
```

6.
```
  906        908        509        406        606
- 153      - 387      - 193      - 174      - 365
```

7.
```
  404        601        304        701        209
-  81      - 120      - 113      -  90      - 145
```

Regroup a hundred and a ten. Subtract.

8.

H	T	O
	9	
4	~~10~~	10
~~5~~	~~0~~	0
− 2	3	5
2	6	5

H	T	O
	9	
5	~~10~~	12
~~6~~	~~0~~	2
− 2	2	6
3	7	6

$$500 - 145$$

$$700 - 339$$

$$900 - 567$$

9.
$$300 - 114 \qquad 500 - 316 \qquad 800 - 427 \qquad 400 - 138 \qquad 300 - 199$$

10.
$$700 - 458 \qquad 900 - 624 \qquad 800 - 112 \qquad 500 - 248 \qquad 600 - 335$$

Write <, >, or =.

11. $255 \bigcirc 560 - 100$ $\qquad$ $655 \bigcirc 900 - 300$ $\qquad$ $650 - 150 \bigcirc 343$

Problem Solving Reasoning — Solve.

12. A soccer league needed to sell **650** candles to raise money for new uniforms. The players already sold **315** candles. How many more do they need to sell?

13. Sadie drove to the beach. When she started her trip the car showed **672** miles. When she returned, she read **708** miles. How many miles did she travel? Do you add or subtract? Why?

Test Prep ★ Mixed Review

14 Maria had $4.56. She earned $3.50 more. How much money does Maria have in all?

A $7.16 $\qquad$ C $8.06

B $7.96 $\qquad$ D $8.16

15 The pilot flew 2,859 miles in a week. The following week he flew 1,042 miles. How many miles did he fly in all?

F 3,891 $\qquad$ H 3,987

G 3,901 $\qquad$ J 3,991

Subtraction with Money

You can use what you learned about subtracting hundreds, tens, and ones to subtract money.

Example.

$$\begin{array}{r} \$2.37 \\ -\ \ .64 \\ \hline \end{array}$$

1. Subtract the pennies.	2. Regroup. Subtract the dimes.	3. Subtract the dollars.
$$\begin{array}{r} \$2.37 \\ -\ \ .64 \\ \hline 3 \end{array}$$	$$\begin{array}{r} {}^{1}\ {}^{13} \\ \$\cancel{2}.\cancel{3}7 \\ -\ \ .64 \\ \hline 73 \end{array}$$	$$\begin{array}{r} {}^{1}\ {}^{13} \\ \$\cancel{2}.\cancel{3}7 \\ -\ \ .64 \\ \hline \$1.73 \end{array}$$

Use a **$** and **.** in the answer.

Complete the table.

	Had	Bought	Change
1.	$2.50	$2.39	$$\begin{array}{r} \$2.50 \\ -\ 2.39 \\ \hline \$\ .11 \end{array} \quad \$.11$$
2.	$3.00	$2.57	
3.	$5.00	$2.81	
4.	$7.75	$6.84	

Do the items cost *more than*, *less than*, or *exactly* ten dollars?

5.

_____ _____ _____ _____

To find the missing number, we subtract the given number from the total.

```
  9   7   7          977
−   4   9   2      − 485
  4   8   5          492
```

To find the missing total, we add the given number and the difference.

```
  9   3   8          792
−   7   9   2      + 146
  1   4   6          938
```

Complete.

6.

```
  9   6   4              ____ ____  8        $5 . 3   7
−  ____ ____ ____      −  3    7   6        − ____ . ____  5
  5   8   1              2    7  ____        $1 . 7   2
```

Solve.

7. Ahmed buys a tie and a pair of socks. The pair of socks cost **$6.50** less than the tie. The tie costs **$9.49**. What is the price of the pair of socks?

_____

8. Elena buys a video for **$9.20**. She gives the clerk **$10.00**. She gets **3** quarters as change. Did she get the correct change?

_____

✓ Quick Check

Subtract.

1.
```
  7 3 5
− 1 6 8
```

2.
```
  4 7 2
− 2 9 3
```

3.
```
  5 0 3
− 1 8 2
```

Work Space.

4.
```
  8 0 0
− 4 3 7
```

5.
```
  $4 . 0 6
− 2 . 3 3
```

6.
```
  $7 . 8 0
− 5 . 6 7
```

Sometimes you can act out or model a problem to help you solve it. Objects that are easy to find and use can help you act out the problem.

> **Problem**
>
> John and three friends ordered a square pizza. John wants to cut the pizza equally into **4** square pieces. How many times does he need to cut the pizza?

1 Understand   As you reread the problem, ask yourself questions.

- How many people are sharing pizza?

  John and his 3 friends make 4 people.

- What shape will each piece be?

  He wants each piece to be square in shape.

2 Decide   Choose a method for solving the problem.

- Use a square piece of paper to act out the problem.

- What does the square piece of paper represent?

  _____

- What could you do to show a cut?

  _____

Pretend the square piece of paper is the pizza

First fold

3 Solve   Use your model.

- How many times do you need to fold the square of paper to get **4** small squares? _____

- How many times will the pizza need to be cut in half to make **4** small square pieces? _____

4 Look back   Draw a line on the folds in the paper to check your answer.

- How did folding the paper help you decide how many times to cut the pizza in half?

  _____

Use the Act It Out Strategy or any other strategy you have learned.

1. John received **5** coins as change after buying the pizza. The coins were worth **50** cents. What coins could he have been given?

Think: Which facts are important?

_____

_____

Answer: _____

_____

2. JANE'S PIZZA PARLOR is written on the pizza box. The letters are in different colors. J is green, A is blue, N is red. If the color pattern continues, what is the color of the last letter on the box?

Think: How can you use the Act It Out Strategy.

_____

Answer: _____

3. Julie made rows of counters with a box of **100** counters. Each row she made had one more counter than the row before it. The first row had **1** counter and the last row had **6**.

(a) How many counters did Julie use? _____

(b) How many were left in the box? _____

4. There are orange juice and grape juice boxes in the cooler. There are **12** juice boxes in all. There are two times as many grape juice boxes as orange juice boxes. How many orange juice boxes are there? How many grape juice boxes?

_____

_____

Extend Your Thinking

5. If you had cut the square pizza in half on the diagonal, and then in half again, what would be the shape of each small pizza?

_____

6. Look at problem **3** again. When Julie completed the pattern with the counters, what shape did she get?

_____

Name _____

STANDARD

Estimating can also be used to check differences.

Example
$$48$$
$$-37$$

48 rounds to → 5 0
− 3 7 rounds to → − 4 0
The estimated difference is about **1 0**

$$48$$
$$-37$$
The actual difference is **1 1**

Round to the nearest ten. Estimate each difference.

1. 7 8 →
− 1 5 → − _____

67 →
− 2 8 → − _____

5 4 →
− 1 6 → − _____

2. 8 6 →
− 1 9 → − _____

3 2 →
− 9 → − _____

4 8 →
− 3 2 → − _____

Round to the nearest hundred. Estimate each difference.

3. 2 9 1 →
− 9 7 → − _____

4 2 6 →
− 1 2 3 → − _____

5 3 9 →
− 1 2 1 → − _____

Use estimation to find the correct answers.
Watch the signs.

4. 8 0
− 1 9   A. **71**   B. **99**   C. **61**   D. **51**

5. 6 8
+ 2 9   A. **87**   B. **97**   C. **39**   D. **49**

6. 1 9 2
− 1 8 9   A. **13**   B. **181**   C. **21**   D. **3**

7. 5 6
3 3
+ 8   A. **79**   B. **97**   C. **41**   D. **87**

Solve. Use estimating to check your answers.

	Actual Work	Estimates

8. Kateri cut **45** strips of colored paper for an art project. She needs **60** strips in all. How many more strips must she cut?

_____

9. Chum took **32** hickory nuts, **49** acorns, and **28** horse chestnuts to a meeting of the Science Club. How many nuts did he take to the meeting?

_____

Problem Solving Reasoning **Solve.**

10. Ali needs **44** cups for a science project. He has **24** cups at school. He brings **20** cups from home. Should he add or estimate to find out if he has enough cups? Why?

_____

11. Letoya adds **237** and **415**. She gets **852**. Is her answer correct? How do you know? Estimate to find if her answer is reasonable.

_____

Test Prep ★ Mixed Review

12 Juan has 847 baseball cards. Which number shows how many cards Juan has, rounded to the nearest ten?

A 800
B 840
C 850
D 900

13 Ward's Farm has 285 apple trees and 132 pear trees. How many more apple trees than pear trees does the farm have?

F 143
G 153
H 317
J 417

Subtracting with thousands is like subtracting with hundreds.

> 1. Subtract the ones.
> 2. Subtract the tens.
> 3. Subtract the hundreds.
> 4. Subtract the thousands.
>   Regroup when needed.

Here are some examples.

Table Form:

Th	H	T	O
	6	16	
8	7̶	6̶	5
− 2	5	8	3
6	1	8	2

Short Form:

$$\begin{array}{r} \overset{8\ 10}{7,9\not{0}6} \\ -\ 1,856 \\ \hline 6,050 \end{array}$$

Sometimes there are not enough hundreds.
Regroup **1** thousand as **10** hundreds.
Then subtract.

Th	H	T	O
4	16		
5̶	6̶	3	9
− 2	7	1	0
2	9	2	9

$$\begin{array}{r} \overset{4\ 10\ \ 5\ 13}{\$5\not{0}.6\not{3}} \\ -\ 49.28 \\ \hline \$1.35 \end{array}$$

Subtract.

1.
$$\begin{array}{r} 9,250 \\ -\ 7,140 \\ \hline \end{array} \qquad \begin{array}{r} \$75.20 \\ -\ 63.80 \\ \hline \end{array} \qquad \begin{array}{r} 7,725 \\ -\ 6,317 \\ \hline \end{array} \qquad \begin{array}{r} 2,367 \\ -\ 1,400 \\ \hline \end{array} \qquad \begin{array}{r} \$33.20 \\ -\ 20.32 \\ \hline \end{array}$$

2.
$$\begin{array}{r} 8,729 \\ -\ \ \ \ 488 \\ \hline \end{array} \qquad \begin{array}{r} 2,900 \\ -\ 1,875 \\ \hline \end{array} \qquad \begin{array}{r} 2,767 \\ -\ 1,829 \\ \hline \end{array} \qquad \begin{array}{r} \$96.00 \\ -\ 84.28 \\ \hline \end{array} \qquad \begin{array}{r} 9,080 \\ -\ 2,098 \\ \hline \end{array}$$

3.
$$\begin{array}{r} \$84.21 \\ -\ 27.19 \\ \hline \end{array} \qquad \begin{array}{r} 2,898 \\ -\ 1,980 \\ \hline \end{array} \qquad \begin{array}{r} 7,532 \\ -\ 4,685 \\ \hline \end{array} \qquad \begin{array}{r} \$50.00 \\ -\ \ 2.72 \\ \hline \end{array} \qquad \begin{array}{r} 3,780 \\ -\ \ \ \ 99 \\ \hline \end{array}$$

**Problem Solving
Reasoning**   Solve.

Books Sold

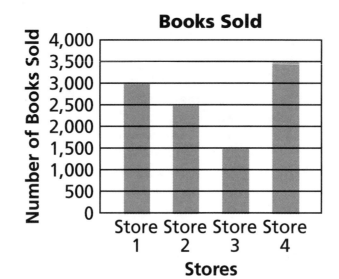

4. Which store sold the most books? Which sold the least books? How did you find out?

_____

_____

5. How many more books must Store 3 sell to sell a total of 2,500 books?

_____

 Quick Check

Round to the nearest ten. Estimate the difference.   Work Space.

1.   6 7 →
     − 4 5 → − _____

2.   4 3 →
     − 2 1 → − _____

Round to the nearest hundred. Estimate the difference.

3.   8 6 7 →
     − 2 4 5 → _____

4.   5 3 5 →
     − 3 1 9 → − _____

Subtract.

5.   5 , 0 7 3
     − 1 , 2 4 5

6.   9 , 6 7 4
     − 5 , 1 2 8

7.   6 , 2 7 0
     − 3 , 5 2 7

The map shows the number of miles between some cities in New Mexico. Use the map to help you estimate and solve the problems.

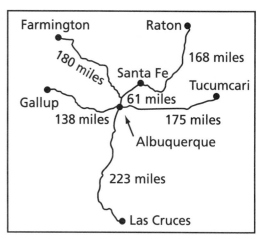

Mr. and Mrs. Davis are driving from Santa Fe to Tucumcari. They don't like to drive more than **300** miles a day. Can they make the trip in one day?

First find the total distance of the trip. Then compare that distance to **300**.

> **6 1** miles (Santa Fe to Albuquerque)
> **+ 1 7 5** miles (Albuquerque to Tucumcari)
> **2 3 6** miles (Total distance traveled)

236 < 300   They can make the trip in one day.

Tips to Remember:

1. Understand	2. Decide	3. Solve	4. Look back

- Think about what the problem is asking you to do. What information does the problem give you? What do you need to find out?
- What information can you get from the map?
- Try to remember a real life situation that might help you answer the problem.

Solve.

1. If the Davises drive from Albuquerque to Raton would they drive more than **300** miles?

Think: Do you need to find an actual answer or an estimate to answer this question?

_____

_____

Answer: _____

2. It costs **$17.39** to fill the tank with gas. Mrs. Davis uses a **$20** bill to pay for the gas. How much change will she get?

Think: Do you need to estimate or find the actual difference to make sure the change is correct?

_____

Answer: _____

Solve.

3. The sign for the Navajo Museum says tours start at noon, **2:00** P.M., and **4:00** P.M. How many tours do they have each afternoon?

_____

4. It is **11:30** A.M. and the Davises are an hour away from the museum. What is the earliest tour they can take? Use the picture Mrs. Davis made to help you decide.

_____

5. The Davises decided to stop and eat lunch before the hour drive to the museum. Lunch took a little over an hour. Will they still make the same tour time?

_____

6. Museum tours cost **$4.95** per person. Mr. and Mrs. Davis each have a dollar off coupon. Mrs. Davis gave the cashier **$10**. How much change will she receive?

_____

7. Which of the cities on the map are more than **450** miles apart?

_____

_____

_____

8. What problems did Mrs. Davis' picture help you solve?

_____

_____

Extend Your Thinking

9. Use the map to find two cities that are less than **300** miles apart, but more than **175** miles apart. What are the cities?

_____

_____

_____

10. Look back at problem **7**. Did you find an estimate or find an exact answer to solve this problem? Why?

_____

_____

_____

Subtract.

1. $\$8.28$
   -6.89

2. 607
   -429

3. $\$2.49$
   -1.27

4. $\$7.08$
   $-.59$

5. 421
   -9

6. $\$7.04$
   -1.19

7. 639
   -157

8. 809
   -276

9. $\$4.58$
   -1.96

10. $\$18.00$
    -16.91

11. 988
    -709

12. 208
    -29

13. 873
    -625

14. 470
    -235

15. $1,638$
    -58

16. $\$9.80$
    $-.99$

17. $1,800$
    -199

18. 500
    -224

19. $1,700$
    -469

20. $5,300$
    $-4,179$

Round to the nearest ten. Estimate the difference.

21. $56 \rightarrow$ ____
    $-28 \rightarrow -$ ____

22. $89 \rightarrow$ ____
    $-31 \rightarrow -$ ____

23. $182 \rightarrow$ ____
    $-54 \rightarrow -$ ____

24. Al has **3** pennies. Sal has **3** nickels. Hal has **3** quarters. If the friends share their coins, what coins would each friend have? How much money would they each have?

_____

25. Mr. Tanaka puts **8** jars side by side on the bottom row. He puts **7** jars on top of the **8** jars. Then he puts **6** jars on top of the **7** jars. How many more rows will he need until there is **1** jar on the top row?

_____

Name _____

1 Earl bought balloons for a party. He got 26 red, 48 blue, and 31 white balloons. How many balloons did Earl buy in all?

A 115

B 105

C 95

D 85

E NH

2 On Saturday 1,539 people visited the zoo. On Sunday 2,078 visited the zoo. How many people visited the zoo on both days?

F 539

G 3,507

H 3,517

J 3,627

K NH

3 Lake Ontario is 804 feet deep, and Lake Huron is 752 feet deep. How many feet deeper is Lake Ontario than Lake Huron?

A 32

B 52

C 102

D 142

E NH

4 Which number means 200,000 + 50,000 + 4,000 + 8?

F 254,800

G 254,008

H 25,480

J 2,548

5 The area of the state of Iowa is 56,276 square miles. What is the value of the digit 5 in the number?

A 5 tens

B 5 thousands

C 5 hundreds

D 5 ten thousands

6 A giant sequoia tree in California is 276 feet tall. What is 276 rounded to the nearest ten?

F 300

G 280

H 270

J 200

UNIT 4 • TABLE OF CONTENTS

Multiplication to 5

CALIFORNIA STANDARDS	Lesson	Page
NS 2.2; A/F 1.1	**1** Algebra • **Addition and Multiplication**	89–90
NS 2.2; A/F 1.1	**2** Algebra • **Multiplying with 2**	91–92
A/F 1.1, 1.5	**3** Algebra • **Commutative and Associative Properties of Multiplication**	93–94
NS 2.2, 2.6; A/F 1.1 2.2	**4** Algebra • **Multiplying with 1 and 0**	95–96
NS 2.2; A/F 1.1, 1.5	**5** Algebra • **Multiplying with 5**	97–99
NS 2.2; A/F 1.1	**6** Algebra • **Multiplying with 4**	100–102
MR 2.3	**7** Problem Solving Strategy: **Make a List**	103–104
NS 2.2; A/F 1.1	**8** Algebra • **Multiplying with 3**	105–106
NS 2.2; A/F 1.1	**9** Algebra • **Multiplying with 10**	107–108
NS 2.8; MR 2.3	**10** Problem Solving Application: **Use a Pictograph**	109–110
	• Unit 4 Review	111
	• Cumulative Review ★ Test Prep	112

Dear Family,

Our class will spend the next few weeks learning about multiplication of whole numbers and the properties of multiplication.

You can expect to see homework that provides practice with using multiplication properties to learn multiplication facts. Here is a sample of the commutative and associative properties of multiplication.

Using the Commutative Property of Multiplication

The commutative property is also called the order property. When multiplying, changing the order of the factors does not change the product.

Example: $6 \times 9 = 54$ $9 \times 6 = 54$
└─── same ───┘

Therefore, if your student knows the multiplication fact $3 \times 4 = 12$, he or she will also know that $4 \times 3 = 12$.

Using the Associative Property of Multiplication

The associative property is also called the grouping property. When multiplying three or more factors, changing the grouping of the factors does not change the product. Parentheses are used to show the grouping.

Example: $1 \times (9 \times 3) = (1 \times 9) \times 3$

$1 \times 27 = 9 \times 3$

$27 = 27$
same

During this unit, students need to continue practicing multiplication facts.

Sincerely,

Addition and Multiplication

4 groups of **2**

2 + 2 + 2 + 2 = 8

We can write an addition sentence to describe the groups. We can also write a multiplication sentence to describe them.

4 twos = **8**

4 × 2 = 8

factor × factor = product

We read this as "Four times two equals eight."

Try these. Complete the number sentences.

1.

2 + 2 + 2 = _____

3 twos = **_____**

Multiplication Sentence

3 × 2 = _____

3 groups of **2 = _____**

2.

2 + 2 + 2 + 2 + 2 + 2 = _____

6 twos = **_____**

6 × 2 = _____

6 groups of **2 = _____**

3.

2 + 2 + 2 + 2 + 2 = _____

5 twos = **_____**

5 × 2 = _____

5 groups of **2 = _____**

4.

2 + 2 + 2 + 2 + 2 + 2 + 2 = _____

7 twos = **_____**

7 × 2 = _____

7 groups of **2 = _____**

Complete.

5.

2 + 2 + 2 + 2 + 2 + 2 + 2 + 2 = _____

8 groups of 2 = _____

___8___ × ___2___ = _____

6.

2 + 2 = _____

2 groups of 2 = _____

_____ × _____ = _____

7.

0 = _____

0 groups of 2 = _____

_____ × _____ = _____

| Problem Solving |
| Reasoning |

Solve.

8. Ayesha puts **2** rows of cards on the table. There are **2** cards in each row. Draw a picture to show how the cards look. How many cards are on the table?

_____

9. Dina writes:
2 + 2 + 2 + 2 + 2 + 2 = 12
How can she write the addition sentence as a multiplication sentence?

_____

Test Prep ★ Mixed Review

10 Mrs. Baron's class sold 2,418 raffle tickets. What is the value of 1 in 2,418?

A one

B ten

C one hundred

D one thousand

11 A zoo purchased 5,855 pounds of grain to feed the animals. What is that number rounded to nearest thousand?

F 5,000

G 5,800

H 5,900

J 6,000

Name _____

number of groups

number of turtles in each group

number of turtles in all

3 × **2** = **6** multiplication sentence

factors   product

factor × factor = product

You can use an array to model multiplication another way.

2 groups { • • • • • • • •

4 in a group

2 × **4** = 8

number   number   in all
of groups in a group

4 ← **number in a group**
× 2 ← **number of groups**
8 ← **in all**

The number line shows the multiplication facts for **2**.

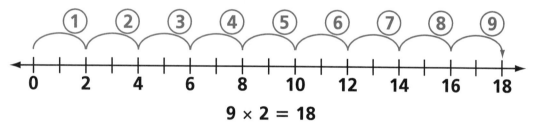

9 × 2 = 18

Write the product or missing factor.

1. 2 × _____ = 4   3 × _____ = 6   0 × 2 = _____

2. 2 × _____ = 2   5 × _____ = 10   1 × 2 = _____

3. 2 × _____ = 8   9 × _____ = 18   2 × 2 = _____

4. 2 × _____ = 6   7 × _____ = 14   3 × 2 = _____

5. 2 × _____ = 10   4 × _____ = 8   4 × 2 = _____

6. 2 × _____ = 14   6 × _____ = 12   5 × 2 = _____

7. 2 × _____ = 18   2 × _____ = 4   6 × 2 = _____

Look at the arrays. Write the multiplication two ways.

8. ● ●
   ● ●
   ● ●

$3 \times 2 = \boxed{}$

$\begin{array}{r} 2 \\ \times\, 3 \\ \hline \end{array}$

9. ● ● ● ● ●
   ● ● ● ● ●
   ● ● ● ● ●

$\underline{} \times \underline{} = \boxed{}$

$\begin{array}{r} \times \\ \hline \end{array}$

Write the product or missing factor.

10.

$\begin{array}{r} 2 \\ \times\, 3 \\ \hline \end{array}$
$\begin{array}{r} 2 \\ \times\, 5 \\ \hline \end{array}$
$\begin{array}{r} 6 \\ \times\, 2 \\ \hline \end{array}$
$\begin{array}{r} \boxed{9} \\ \times\, \boxed{} \\ \hline 18 \end{array}$
$\begin{array}{r} \boxed{} \\ \times\, 2 \\ \hline 14 \end{array}$
$\begin{array}{r} \boxed{} \\ \times\, 6 \\ \hline 12 \end{array}$
$\begin{array}{r} \boxed{} \\ \times\, 8 \\ \hline 16 \end{array}$

11.

$\begin{array}{r} 8 \\ \times\, 2 \\ \hline \end{array}$
$\begin{array}{r} 2 \\ \times\, 0 \\ \hline \end{array}$
$\begin{array}{r} 2 \\ \times\, 7 \\ \hline \end{array}$
$\begin{array}{r} \boxed{} \\ \times\, 2 \\ \hline 2 \end{array}$
$\begin{array}{r} \boxed{9} \\ \times\, \boxed{} \\ \hline 18 \end{array}$
$\begin{array}{r} \boxed{2} \\ \times\, \boxed{} \\ \hline 10 \end{array}$
$\begin{array}{r} \boxed{} \\ \times\, 4 \\ \hline 8 \end{array}$

Problem Solving Reasoning

Solve.

12. The Flower Depot sells **1** flowerpot for **$2**, **2** flowerpots for **$4**, and **3** for **$6**. If the pattern continues how much do **5** flowerpots cost?

_____

13. Irma and Ito went shopping at the Flower Depot. Irma bought **6** pots and Ito bought **9** pots. Each pot costs **$2**. Circle the statement that helps you know who spent more money.

$6 \times 2 < 18$ $2 \times 6 > 9$

14. During a game, Ping scores **4** baskets. For each basket she gets **2** points. Did Ping score more or less than **10** points?

_____

15. I am a number. If you multiply me by **2**, you get **18**. What number am I? Is **18** a sum or a product?

_____

Test Prep ★ Mixed Review

16 Eva has to put 345 new books on the shelves. She has already put 182 books on the shelves. How many more books does she have to put on the shelves?

  A 547   **C** 243

  B 527   **D** 163

17 Leia paid $6.25 for some art supplies. She gave the clerk a $10.00 bill. How much change will Leia receive?

  F $2.75   **H** $3.85

  G $3.75   **J** $4.75

Commutative and Associative Properties of Multiplication

You can use what you know about the properties of addition, to learn about the properties of multiplication.

Commutative Property of Addition

$3 + 2 = 5$ $2 + 3 = 5$

← same →

Changing the **order** of the addends does not change the sum.

Commutative Property of Multiplication

4 twos   2 fours
$4 \times 2 = 8$ $2 \times 4 = 8$

← same →

Changing the **order** of the factors does not change the product.

Find the products. Then show the commutative property of multiplication.

1. $5 \times 2 = $ ____ $7 \times 2 = $ ____ $3 \times 2 = $ ____

$2 \times 5 = $ ____ $2 \times 7 = $ ____   ____ $\times$ ____ $= $ ____

2. $4 \times 2 = $ ____ $9 \times 2 = $ ____ $6 \times 2 = $ ____

____ $\times$ ____ $= $ ____   ____ $\times$ ____ $= $ ____   ____ $\times$ ____ $= $ ____

3. $1 \times 2 = $ ____ $2 \times 4 = $ ____ $2 \times 7 = $ ____

____ $\times$ ____ $= $ ____   ____ $\times$ ____ $= $ ____   ____ $\times$ ____ $= $ ____

4. $2 \times 8 = $ ____ $2 \times 5 = $ ____ $2 \times 9 = $ ____

____ $\times$ ____ $= $ ____   ____ $\times$ ____ $= $ ____   ____ $\times$ ____ $= $ ____

Find the products.

5. $4 \times 2 = $ ____ $2 \times 5 = $ ____ $6 \times 2 = $ ____

$2 \times 4 = $ ____ $5 \times 2 = $ ____ $2 \times 6 = $ ____

Associative Property of Addition

Add these first

$$(1 + 4) + 5 = 1 + (4 + 5)$$

$$5 + 5 = 1 + 9$$

$$10 = 10$$

Changing the **grouping** of the addends does not change the sum.

Associative Property of Multiplication

Multiply these first

$$(2 \times 3) \times 4 = 2 \times (3 \times 4)$$

$$6 \times 4 = 2 \times 12$$

$$24 = 24$$

Changing the **grouping** of the factors does not change the product.

Complete. Always work in the parentheses first.

6. $(2 \times 3) \times 1 =$

$\underline{6} \times \underline{1} = \underline{}$

or

$2 \times (3 \times 1) =$

$\underline{2} \times \underline{} = \underline{6}$

$(4 \times 2) \times 1 =$

$\underline{} \times \underline{} = \underline{}$

or

$4 \times (2 \times 1) =$

$\underline{} \times \underline{} = \underline{}$

$(5 \times 1) \times 2 =$

$\underline{} \times \underline{} = \underline{}$

or

$5 \times (1 \times 2) =$

$\underline{} \times \underline{} = \underline{}$

Problem Solving Reasoning **Solve.**

7. Write two number sentences using the factors **4** and **2**. Is the product the same? Why?

_____

_____

8. Raul says **1 × 2 × 3 = 6**. Fran says **3 × 1 × 2** is **8**. Is she correct? What property can help you find out?

_____

 Quick Check

Complete.

1. $2 + 2 + 2 + 2 + 2 =$ _____

$5 \times 2 =$ _____

2. $2 + 2 =$ _____

$2 \times 2 =$ _____

3. _____ $\times 2 = 6$

4. _____ $\times 2 = 16$

5. $(2 \times 2) \times 4 =$ _____

$2 \times (2 \times 4) =$ _____

6. $\begin{array}{r} 9 \\ \times 2 \\ \hline \end{array}$ $\begin{array}{r} 2 \\ \times 9 \\ \hline \end{array}$

Work Space.

Here are some special properties to remember when multiplying with 1 and 0.

1 × 4 = 4
1 group of **4** balloons

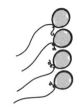

4 × 1 = 4
4 groups of **1** balloon

1 × 3 = 3
1 group of **3** balloons

1 times a given number equals that number.

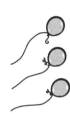

3 × 1 = 3
3 groups of **1** balloon

Any given number times **1** equals that number.

1 × 4 = 4 and **4 × 1 = 4**
1 × 3 = 3 and **3 × 1 = 3**

These are examples of the commutative property of multiplication, because changing the order of the factors does not change the product.

2 zeros

2 × 0 = [0]

Any number times **0** equals **0**.

There are no groups of **4**.

0 fours

0 × 4 = [0]

0 times any number equals **0**.

Use the commutative property to write a related multiplication fact.

1. **5 × 1 = 5** so _____   **1 × 8 = 8** so _____   **4 × 1 = 4** so _____

2. **1 × 6 = 6** so _____   **7 × 1 = 7** so _____   **1 × 3 = 3** so _____

Write the products.

3. 1 × 0 = _____   1 × 1 = _____   6 × 1 = _____

4. 2 × 1 = _____   0 × 2 = _____   1 × 8 = _____

5. 3 × 1 = _____   1 × 3 = _____   7 × 0 = _____

6. 4 × 0 = _____   1 × 4 = _____   5 × 1 = _____

7. 5 × 0 = _____   1 × 5 = _____   0 × 3 = _____

8. 6 × 1 = _____   0 × 6 = _____   1 × 9 = _____

Find the products.

9.

6	1	3	5	1	2	0	7	8	0
$\times\,0$	$\times\,9$	$\times\,1$	$\times\,0$	$\times\,1$	$\times\,1$	$\times\,4$	$\times\,1$	$\times\,1$	$\times\,6$

Complete the multiplication table.

10.

×	0	1	2	3	4	5	6	7	8	9
0	0	0								
1	0	1								
2	0	2	4							

Write + or ×.

11. 1 ☐ 1 = 2   1 ☐ 8 = 8   6 ☐ 1 = 7

12. 3 ☐ 0 = 3   0 ☐ 5 = 0   1 ☐ 1 = 2

13. 7 ☐ 1 = 7   1 ☐ 4 = 5   9 ☐ 0 = 9

Problem Solving Reasoning Solve.

14. Tina planted **1** row of carrots. The row had **8** carrot plants. How many carrot plants did Tina have? How do you know?

_____

_____

15. Max has **5** horses. He buys horse shoes for all their hoofs. How can you find the total number of horseshoes by skip-counting? by multiplying?

_____

Test Prep ★ Mixed Review

16 Manuel used 300 blocks to build a tower. His sister used 157 blocks to build a tower. How many fewer blocks did Manuel's sister use?

A 43   C 153

B 143   D 253

17 A store usually sells a sofa for $879. It is on sale for $629. About how much money would you save buying the sofa on sale?

F $1400   H $300

G $400   J $100

You can use skip-counting to multiply with 5.

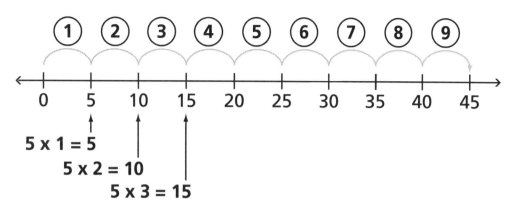

$5 \times 1 = 5$

$5 \times 2 = 10$

$5 \times 3 = 15$

$\begin{array}{r} 1 \\ \times 5 \\ \hline 5 \end{array}$ fish in a group
groups
fish in all

$\begin{array}{r} 5 \\ \times 2 \\ \hline 10 \end{array}$ cherries in a group
groups
cherries in all

Use the number line above.

1. What pattern do you see in the ones place of the products?

_____

2. If you skip-count one more time what will the next product be? _____

Use the commutative property. Write related multiplication facts.

3.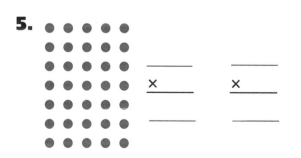

$4 \times 5 = 20$

_____ × _____ = _____

4.

$\begin{array}{r} 5 \\ \times 3 \\ \hline 15 \end{array}$ $\begin{array}{r} \\ \times \\ \hline \end{array}$

5.

× _____   × _____

_____   _____

6.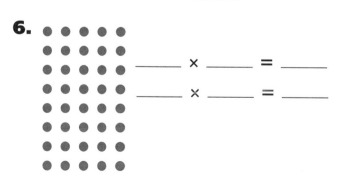

_____ × _____ = _____

_____ × _____ = _____

Find the products.

7. $3 \times 5 =$ _____ $4 \times 1 =$ _____ $8 \times 5 =$ _____ $2 \times 7 =$ _____

8. $4 \times 2 =$ _____ $1 \times 5 =$ _____ $7 \times 1 =$ _____ $8 \times 2 =$ _____

Find the products.

9.
$$\begin{array}{cccccccc} 5 & 8 & 6 & 5 & 2 & 7 & 5 & 5 \\ \times 2 & \times 5 & \times 5 & \times 5 & \times 5 & \times 5 & \times 6 & \times 0 \end{array}$$

10.
$$\begin{array}{cccccccc} 5 & 9 & 6 & 5 & 5 & 0 & 5 & 3 \\ \times 9 & \times 5 & \times 2 & \times 4 & \times 1 & \times 5 & \times 8 & \times 5 \end{array}$$

Skip count to tell how much. Write a multiplication sentence.

11.

_____ $\times$ _____ ¢ = _____ ¢

12.

_____ $\times$ _____ ¢ = _____ ¢

Use >, <, or =.

13. $5 \times 3 \bigcirc 3 \times 2$ $5 \times 0 \bigcirc 0 \times 2$ $2 \times 2 \bigcirc 1 \times 4$

14. $0 \times 5 \bigcirc 0 \times 1$ $1 \times 0 \bigcirc 0 \times 0$ $6 \times 5 \bigcirc 9 \times 2$

15. $2 \times 3 \bigcirc 5 \times 1$ $2 \times 9 \bigcirc 5 \times 5$ $2 \times \$0.50 \bigcirc 1 \times \$.05$

16. $8 \times 1 \bigcirc 2 \times 5$ $2 \times 3 \bigcirc 3 \times 2$ $5 \times \$.05 \bigcirc 3 \times \$.05$

Match.

17.			**18.**			**19.**		
5×2	6		6×5	35		5×0	5	
0×1	30		9×1	10		2×8	4	
2×3	10		7×5	30		5×1	16	
5×6	0		4×5	0		1×4	8	
1×9	20		2×5	9		5×3	0	
5×4	35		3×2	20		2×4	40	
5×7	9		1×0	6		5×8	15	

**Problem Solving
Reasoning**

Solve.

20. A number sentence has a product of **25** and a factor of **5**. What is the missing factor?

_____

21. A box contains **6** rows. In each row there are **5** cans. Write a number sentence that tells how many cans in all.

_____

22. Ruby makes **5** piles of pennies. Each pile has **7** pennies. How many pennies does Ruby have? How did you find the answer?

_____

_____

23. Jay and **4** friends share some baseball cards equally. Each one got **9** cards. How many cards were there in all?

_____

Test Prep ★ Mixed Review

24 Lucia wants to buy a notebook that costs $5.85 and a ruler that costs $1.19. How much will Lucia spend on these items?

A $3.66   C $6.94

B $4.76   D $7.04

25 The workers washed 471 windows on Monday and 364 windows on Tuesday. About how many windows did they wash both days?

F 100   H 900

G 200   J 1000

You can use what you know about multiplying with 2 to help you multiply with 4.

Find **4 × 6.**

Think: **2 × 6 = 12**

Then double the product.

So, **4 × 6 = 24**

You can use the commutative property to find related multiplication sentences. Since **4 × 6 = 24** then **6 × 4 = 24**.

4 × 6 = 24 and **6 × 4 = 24** are related multiplication sentences.

Complete. Write related multiplication sentences.

1.

_____ × _____ = _____

_____ × _____ = _____

2.
_____ × _____ = _____

_____ × _____ = _____

3.
_____ × _____ = _____

_____ × _____ = _____

4.
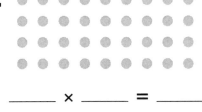
_____ × _____ = _____

_____ × _____ = _____

Name _____

Find the products.

5. $2 \times 7 =$ _____ $2 \times 5 =$ _____ $2 \times 9 =$ _____

$4 \times 7 =$ _____ $4 \times 5 =$ _____ $4 \times 9 =$ _____

6.

$\begin{array}{r} 1 \\ \times 4 \\ \hline \end{array}$ $\begin{array}{r} 3 \\ \times 4 \\ \hline \end{array}$ $\begin{array}{r} 9 \\ \times 4 \\ \hline \end{array}$ $\begin{array}{r} 4 \\ \times 0 \\ \hline \end{array}$ $\begin{array}{r} 4 \\ \times 6 \\ \hline \end{array}$ $\begin{array}{r} 2 \\ \times 4 \\ \hline \end{array}$ $\begin{array}{r} 4 \\ \times 4 \\ \hline \end{array}$ $\begin{array}{r} 5 \\ \times 4 \\ \hline \end{array}$ $\begin{array}{r} 4 \\ \times 8 \\ \hline \end{array}$

Find the missing factors.

7. $4 \times$ _____ $= 24$ $4 \times$ _____ $= 32$ $4 \times$ _____ $= 16$

8. _____ $\times 4 = 28$ _____ $\times 4 = 8$ _____ $\times 4 = 36$

Shade those blocks that contain products that are even numbers.

Remember that even numbers end in the digits 2, 4, 6, 8, 0.

9.

1×1	4×6	$2 \times 2 \times 3$	6×2	7×1
$5 \times 3 \times 1$	$\begin{array}{r} 2 \\ \times 8 \\ \hline \end{array}$	5×9	$5 \times 1 \times 7$	$\begin{array}{r} 9 \\ \times 1 \\ \hline \end{array}$
$1 \times 1 \times 3$	5×6	9×2	9×5	$1 \times 5 \times 1$
$\begin{array}{r} 5 \\ \times 9 \\ \hline \end{array}$	2×8	$3 \times 1 \times 5$	5×5	7×1
5×7	3×4	$2 \times 3 \times 1$	$\begin{array}{r} 6 \\ \times 2 \\ \hline \end{array}$	$1 \times 5 \times 3$

Use the pictures and the commutative property to write a number sentence.

10. ◯◯◯◯   ◉◉◉◉   ⬭

$4 \times 0 =$ ___ $0 \times 4 =$ ___   ___ $\times$ ___ $=$ ___   ___ $\times$ ___ $=$ ___

Find the products.

11.

6	3	1	0	4	4	4	4
× 4	× 4	× 4	× 4	× 7	× 5	× 2	× 8

Find the missing factors.

12.

$$\begin{array}{c} 4 \\ \times \boxed{} \\ \hline 20 \end{array} \qquad \begin{array}{c} 1 \\ \times \boxed{} \\ \hline 4 \end{array} \qquad \begin{array}{c} \boxed{} \\ \times \; 4 \\ \hline 24 \end{array} \qquad \begin{array}{c} 4 \\ \times \boxed{} \\ \hline 16 \end{array} \qquad \begin{array}{c} \boxed{} \\ \times \; 9 \\ \hline 36 \end{array} \qquad \begin{array}{c} \boxed{} \\ \times \; 2 \\ \hline 8 \end{array}$$

Complete.

13. $4 \times 5 \bigcirc 5 \times 3$ $\qquad 6 \times 2 \bigcirc 4 \times 6$

$4 \times 4 \bigcirc 5 \times 5$ $\qquad 4 \times 8 \bigcirc 5 \times 7$

Problem Solving Reasoning Solve.

14. A park ranger sees **9** deer running through a field. How many legs does she see? How do you know?

_____

15. Mr. Hu's class lines up in **5** equal lines. There are **20** students. How many students are in each line? Write a number sentence.

_____

✓ Quick Check

Multiply.

1. $3 \times 1 =$ _____ $\qquad$ **2.** $0 \times 8 =$ _____

3. $5 \times 7 =$ _____ $\qquad$ **4.** $3 \times 5 =$ _____

5. $\begin{array}{c} 5 \\ \times 1 \\ \hline \end{array}$ $\qquad$ **6.** $\begin{array}{c} 9 \\ \times 5 \\ \hline \end{array}$ $\qquad$ **7.** $\begin{array}{c} 4 \\ \times 9 \\ \hline \end{array}$

8. $\begin{array}{c} 7 \\ \times 4 \\ \hline \end{array}$ $\qquad$ **9.** $\begin{array}{c} 4 \\ \times 6 \\ \hline \end{array}$ $\qquad$ **10.** $\begin{array}{c} 4 \\ \times 4 \\ \hline \end{array}$

Work Space.

Sometimes you can make a list to solve a problem. The list helps you organize your thinking and keep track of the information.

Problem

Steve gave these clues to his friends. Two numbers have a sum of **11** and a product of **30**. What are the numbers?

---

1 **Understand** As you reread the clues, ask yourself questions.

- What do the words **sum** and **product** mean?

  The sum is the answer to an addition problem. The product is the answer to a multiplication problem.

- What is the sum and product of the numbers?

  The sum is 11. The product is 30.

---

2 **Decide** Choose a method for solving the problem.

- Make a list to help you solve the problem. Begin with two numbers with a sum of **11**.

Two Numbers with a Sum of 11
4, 7

---

3 **Solve** Use the list to find the answer.

- List pairs of numbers with a sum of **11**. Then check to see if the product of the **2** numbers is **30**.

Two Numbers with a Sum of 11	Product of the Numbers
4, 7	28
3, 8	24
2, 9	18
5, 6	30

---

4 **Look back** Check your answer.

Answer _____

- What other problem-solving strategy can you use?

  _____

- How does the list help you?

  _____

Use the Make a List Strategy or any other strategy you have learned.

1. Tim says his mystery number is less than **20**. If you count by **3's** you will say his mystery number. If you count by **5's** you will also say his mystery number. What is Tim's mystery number?

Think: What are the important clues for Tim's mystery number?

_____

Answer: _____

2. Earl says the difference between his two mystery numbers is **5**. The product of the two numbers is **24**. What are Earl's two mystery numbers?

Think: What are the important clues for the mystery number?

_____

Answer: _____

3. José is making a banner with yellow, blue, and white stripes. The pattern is repeated **5** times across the banner. What color will the stripe in the middle of the banner be?

_____

4. Lionel says the **2** digits in his mystery number have a sum of **6**. You say this mystery number if you count by **3's** or count by **4's**. What is Lionel's mystery number?

_____

5. Ajai's mystery number is an even number. The number is greater than **30** and less than **50**. The sum of the digits is **6**. What is the mystery number?

_____

6. The boys think they can write **3** number mysteries each half hour. If they start at **11:00** A.M. and stop at **2:00** P.M., how many number mysteries do they think they can write?

_____

Extend Your Thinking

7. In which problems above did you make a list to help you find the answers?

_____

8. Write your own number mystery problem. Then give the problem to friends to solve.

_____

_____

Use the commutative property to find the
facts for 3 that you already know.

0 × 3 = 0	so	**3 × 0 = 0**
1 × 3 = 3	so	**3 × 1 = 3**
2 × 3 = 6	so	**3 × 2 = 6**
4 × 3 = 12	so	**3 × 4 = 12**
5 × 3 = 15	so	**3 × 5 = 15**

Here are some other multiplication facts for 3.

3 pears in each group
7 groups
21 pears in all

3
× 7
___
21   **3 × 7 = 21**

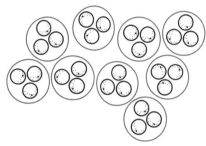

3 oranges in each group
9 groups
27 oranges in all

3
× 9
___
27   **3 × 9 = 27**

Complete. Write a number sentence.

1.

_____
×_____
_____   _____ × _____ = _____

2.

_____
×_____
_____   _____ × _____ = _____

Complete the number sentence.

3. 3 × 5 = _____   _____ × 3 = 24   _____ × 3 = 27

4. 3 × 6 = _____   _____ × 3 = 18   _____ × 3 = 21

5. 3 × 7 = _____   _____ × 3 = 12   _____ × 3 = 15

Use <, >, or =.

6. 3×4 ◯ 2×10 3×6 ◯ 2×7

7. 5×3 ◯ 4×4 4×2 ◯ 3×3

8. 4×8 ◯ 3×9 5×6 ◯ 8×3

Complete this multiplication table.

9.

×	0	1	2	3	4	5	6	7	8	9
0	0	0								
1		1								
2			4							
3				9						
4					16					
5						25				

Problem Solving Reasoning Solve.

10. Ken sets the dinner table for his family of **6**. Everyone gets a knife, a fork, and a spoon. How many of these items does Ken need to set the table?

11. An amusement park sells tickets for rides. You can buy **3** tickets for a dollar. How many tickets can you buy with **8** dollars? How did you find the answer?

Test Prep ★ Mixed Review

12 Which shows these four numbers in order from least to greatest?

1,401, 699, 2,033, 845

A 2,300, 1,401, 845, 699

B 2,300, 699, 845, 1,401

C 845, 699, 2,033, 1,401

D 699, 845, 1,401, 2,033

13 Which number is greater than **42,605**?

F 39,777

G 44,100

H 38,546

J 41,986

You can skip count on a number line to multiply with **10**.

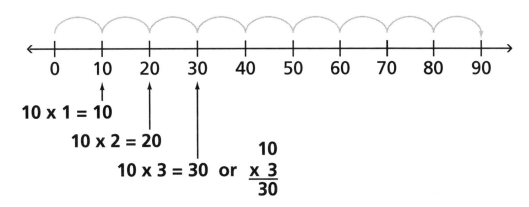

10 x 1 = 10

10 x 2 = 20

10 x 3 = 30 or $\begin{array}{r} 10 \\ \times\ 3 \\ \hline 30 \end{array}$

To find the value of a group of dimes you skip count by **10**.

10¢   20¢   30¢   40¢   50¢   60¢   70¢   80¢   90¢

1. When you multiply with **10** what pattern do you see
in the ones place of the product?

_____

2. Write the multiplication fact in two ways.

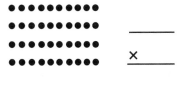

$\times$ _____

_____

_____ $\times$ _____ = _____

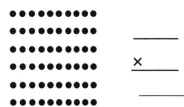

$\times$ _____

_____

_____ $\times$ _____ = _____

Multiply.

3.
$\begin{array}{r} 10 \\ \times\ 9 \\ \hline \end{array}$
$\qquad$
$\begin{array}{r} 10 \\ \times\ 5 \\ \hline \end{array}$
$\qquad$
$\begin{array}{r} 10 \\ \times\ 8 \\ \hline \end{array}$
$\qquad$
$\begin{array}{r} 10 \\ \times\ 7 \\ \hline \end{array}$
$\qquad$
$\begin{array}{r} 10 \\ \times\ 0 \\ \hline \end{array}$

Multiply.

10.

x	3
9	
2	
0	
7	

x	5
5	
4	
1	
2	

x	4
2	
6	
5	
7	

x	10
3	
5	
2	
1	

Write the product in the outside section.

11.

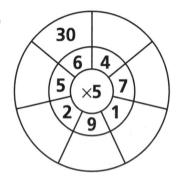

12.

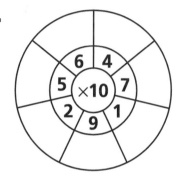

| Problem Solving |
| Reasoning |

Solve.

13. Travis has **5** dimes. Mina has **2** quarters. Do they have the same amount of money? How do you know?

_____

14. Juan places **3** groups of **10** counters on his desk. Write the number sentence Juan is trying to solve. Find the product.

_____

✓ Quick Check

Multiply.

1. 3 × 9 = _____

2. 6 × 3 = _____

3. 8 × 3 = _____

4. 10 × 4 = _____

5. 6 × 10 = _____

6. 3 × 10 = _____

7.   5
  × 3

8.   6
  × 3

9.   3
  × 3

10.   3
  × 8

11.   10
  × 1

Work Space.

Pictographs show data with symbols.
Students voted for the juice they like the best.
The pictograph shows how they voted.

In this lesson, you will need to use the
pictograph to solve problems.

Tips to Remember:

1. Understand   2. Decide   3. Solve   4. Look back

- Ask yourself: Have I solved a problem like this before?
- Think about the strategies you have learned that can help you solve a problem.
- If needed, write the problem as a number sentence. Ask yourself: What numbers should I use? What operations should I use?

Favorite Juices	
grape	▽ ▽ ▽ ▽
apple	▽ ▽ ▽ ▽ ▽ ▽ ▽
tomato	▽ ▽
orange	▽ ▽ ▽ ▽

Key   Each ▽ = 4 votes

Use the pictograph to solve the problems.

1. How many more votes did the most popular juice have than the least popular juice?

   Think: To compare the number of votes, do you add, subtract, multiply, or divide?

   _____

   Answer: _____

2. Which two types of juice had close to the same amount of votes?

   Think: Which two rows of glasses in the pictograph are about the same length?

   _____

   Answer: _____

3. Which types of juices received more than **15** votes?

   _____

4. How many students voted?

   _____

Favorite Ice Cream Flavors

butterscotch	🍦 🍦
vanilla	🍦 🍦 🍦 🍦
strawberry	🍦 🍦 🍦
chocolate	🍦 🍦 🍦 🍦 🍦 🍦

Key Each 🍦 = 5 votes

5. How many people chose chocolate ice cream as their favorite flavor?

_____

6. Which ice cream flavor received twice as many votes as butterscotch?

_____

7. Eric wanted to buy a **3**-scoop ice cream cone. He chose vanilla, chocolate and strawberry flavors. How many different ways could the scoops be arranged on the ice cream cone?

_____

8. The cost of the **3**-scoop ice cream cone was **$2.19** plus **7¢** tax. Eric paid for the ice cream cone with a **$5** bill. How much change should he receive?

_____

Extend Your Thinking

9. If each glass in the Favorite Juice pictograph represented **2** votes, how would the look of the graph change?

_____

_____

_____

_____

10. How is a pictograph like a bar graph? How is a pictograph different from a bar graph?

_____

_____

_____

_____

_____

Find the products.

1. $4 \times 0 =$ _____   **2.** $7 \times 3 =$ _____   **3.** $3 \times 2 =$ _____

4. $5 \times 1 =$ _____   **5.** $4 \times 3 =$ _____   **6.** $4 \times 4 =$ _____

7. 6   **8.** 7   **9.** 5   **10.** 5   **11.** 3   **12.** 1
   $\times 2$ $\times 4$ $\times 3$ $\times 4$ $\times 4$ $\times 4$

Fill in the table.

		0	1	7	3	4	6	5	10
13.	× 3	0							
14.	× 4			28					
15.	× 5				15				

Find the product. Show the commutative property.

16. $3 \times 5 =$ _____

_____ × _____ = _____

17. $7 \times 2 =$ _____

_____ × _____ = _____

Complete. Show the associative property.

18. $(4 \times 2) \times 2 =$ or $4 \times (2 \times 2) =$

_____ × _____ = _____   _____ × _____ = _____

Solve.

19. Which color shoe had the most sales? How many pairs of this color were sold?

_____

20. How many pairs of shoes were sold in all? How did you find the answer?

_____

Shoes Sold	
blue	🥾🥾🥾🥾🥾
black	🥾🥾🥾
white	🥾🥾🥾🥾🥾🥾
red	🥾
Key Each 🥾	2 pairs of shoes

1 Zora bought a book about model airplanes and a model kit. She paid $.65 tax for her purchase.

What was the total amount of money Zora spent?

A $3.00   **C** $11.99   **E** NH

B $13.63   **D** $12.99

2 Jared and Bethanie were both born in February. Jared was born in 1976. Bethanie was born in 1994. How many years older is Jared than Bethanie?

F 70 years   **J** 22 years

G 19 years   **K** NH

H 18 years

3 The students in one class read for 4,600 minutes during one month. The students in another class read for 4,900 minutes during that same month. How many minutes did they read altogether during the month?

A 300   **D** 9,500

B 9,600   **E** NH

C 8,300

4 Chan and Kendra are each trying to plan a schedule to practice their skit for the school variety show. They want to practice as many hours as possible in one week.

Chan's Plan

Sun	Mon	Tues	Wed	Thu	Fri	Sat
	3 hr		3 hr			

Kendra's Plan

Sun	Mon	Tues	Wed	Thu	Fri	Sat
		2 hr	2 hr	2 hr		

Whose plan will give them more practice time?

F Chan's Plan

G Monday

H Tuesday

J Kendra's Plan

K NH

5 Which is another way to write 4 + 4 + 4 + 4 + 4?

A 5 + 4

B 20 + 4

C 5 × 4

D 4 × 4 × 4 × 4 × 4

6 Mariko walks her dog for 10 minutes each morning. Which could you use to find how many minutes Mariko walks her dog in one week?

F 7 × 10   **H** 10 ÷ 7

G 7 + 10   **J** NH

UNIT 5 • TABLE OF CONTENTS

Multiplication and Division to 5

CALIFORNIA STANDARDS	Lesson	Page
	1 Understanding Division	115–116
NS 2.3; A/F 1.1	**2** Algebra • Inverse Operations	117–118
NS 2.3; A/F 1.1	**3** Algebra • Fact Families	119–120
NS 2.6	**4** Dividing with 1 and 0	121–122
NS 2.3	**5** Dividing with 5	123–124
NS 2.2, 2.3; A/F 1.1	**6** Algebra • Related Facts: Multiplying and Dividing with 5	125–126
MR 2.3, 3.2	**7** Problem Solving Strategy: Draw a Picture	127–128
NS 2.2, 2.3; A/F 1.1	**8** Related Facts: Multiplying and Dividing with 4	129–131
NS 2.2, 2.3; A/F 1.1	**9** Algebra • Related Facts: Multiplying and Dividing with 3	132–134
NS 2.7, 2.8; A/F 2.1	**10** Algebra • Unit Cost	135–136
MR 2.3, 3.2, 3.3	**11** Algebra • Problem Solving Application: Choose the Operation	137–138
	• Unit 5 Review	139
	• Cumulative Review ★ Test Prep	140

We will be using this vocabulary:

quotient the answer in a division problem

divisor the number to divide by in a division problem

dividend the number that is divided in a division problem.

inverse the opposite. For example, multiplication is the inverse of division.

unit cost the price for one of an item

Dear Family,

During the next few weeks, our math class will be learning division of whole numbers and practicing related multiplication and division facts. Students will be introduced to unit cost.

The homework you might expect to see provides practice in completing number sentences for related facts. Here is a sample you may want to keep handy to give help if needed.

Writing Fact Families for Multiplication and Division

Since multiplication and division are related operations, we can write number sentences called fact families.

We can describe the array with multiplication sentences:

3 groups of 5

$3 \times 5 = 15$

5 groups of 3

$5 \times 3 = 15$

We can describe the array with division sentences:

$15 \div 5 = 3$

$15 \div 3 = 5$

These four number sentences make up a fact family.

$3 \times 5 = 15$ $15 \div 3 = 5$
$5 \times 3 = 15$ $15 \div 5 = 3$

During this unit, students will need to continue practicing their multiplication and division facts. Provide opportunities for them to practice finding unit cost.

Sincerely,

Name _____

There are **10** dots in the box.

Use loops to make as many groups of **2** dots each as you can.

How many groups do you have? _____

We can write this as a **division sentence.**

$$10 \div 2 = 5 \leftarrow \text{quotient}$$

dots in   dots in   groups
all   each
    group

We read this as "Ten divided by two equals five."

Make groups of 2. Complete the division sentences.

1.

6 ÷ 2 = _____

2.

8 ÷ 2 = _____

3.

12 ÷ 2 = _____

4.

16 ÷ 2 = _____

5.

2 ÷ 2 = _____

6.

14 ÷ 2 = _____

7.

18 ÷ 2 = _____

8.

4 ÷ 2 = _____

We can show division in another way.

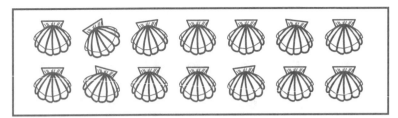

Loop groups of **2**. How many groups of **2** are in **14**? _____

Write: **14 ÷ 2 = 7** ← quotient   or   divisor ——┐   7 ← quotient

divisor ┌── divisor   2) 1 4

↑ dividend   ↑ dividend

Make groups of 2. Complete the divisions.

9.

2) 4   4 ÷ 2 = ☐

10. 2) 1 0   10 ÷ 2 = ☐

11. 2) 1 8   18 ÷ 2 = ☐

12. 2) 2   2 ÷ 2 = ☐

Problem Solving Reasoning   Solve.

13. Tiffany collected **14** ladybugs for science class. She needs to put **2** in each jar. How many jars does she need?

_____

14. Lowell draws **18** circles. He loops groups of **2**. How many groups of **2** does he have? How do you know?

_____

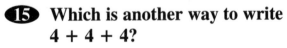

15 Which is another way to write 4 + 4 + 4?

     A 4 × 4
     B 4 × 3
     C 3 × 4
     D 8 − 4

16 What number goes in the box to make the number sentence true?

$3 \times 5 = 5 \times$ ☐

     F 2
     G 3
     H 8
     J 15

Inverse Operations

Dividing by **2** undoes multiplying by **2**.

 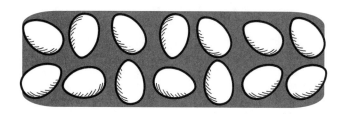

$2 \times 3 = 6$ $2 \times 7 = 14$

$6 \div 2 = 3$ $14 \div 2 = 7$

We say that multiplying by a number and dividing by that number are **inverse operations**.

You know that $6 \div 2 = 3$ because $2 \times 3 = 6$.

Complete.

1. $4 \div 2 = 2$ $14 \div 2 = $ ____ $12 \div 2 = $ ____

     because   because   because

     $2 \times 2 = $ ____ $2 \times $ ____ $= $ ____ $2 \times $ ____ $= $ ____

2. $18 \div 2 = $ ____ $10 \div 2 = $ ____ $2 \div 2 = $ ____

     because   because   because

     ____ $\times$ ____ $= $ ____   ____ $\times$ ____ $= $ ____   ____ $\times$ ____ $= $ ____

Complete these related multiplication and division facts.

3. $\begin{array}{r} 2 \\ \times\, 2 \\ \hline \end{array}$ $2\,\overline{)\,4}$ $\begin{array}{r} 3 \\ \times\, 2 \\ \hline \end{array}$ $2\,\overline{)\,6}$ $\begin{array}{r} 4 \\ \times\, 2 \\ \hline \end{array}$ $2\,\overline{)\,8}$

4. $\begin{array}{r} 6 \\ \times\, 2 \\ \hline \end{array}$ $2\,\overline{)\,12}$ $\begin{array}{r} 7 \\ \times\, 2 \\ \hline \end{array}$ $2\,\overline{)\,14}$ $\begin{array}{r} 8 \\ \times\, 2 \\ \hline \end{array}$ $2\,\overline{)\,16}$

Because they are inverse operations, we can check division by multiplying.

$18 \div 2 = 9$ because $2 \times 9 = 18$ $\begin{array}{r} 9 \\ 2\overline{)18} \end{array}$ because $\begin{array}{r} 9 \\ \times 2 \\ \hline 18 \end{array}$

Divide, and check by multiplying.

5. $18 \div 2 =$ _____ $10 \div 2 =$ _____ $16 \div 2 =$ _____

_____ $\times 9 =$ _____   _____ $\times 5 =$ _____   _____ $\times 8 =$ _____

6. $8 \div 2 =$ _____ $14 \div 2 =$ _____ $12 \div 2 =$ _____

_____ $\times 4 =$ _____   _____ $\times 7 =$ _____   _____ $\times 6 =$ _____

Divide. Write >, <, or =.

7. $12 \div 2 \bigcirc 14 \div 2$ $18 \div 2 \bigcirc 16 \div 2$

8. $6 \div 2 \bigcirc 4 \div 2$ $8 \div 2 \bigcirc 10 \div 2$

Problem Solving
Reasoning

Solve.

9. Kateri writes $6 \div 2 = 3$. What two multiplication sentences can she use to check her answers?

_____

10. Ramon has **8** birds in **2** cages. Each cage has the same number of birds in it. How many birds are in each cage? Check your answer.

_____

Test Prep ★ Mixed Review

11 What number goes in the box and makes this sentence true?

$26 \times 1 = \boxed{}$

A 25
B 26
C 27
D 28

12 Mario bought 4 boxes of pencils. There were 5 pencils in each box. How many pencils did he buy altogether?

F 1
G 9
H 15
J 20

Name _____

Multiplication and division are related operations.

Look at this picture. We can write these multiplication and division sentences about the picture.

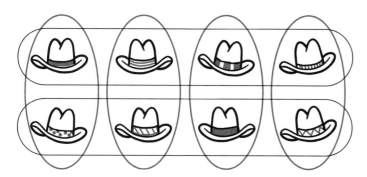

$4 \times 2 = 8$, so $8 \div 2 = 4$

$2 \times 4 = 8$, so $8 \div 4 = 2$

We call these four number sentences a fact family.

Complete the number sentences.
Write the related facts.

1. $16 \div 2 =$ _____

$16 \div 8 =$ _____

$8 \times 2 =$ _____

$2 \times 8 =$ _____

$14 \div 2 =$ _____

$14 \div 7 =$ _____

$7 \times 2 =$ _____

$2 \times 7 =$ _____

$2 \div 2 =$ _____

$2 \div 1 =$ _____

_____ $\times 2 =$ _2_

_____ $\times$ _____ $=$ _____

2. $12 \div 2 =$ _____

_____ $\div$ _6_ $=$ _____

_____ $\times$ _2_ $=$ _____

_____ $\times$ _____ $=$ _12_

$10 \div 2 =$ _____

_____ $\div$ _5_ $=$ _____

_____ $\times$ _____ $=$ _10_

_____ $\times$ _____ $=$ _____

$18 \div 2 =$ _____

_____ $\div$ _____ $=$ _2_

_____ $\times$ _2_ $=$ _____

_2_ $\times$ _____ $=$ _____

3. $12 \div 6 =$ _____

_____ $\div$ _____ $=$ _____

_____ $\times$ _____ $=$ _____

_____ $\times$ _____ $=$ _____

$6 \div 2 =$ _____

_____ $\div$ _____ $=$ _____

_____ $\times$ _____ $=$ _____

_____ $\times$ _____ $=$ _____

$16 \div 8 =$ _____

_____ $\div$ _____ $=$ _____

_____ $\times$ _____ $=$ _____

_____ $\times$ _____ $=$ _____

Write the related facts.

4.   3 × 2 = ☐

____ × ____ =

____ ÷ ____ =

____ ÷ ____ =

2 × 6 = ☐

____ × ____ =

____ ÷ ____ =

____ ÷ ____ =

8 × 2 = ☐

____ × ____ =

____ ÷ ____ =

____ ÷ ____ =

5.   4 × 2 = ☐

____ × ____ =

____ ÷ ____ =

____ ÷ ____ =

2 × 7 = ☐

____ × ____ =

____ ÷ ____ =

____ ÷ ____ =

2 × 2 = ☐

____ ÷ ____ =

Problem Solving Reasoning   Solve.

6. Jen wrote the division sentence **10 ÷ 2 = 5.** Write three sentences that belong in the same fact family.

_____

7. Explain how knowing **8 × 2 = 16** can help you find **16 ÷ 2 = ____.**

_____

✓ Quick Check

Make groups of 2. Write the quotient.

Work Space.

1.

10 ÷ 2 = _____

2. ●●●●●●●●
●●●●●●●●

16 ÷ 2 = _____

3. Complete.

14 ÷ 2 = ____ because 2 × ____ = 14

Complete the related facts.

4.   18 ÷ 2 = 9

18 ÷ ____ = 2

2 × ____ = 18

9 × ____ = 18

5.   12 ÷ 2 = 6

12 ÷ ____ = 2

____ × 2 = 12

2 × ____ = ____

Name _____

There are **2** ones in **2**.

$$1\overline{)2}^{\,2} \qquad 2 \div 1 = 2$$

$$1\overline{)3}^{\,3} \qquad 3 \div 1 = 3$$

| A number divided by **1** equals that number. |

There is **1** four in **4**.

$$4\overline{)4}^{\,1} \qquad 4 \div 4 = 1$$

$$2\overline{)2}^{\,1} \qquad 2 \div 2 = 1$$

| A number divided by itself equals **1**. |

Find the quotients.

1. $1\overline{)5}$ $\qquad 4\overline{)4}$ $\qquad 3 \div 1 = \boxed{}$ $\qquad 2 \div 2 = \boxed{}$ $\qquad 3\overline{)3}$ $\qquad 1\overline{)2}$

2. $1\overline{)8}$ $\qquad 1\overline{)1}$ $\qquad 7 \div 7 = \boxed{}$ $\qquad 6 \div 1 = \boxed{}$ $\qquad 8\overline{)8}$ $\qquad 5\overline{)5}$

There are **0** threes in **0**.

$$3\overline{)0}^{\,0} \qquad 0 \div 3 = 0$$

$$2\overline{)0}^{\,0} \qquad 0 \div 2 = 0$$

| **0** divided by a nonzero number is **0**. |

How many zeros are in **8**?

$$0\overline{)8} \qquad 8 \div 0 = \boxed{}$$

| Think: What number times **0** equals **8**? There is none! There is no division by **0**. |

 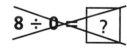

Find the quotients. If there is no answer, cross out the problem.

3. $2\overline{)0}$ $\qquad 4\overline{)0}$ $\qquad 0 \div 2 = \boxed{}$ $\qquad 3 \div 0 = \boxed{}$ $\qquad 1\overline{)0}$ $\qquad 4\overline{)4}$

4. $1\overline{)4}$ $\qquad 0\overline{)7}$ $\qquad 0 \div 1 = \boxed{}$ $\qquad 0 \div 3 = \boxed{}$ $\qquad 6\overline{)6}$ $\qquad 0\overline{)1}$

Solve. Work the problems in the spaces to the right.

5. Vaing paid **16¢** for **2** marbles. Both marbles cost the same amount. How much did she pay for **1** marble?

6. Joao's mother gave out **18** favors at a party. She gave each child **2** favors. How many children came to the party?

7. Diego hung **14** papers on the bulletin board. He put **2** papers in each row. How many rows of papers did he make?

8. Sarai has **16** postcards. If she could fit **2** on a page of her scrapbook, how many pages does she need?

9. David received **6** new books. He plans to read **1** each week. How long will it take him to read all his new books?

10. Write a problem for **12 ÷ 2 =** ☐ . Then solve it.

| Problem Solving Reasoning | **Solve.** |

11. I am a number. If you divide me by **8**, you get **1** as a quotient. What number am I? Explain how you got the answer.

_____

_____

12. Mei-Ling has **0** dog cookies and **7** dogs to share them. Loop the division sentence that tells the story.

$$7 ÷ 0 = 0$$

$$0 ÷ 7 = 0$$

Test Prep ★ Mixed Review

13 What number goes in the box to make the number sentence true?

$(4 × 7) × 2 = 4 × ($ ☐ $× 2)$?

A 3   **C** 9

B 7   **D** 11

14 Carlo's car wash cleaned 1,478 cars in June and 2,056 in July. How many cars were washed in both months?

F 4,424   **H** 3,324

G 3,534   **J** 578

Draw **15** dots in the box.

Divide the dots into groups of **5.**
How many groups do you have?

This shows that **15 ÷ 5 = 3.**

quotient

Loop the groups of 5. Complete the number sentences.

1. • • • • •   5 ÷ 5 = _____   • • • • •   10 ÷ 5 = _____
                                            • • • • •

2. (dots)   25 ÷ 5 = _____   (dots)   45 ÷ 5 = _____

3. (dots)   20 ÷ 5 = _____   (dots)   35 ÷ 5 = _____

4. (dots)   15 ÷ 5 = _____   0 ÷ 5 = _____

5. (dots)   30 ÷ 5 = _____   (dots)   40 ÷ 5 = _____

Find the quotients.

6. $5 \div 5 =$ _____ $10 \div 5 =$ _____ $15 \div 5 =$ _____

7. $5\overline{)5}$ $5\overline{)15}$ $5\overline{)20}$

8. $30 \div 5 =$ _____ $35 \div 5 =$ _____ $40 \div 5 =$ _____

Dividing by **5 undoes** multiplying by **5**.
So we can check division by multiplying:

$10 \div 5 = 2$ because $5 \times 2 = 10$

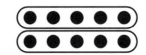

Find the quotients. Check by multiplying.

9. $5 \div 5 =$ _____ because _____ × _____ = _____ $5\overline{)5}$

10. $25 \div 5 =$ _____ because _____ × _____ = _____ $5\overline{)25}$

11. $30 \div 5 =$ _____ because _____ × _____ = _____ $5\overline{)30}$

12. $10 \div 5 =$ _____ because _____ × _____ = _____ $5\overline{)10}$

Problem Solving
Reasoning

Solve.

13. Brenda has **20¢**. She has only nickels. How many nickels does she have? How do you know?

_____

14. Mr. Lee has **12** fish to put in **4** fish bowls. Will he put **2** or **3** fish in each bowl? How do you know?

_____

Test Prep ★ Mixed Review

15 What number goes in the box and makes this sentence true?

$17 \times 0 = \boxed{}$

A 17
B 16
C 1
D 0

16 Mei bought 2 packages of stickers. There were 8 stickers in each package. How many stickers did she buy in all?

F 6
G 10
H 14
J 16

Here are the fact families for **5.**

Write a multiplication fact for each picture.
Then complete the fact family.

1.

___3___ × ___5___ = _____

_____ × _____ = _____

_____ ÷ _____ = _____

_____ ÷ _____ = _____

2.

_____ × _____ = _____

_____ × _____ = _____

_____ ÷ _____ = _____

_____ ÷ _____ = _____

3.

_____ × _____ = _____

_____ × _____ = _____

_____ ÷ _____ = _____

_____ ÷ _____ = _____

4.

_____ × _____ = _____

_____ × _____ = _____

_____ ÷ _____ = _____

_____ ÷ _____ = _____

Write the related division facts for each
multiplication sentence.

5. 5 × 8 = _____

___40___ ÷ ___8___ = ___5___

___40___ ÷ ___5___ = ___8___

6. 5 × 9 = _____

_____ ÷ _____ = _____

_____ ÷ _____ = _____

7. 5 × 7 = _____

_____ ÷ _____ = _____

_____ ÷ _____ = _____

8. 5 × 6 = _____

_____ ÷ _____ = _____

_____ ÷ _____ = _____

Write the related facts.

9.

$4 \times 5 = \boxed{}$

_____ $\times$ _____ $=$

_____ $\div$ _____ $=$

_____ $\div$ _____ $=$

$6 \times 5 = \boxed{}$

_____ $\times$ _____ $=$

_____ $\div$ _____ $=$

_____ $\div$ _____ $=$

$5 \times 5 = \boxed{}$

_____ $\div$ _____ $=$

10.

$9 \times 5 = \boxed{}$

_____ $\times$ _____ $=$

_____ $\div$ _____ $=$

_____ $\div$ _____ $=$

$3 \times 5 = \boxed{}$

_____ $\times$ _____ $=$

_____ $\div$ _____ $=$

_____ $\div$ _____ $=$

$5 \times 7 = \boxed{}$

_____ $\times$ _____ $=$

_____ $\div$ _____ $=$

_____ $\div$ _____ $=$

Problem Solving Reasoning | **Solve.**

11. When you multiply two numbers you get **45**. When you divide **45** by one of these numbers you get **9**. What are the two numbers?

_____

12. Mrs. Greene can ride **5** miles on her bicycle in one hour. How long will it take her to ride **20** miles? How do you know?

_____

✓ Quick Check

Find the quotient.

1. $0 \div 3 =$ _____

2. $6 \div 1 =$ _____

3. $0 \div 5 =$ _____

4. $9 \div 1 =$ _____

5. $45 \div 5 =$ _____

6. $20 \div 5 =$ _____

Work Space.

Write the related facts.

7. $35 \div 5 =$ _____

_____ $\div$ _____ $=$ _____

_____ $\times$ _____ $=$ _____

_____ $\times$ _____ $=$ _____

Problem Solving Strategy: Draw A Picture

Sometimes it helps to draw a picture to solve a problem.

Problem

Three students had a sack race at the school carnival. At the end of the race, Greta had gone **8** feet. Jacob had gone twice as far as Greta. Emily had gone half as far as Greta. In what order did the students finish the race?

---

1 **Understand**   As you reread the problem, ask yourself questions.

• How many people were in the race?

   Three people, Emily, Jacob, and Greta.

• What does twice as far mean?

   Twice as far means the distance multiplied by 2.

• What does half as far mean?

   Half as far means divide the distance by 2.

---

2 **Decide**   Choose a method for solving.

• Draw a picture to help you solve this problem.

   Greta went 8 feet in the race.

   **Jacob went twice as far, or
   2 × 8 = 16 feet.**

   **Emily went half as far, or
   8 ÷ 2 = 4 feet.**

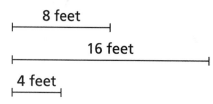

8 feet

16 feet

4 feet

---

3 **Solve**   Look at the picture to decide who came in first, second, and third.

• Jacob came in first

• Who came in second? _____

• Who came in third? _____

---

4 **Look back**   Check that your picture goes with the problem.

• Explain how the picture helped you solve the problem.

   Answer _____

Solve. Use the Draw a Picture Strategy or any other strategy you have learned.

1. At the carnival, the artist takes a half hour to paint one face. The artist works from **9 A.M.** to **5 P.M.** He will close for **1** hour at lunch time. How many faces can he paint in a day?

   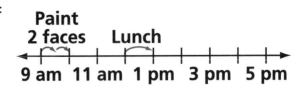

   Think: How can drawing a time line help you solve this problem?

   _____

   Answer: _____

2. There are **12** children in line at the snack bar. There are **4** children ahead of Sandy. How many children are behind her?

   _____

3. Marta paid for her snack order and received 9 coins as change. The coins totaled **75¢**. What coins did Marta get?

   _____

4. A picnic table can seat **5** people on each side and **1** person at each end. The Jefferson family put two picnic tables together end-to-end to make one long table. How many people can sit at the tables?

   _____

5. The picnic tables are arranged in rows of **5**. Each table is **6** feet long. There are **3** feet between each picnic table. How long is one row of tables?

   _____

   _____

Extend Your Thinking

6. Look back at the problem about the sack race. If Emily went twice as far as Jacob, how would the picture change? How would the order change?

   _____

7. In which of the problems above did you choose to draw a picture to solve the problem?

   _____

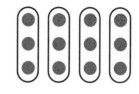

We know that **4 × 3 = 12**, so **12 ÷ 4 = 3**.

Here is another way to write **12 ÷ 4 = 3**:

$$\text{divisor} \rightarrow 4\overline{)1\,2} \quad \overset{3}{} \leftarrow \text{quotient}$$

Find the quotients. Check by multiplying.

1. 36 ÷ 4 = _____ because _____ × _____ = _____   4)̄3 6

2. 28 ÷ 4 = _____ because _____ × _____ = _____   4)̄2 8

3. 32 ÷ 4 = _____ because _____ × _____ = _____   4)̄3 2

4. 24 ÷ 4 = _____ because _____ × _____ = _____   4)̄2 4

5. 16 ÷ 4 = _____ because _____ × _____ = _____   4)̄1 6

6. 4 ÷ 4 = _____ because _____ × _____ = _____   4)̄4

7. 12 ÷ 4 = _____ because _____ × _____ = _____   4)̄1 2

8. 8 ÷ 4 = _____ because _____ × _____ = _____   4)̄8

9. 20 ÷ 4 = _____ because _____ × _____ = _____   4)̄2 0

Find the quotients. Related facts can help you.

10. 4 ÷ 4 = _____   28 ÷ 4 = _____   12 ÷ 4 = _____   4 ÷ 1 = _____

11. 4)̄8   4)̄3 2   4)̄1 6   4)̄2 0

12. 32 ÷ 8 = _____   24 ÷ 6 = _____   16 ÷ 4 = _____   12 ÷ 3 = _____

13. 9)̄3 6   8)̄3 2   5)̄2 0   7)̄2 8

Write the related multiplication and division facts.

14.

_____ × _____ = _____

_____ ÷ _____ = _____

_____ × _____ = _____

_____ ÷ _____ = _____

Find the product and quotient. In the space next to each problem, check your work with the inverse operation.

15.
$$\begin{array}{r} 8 \\ \times\,4 \\ \hline \end{array}$$
$4\overline{)32}$

$$\begin{array}{r} 4 \\ \times\,1 \\ \hline \end{array}$$
$\overline{)}$

$4\overline{)28}$
× ___

16.
$$\begin{array}{r} 4 \\ \times\,3 \\ \hline \end{array}$$
$\overline{)}$

$$\begin{array}{r} 5 \\ \times\,4 \\ \hline \end{array}$$
$\overline{)}$

$4\overline{)0}$
× ___

17.
$6\overline{)24}$
× ___

$8\overline{)32}$
× ___

$$\begin{array}{r} 4 \\ \times\,9 \\ \hline \end{array}$$
$\overline{)}$

Work the problems in the spaces to the right.

18. If Pat has **4** sticks and Leroy has **6** times as many, how many sticks does Leroy have?

_____ sticks

19. Setsuko stored **24** pansy plants equally on **4** shelves in her greenhouse. How many plants did she put on each shelf?

_____ plants

20. Mr. Jacobs has **32** books. He wants **4** children to share them equally. How many will each child get?

_____ books

Write the related facts.

21. 4 × 8 = ☐   4 × 1 = ☐   7 × 4 = ☐

____ × ____ =   ____ × ____ =   ____ × ____ =

____ ÷ ____ =   ____ ÷ ____ =   ____ ÷ ____ =

____ ÷ ____ =   ____ ÷ ____ =   ____ ÷ ____ =

22. 6 × 4 = ☐   4 × 5 = ☐   4 × 4 = ☐

____ × ____ =   ____ × ____ =   ____ ÷ ____ =

____ ÷ ____ =   ____ ÷ ____ =

____ ÷ ____ =   ____ ÷ ____ =

Find the product. Use the Associative Property to check.

23. $2 \times 3 \times 2 =$ ____ $2 \times 2 \times 5 =$ ____ $4 \times 2 \times 2 =$ ____

Problem Solving
Reasoning
Solve.

24. Latoya starts with the number **36.** She subtracts **4** again and again until she gets **0.** How many times does she subtract **4?**

_____

25. I am one of two numbers. When you multiply us you get **32.** When you divide by me you get the other number, **8.** What number am I?

_____

Test Prep ★ Mixed Review

26 Luis rode his bike for 3 days. He rode 6 miles each day. How many miles did Luis ride in all?

   A 24   **C** 9

   B 18   **D** 3

27 The workers used 338 red bricks and 244 white bricks. How many bricks were used altogether to build the wall?

   F 94   **H** 582

   G 572   **J** 672

You have learned two ways to write a division equation:

$$27 \div 9 = 3 \quad \text{and} \quad 9\overline{)27} = 3$$

Find the product. Check by division.

1. $3 \times 8 =$ _____ $24 \div 8 =$ _____ $8\overline{)24}$

2. $3 \times 7 =$ _____ $21 \div 7 =$ _____ $7\overline{)21}$

3. $3 \times 6 =$ _____ $18 \div 6 =$ _____ $6\overline{)18}$

4. $3 \times 4 =$ _____ $12 \div 4 =$ _____ $4\overline{)12}$

5. $3 \times 3 =$ _____ $9 \div 3 =$ _____ $3\overline{)9}$

6. $3 \times 2 =$ _____ $6 \div 2 =$ _____ $3\overline{)6}$

7. $3 \times 9 =$ _____ $27 \div 9 =$ _____ $9\overline{)27}$

Write the quotients.

8. $3\overline{)12}$ $3\overline{)3}$ $3\overline{)6}$ $3\overline{)15}$ $3\overline{)0}$

9. $3\overline{)24}$ $3\overline{)21}$ $3\overline{)9}$ $3\overline{)18}$ $3\overline{)27}$

Fill in the blanks.

10. $4 \times 2 =$ _____ $4 \times$ _____ $= 16$ $12 \div 4 =$ _____   _____ $\times 2 = 18$

11. $5 \times 6 =$ _____   _____ $\times 9 = 45$ $32 \div 4 =$ _____ $3 \times$ _____ $= 12$

12. $3 \times 5 =$ _____ $7 \times$ _____ $= 35$ $20 \div 5 =$ _____ $14 \div$ _____ $= 2$

13. $4 \times 9 =$ _____   _____ $\times 4 = 0$ $8 \div 2 =$ _____ $28 \div$ _____ $= 4$

Study the picture and write four related multiplication and division facts.

14.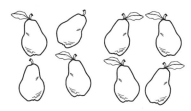

_____ × _____ = _____

_____ ÷ _____ = _____

_____ × _____ = _____

_____ ÷ _____ = _____

Write the related facts for each picture.

15.

_____ × _____ = _____

_____ × _____ = _____

_____ ÷ _____ = _____

_____ ÷ _____ = _____

_____ × _____ = _____

_____ × _____ = _____

_____ ÷ _____ = _____

_____ ÷ _____ = _____

The four equations in each row are related facts. Complete each equation.

16. $2 \times 3 =$ _____ $6 \div 3 =$ _____ $3 \times 2 =$ _____ $6 \div 2 =$ _____

17. $5 \times 3 =$ _____ $15 \div 3 =$ _____ $3 \times 5 =$ _____ $15 \div 5 =$ _____

18. $7 \times 3 =$ _____ $21 \div 3 =$ _____ $3 \times 7 =$ _____ $21 \div 7 =$ _____

Problem Solving Reasoning | **Solve.**

19. Tonweya picked **7** flowers. Anna picked **3** times as many. How many flowers did Anna pick? _____

20. Paula has three nickels. How much money does she have? _____

21. Make up a problem for **15 ÷ 5 =** _____. Then solve it.

_____

Write the related facts.

22.

$3 \times 1 = \boxed{}$

$\underline{} \times \underline{} =$

$\underline{} \div \underline{} =$

$\underline{} \div \underline{} =$

$2 \times 3 = \boxed{}$

$\underline{} \times \underline{} =$

$\underline{} \div \underline{} =$

$\underline{} \div \underline{} =$

$7 \times 3 = \boxed{}$

$\underline{} \times \underline{} =$

$\underline{} \div \underline{} =$

$\underline{} \div \underline{} =$

23.

$4 \times 3 = \boxed{}$

$\underline{} \times \underline{} =$

$\underline{} \div \underline{} =$

$\underline{} \div \underline{} =$

$3 \times 8 = \boxed{}$

$\underline{} \times \underline{} =$

$\underline{} \div \underline{} =$

$\underline{} \div \underline{} =$

$5 \times 3 = \boxed{}$

$\underline{} \times \underline{} =$

$\underline{} \div \underline{} =$

$\underline{} \div \underline{} =$

24.

$3 \times 3 = \boxed{}$

$\underline{} \div \underline{} =$

$6 \times 3 = \boxed{}$

$\underline{} \times \underline{} =$

$\underline{} \div \underline{} =$

$\underline{} \div \underline{} =$

$3 \times 9 = \boxed{}$

$\underline{} \times \underline{} =$

$\underline{} \div \underline{} =$

$\underline{} \div \underline{} =$

Problem Solving Reasoning Solve.

25. Carmen builds an array of cans for a store display. She uses **12** cans. Name two different arrays of cans she can make.

_____

26. Fred has **18** shoes in his closet. How many pairs of shoes is that? How did you find the answer?

_____

Test Prep ★ Mixed Review

27 For a project Maria used 453 toothpicks to build a house and 175 toothpicks to build a garage. How many toothpicks did she use in all?

A 278   C 578

B 528   D 628

28 Four teams meet in the park for practice. There are 10 players on each team. Altogether how many players are in the park for practice?

F 40   H 14

G 20   J 6

This ad is in a newspaper. You want to buy **1** beach towel. How much does one towel cost? You need to find the **unit cost**.

BEACH TOWELS

4 for $32

Here's a way:

You can divide to find the unit cost.

Since **32 ÷ 4 = 8**, then **$32 ÷ 4 = $8**.

One towel costs **$8**.

Unit cost is the price for one of a group of items.

Use the chart. Find the unit cost.

	Item	Price	Unit Cost
1.	diving masks	2 for $16	
2.	beach balls	6 for $24	
3.	shovels	3 for $18	
4.	pails	5 for $30	

Use the ad to solve.

5. What is the cost of **1** box of sidewalk chalk?

_____

6. Which costs more, a kite or a jump rope?

_____

7. You have $2. Do you have enough to buy a sand toy?

_____

8. You have $5. Can you buy a jump rope? What change will you get?

_____

9. Suppose you want **2** boxes of sidewalk chalk. How much will they cost? How did you find out? _____

Toy Sale	
jump ropes	4 for $16
sidewalk chalk	4 boxes for $20
kites	2 for $12
sand toys	6 for $18

Solve the problems in your head. Then show how you got the answer.

10. Sue bought **3** treats for her dog. How much did she pay for each treat if she spent **$15?**

11. How much does one puzzle cost if you can buy **6** puzzles for **$24.**

12. A package of **5** baskets costs **$15.** How much does each basket cost?

13. How much does each baseball cost if **3** baseballs cost **$27.**

14. At **$30** for **5** books, how much will **1** book cost?

Problem Solving Reasoning Solve.

15. A store sells **4** cassette tapes for **$16.** You have **$10.** How many tapes can you buy?

16. Model airplanes are on sale for **3** for **$18.** Pedro wants to buy only **1** airplane. How much will he pay? How do you know?

_____

✓ **Quick Check**

Multiply or divide.

1. $4 \times 7 =$ _____
2. $5 \times 4 =$ _____
3. $36 \div 4 =$ _____
4. $24 \div 4 =$ _____

5. $\begin{array}{r} 4 \\ \times 8 \\ \hline \end{array}$
6. $\begin{array}{r} 2 \\ \times 3 \\ \hline \end{array}$
7. $\begin{array}{r} 3 \\ \times 9 \\ \hline \end{array}$

Work Space.

Find the unit cost.

8. 4 books for $12. _____
9. 5 pillows for $40. _____
10. 3 shovels for $18. _____
11. 4 balls for $36. _____

To solve problems you may need to decide whether to add, subtract, multiply, or divide.

In this lesson you will make decisions about which operations to use to solve problems.

Tips to Remember:

| 1. Understand | 2. Decide | 3. Solve | 4. Look back |

- Read the problem carefully. Ask yourself questions about any part that does not make sense. Reread to find answers.
- Picture the situation described in the problem. Can you use addition, subtraction, multiplication, or division to show what is happening?
- Predict the answer. Then solve the problem. Compare your answer with your prediction.

Game and Movie Rental Fees

2 nights	$3.00
3 nights	$4.00
4 nights	$5.00

Late Fee $2 each night

Solve.

1. Jackson watched two movies. The first movie was **125** minutes long. The second movie was **90** minutes long. How much longer was the first movie?

Think: To compare the lengths of the movies, should you add, subtract, multiply or divide?

_____

Answer: _____

2. LaShana rented a movie for **2** nights. She kept it for **2** extra nights. How much did she pay altogether?

Think: How much did the rental cost? What is the late fee for each night?

_____

Answer: _____

_____

3. Steven rented **3** games for **3** nights and **2** movies for **2** nights. How much do the rentals cost?

_____

Snacks	
Popcorn	$1.29
Juice	$1.39
Soda	$1.39
Raisin Bar	$1.49
Mints	$1.15

4. Cedric bought **2** raisin bars and **2** bags of popcorn. How much did he pay?

_____

5. Cedric paid for the snacks with a **$10** bill. How much change did he get?

_____

6. If you had **$8**, could you purchase one of each item on the Snack Chart? How would you find out?

_____

7. Evan bought some snacks. He gave the clerk **$5** to pay for the snacks. He got **$2.32** in change. What snacks could Evan have bought?

_____

Extend Your Thinking

8. You do not always need numbers to find an answer. For example, Mrs. Adams gave her

░░░░ children, ░░░░ mints each.

How many mints did she buy? What operation would you use to find the answer? Why?

_____

9. Make up you own problem using information from one of the charts. Then let a friend solve your problem.

_____

Find the quotients.

1. $9\overline{)36}$ 2. $5\overline{)20}$ 3. $1\overline{)4}$ 4. $4\overline{)0}$

5. $3\overline{)24}$ 6. $6\overline{)24}$ 7. $5\overline{)20}$ 8. $3\overline{)15}$

9. $4\overline{)28}$ 10. $2\overline{)10}$ 11. $9\overline{)45}$ 12. $7\overline{)14}$

Find the quotients. Check by multiplying.

13. $14 \div 2 =$ _____ because _____ $\times 7 =$ _____

14. $18 \div 2 =$ _____ because _____ $\times 9 =$ _____

15. $4 \div 2 =$ _____ because _____ $\times 2 =$ _____

16. $18 \div 6 =$ _____ because _____ $\times 6 =$ _____

Write 2 multiplication sentences and 2 division sentences for this array.

17.

_____ $\times$ _____ $=$ _____   _____ $\div$ _____ $=$ _____

_____ $\times$ _____ $=$ _____   _____ $\div$ _____ $=$ _____

Solve.

18. Mary bought **2** balloons for **$10**. What was the cost of **1** balloon?

_____

19. If **4** notebooks cost **$12**, how much does **1** notebook cost? How do you know?

_____

20. Kim put **16** pictures in **4** rows. How many pictures were in each row? How did you find out?

_____

21. Six friends want to share **24** bananas equally. How many will each friend get?

_____

1 Juan picked 5 baskets of apples from the tree. There were 7 apples in each basket.

How many apples did Juan pick in all?

A 11

B 40

C 25

D 35

E NH

2 The window washers have to clean 4 rows of windows in the factory. There are 10 windows in each row.

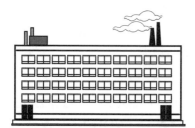

How many windows did they have to wash?

F 20

G 44

H 25

J 30

K NH

3 Lee put 24 stamps into his stamp album. He put 4 stamps on each page.

How many pages did Lee use?

A 3   C 4   E NH

B 8   D 7

4 The sign at the bakery shows that 3 pies cost $27.

3 for $27

How much does one pie cost?

F $9   H $8   K NH

G $6   J $7

5 Which number sentence is in the same family of facts as $6 \times 5 = 30$?

A $6 + 5 = 11$ C $6 - 1 = 5$

B $30 + 5 = 35$ D $30 \div 6 = 5$

6 What number goes in the box and makes this number sentence true?

$4 \times 3 = \boxed{} \times 4$

F 1   H 3

G 7   J 12

UNIT 6 • TABLE OF CONTENTS

Geometry, Data, and Probability

CALIFORNIA STANDARDS	Lesson	Page
M/G 2.1	1 Polygons	143–144
M/G 2.4	2 Right Angles	145–146
M/G 2.3, 2.4	3 Attributes of Quadrilaterals	147–148
M/G 2.2, 2.4	4 Triangles	149–150
M/G 2.1	5 Congruent Figures	151–152
MR 2.3, 3.2, 3.3	6 Algebra • Problem Solving Application: Use a Picture	153–154
M/G 2.5, 2.6	7 3-Dimensional Objects	155–156
MR 1.1, 2.3, 3.2, 3.3; A/F 2.2	8 Algebra • Problem Solving Strategy: Find a Pattern	157–158
MR 2.3	9 Algebra • Ordered Pairs	159–160
S/D/P 1.2, 1.3	10 Collecting and Recording Data	161–162
S/D/P 1.1	11 Events	163–164
S/D/P 1.1, 1.2, 1.3	12 Algebra • Making Predictions	165–166
	• Unit 6 Review	167–168
	• Cumulative Review ★ Test Prep	169–170

Dear Family,

During the next several weeks, our math class will be learning about geometry, collecting and recording data, and probability.

You can expect to see homework that provides additional practice locating points with ordered pairs. Here is a sample that explains ordered pairs. You may wish to keep it handy if help is needed.

Using Ordered Pairs

Ordered pairs of numbers are used to locate points on a grid or map. The order of the numbers is important. Here is the way to find the ordered pair (**3,4**) on the map at the right.

(**3,4**)

This number means go across **3**.   This number means go up **4**.

The ordered pair (**3,4**) names the location of the library.

Note that you cannot change the order of the numbers. The ordered pair (**4,3**) does not name the same point as (**3,4**).

During this unit, students will need to continue using and recognizing plane and solid figures.

Sincerely,

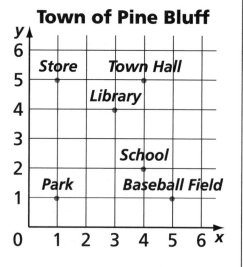

Town of Pine Bluff

Name _____

A **polygon** is a flat closed figure with three or more sides.

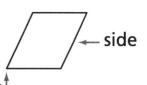

←side

corner↑

These are polygons.	These are not polygons.

Some polygons have special names.

triangle   rectangle   square   pentagon   hexagon   octagon

Is the figure a polygon? Explain why or why not.

1.

_____

2.

_____

3.

_____

_____

Complete the table.

	Figure	Number of Sides	Number of Corners
4.	triangle		
5.	rectangle		
6.	square		
7.	pentagon		
8.	hexagon		
9.	octagon		

Write *true* or *false*.

10. A circle is a flat, closed figure that is not a polygon. _____

11. A triangle is a polygon with **3** sides and **3** corners. _____

12. A pentagon is an open figure with **5** sides and **4** corners. _____

13. A square has **4** sides and is an open figure. _____

14. An octagon is a polygon with **8** sides. _____

15. A hexagon is a closed figure with **7** corners. _____

16. A polygon always has the same number of sides as it has corners. _____

Complete.

17. Which figures at the right are polygons?

_____

18. Which figures at the right are not polygons?

_____

| Problem Solving |
| Reasoning |

Solve.

19. George uses **3** toothpicks to make a polygon. What polygon did he make? How do you know?

_____

_____

20. Alexa draws **3** straight lines. The lines do not touch each other. Did she draw a polygon? How do you know?

_____

_____

Test Prep ★ Mixed Review

21 At the fair **265** red balloons and **439** blue balloons were sold. How many balloons were sold in all?

A 604   C 704

B 605   D 705

22 The grocery store sold **361** pounds of chicken and **194** pounds of beef in a week. How many more pounds of chicken sold?

F 155   H 267

G 167   J 555

The corners of a polygon are called **angles.**

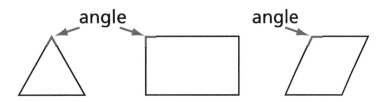

A **right angle** is a square corner.

The corner of a book or a piece of paper is a right angle.

a right angle

greater than a right angle

less than a right angle

How many right angles does the figure have?

1.

    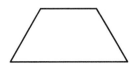   

_____   _____   _____   _____

Is the angle in red a *right angle*, *greater than* a right angle, or *less than* a right angle?

2.

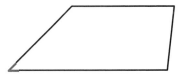   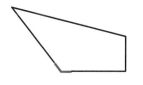

_____   _____   _____

Name three things in the classroom that have a right angle.

3. _____

Look at the clock. When the clock hands show **9:00** they form a right angle.

Name a time when the hands shows the angle.

4. an angle that is greater than a right angle _____

5. an angle that is less than a right angle _____

6. a right angle _____

7. Name a time when the hands form a straight line. _____

| Problem Solving |
| Reasoning |

Solve.

8. Elysse uses **4** right angles to draw a polygon. How many different polygons can she make?

_____

9. I am a capital letter in the alphabet. I have **1** right angle. What letter am I?

_____

10. Suppose you cut a sandwich in half from corner to corner. What polygons might you see?

_____

11. Mr. Brown will meet Mr. Liang at **7:15 P.M.** What angle will the clock show?

_____

Test Prep ★ Mixed Review

12 Juanita bought 5 bags of marbles. There were 8 marbles in each bag. How many marbles did Juanita buy altogether?

A 40

B 30

C 25

D 13

13 Mei put 36 photos in the album. She put 4 photos on each page. How many pages did Mei use in all?

F 6

G 8

H 9

J 32

Name _____   **Attributes of Quadrilaterals**

Line	**Line Segment**	**Parallel Lines**
←————————→	●————————●	←————————→ ←————————→
A **line** is a straight path that goes on forever in two directions.	A **line segment** is part of a line that has **2** endpoints.	**Parallel lines** are lines that are always the same distance apart.

A **quadrilateral** is a polygon with **4** line segments, or sides, and **4** angles.

Some quadrilaterals have opposite sides that are parallel. They are called **parallelograms**.

Quadrilaterals	
Opposite Sides Parallel	**Sides Not Parallel**
▭ ▱ ▭	⬭

Loop the lines that are parallel.

1.

Complete the chart.

	Figure	**Are the sides parallel?**	**Number of equal sides**	**Number of angles**	**Number of right angles**
2.	▭ rectangle				
3.	◻ square				
4.	▱ parallelogram				

5. A rectangle and a square are both polygons and quadrilaterals. How are they the same? How are they different?

_____

Draw the figure.

6.

A quadrilateral with parallel sides that is not a square	A polygon that is not a quadrilateral	A quadrilateral whose sides are of equal length

Problem Solving Reasoning | **Solve.**

7. I am a figure with **4** sides and **4** right angles. Not all of my sides are equal. Both sets of opposite sides are parallel. What figure am I? _____

8. Maggie thinks all quadrilaterals are polygons. Josh thinks all polygons are quadrilaterals. Who is right? Explain.

_____

_____

9. Marisa drew a figure with **4** sides and **4** angles. Only one set of opposite sides are parallel. Could the figure be a square? Explain. _____

_____

10. Jared drew a figure with twice as many sides and corners as a quadrilateral. Name the figure.

_____

✓ Quick Check

Name the polygon.

Work Space.

1.

2.

3.

_____ _____ _____

Is it a right angle? Write *yes* or *no*.

4.

5.

6.

_____ _____ _____

Is it a quadrilateral? Write *yes* or *no*.

7.

8.

9.

_____ _____ _____

Name _____

Triangles can be named by the length of their sides.

Equilateral Triangle	Isosceles Triangle	Scalene Triangle
		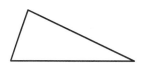
All the sides are the same length.	Two sides are the same length.	No sides are the same length.

Name the triangle.

1.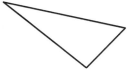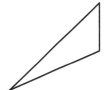

_____ _____ _____ _____

2. A store's sign is the shape of an equilateral triangle. One side measures **21** inches. What is the length of each of the other two sides?

_____

3. A triangle has sides that are **6** inches, **8** inches, and **10** inches long. What kind of triangle is it?

_____

Look at the picture. Write the numbers in each kind of triangle next to the name.

4. equilateral triangle _____

5. isosceles triangle _____

6. scalene triangle _____

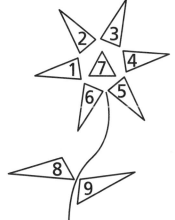

A triangle that has a right angle is called a **right triangle**. Here are some right triangles.

 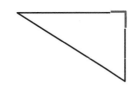 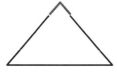 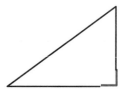

Is the figure a right triangle? Write *yes* or *no*.

6.

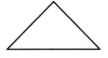

_____   _____   _____   _____

Problem Solving
Reasoning

Solve.

7. Kaity draws a scalene triangle. Two sides measure **5** inches and **3** inches? Can the third side measure **3** inches? Why or why not?

_____

8. Brent sets the table. He takes a square napkin and folds it in half. He makes a triangle. What two names can you use to describe the triangle?

_____

9. Draw a straight line from one corner of the rectangle to another. What kind of triangles did you make?

_____

Test Prep ★ Mixed Review

10 Uri bought 6 packages of pencils. There were 3 pencils in each package. How many pencils did Uri buy in all?

A 3
B 9
C 12
D 18

11 Mrs. Ying has 16 ballet students in her class. They practice in 2 equal-sized rows. How many dancers are in each row?

F 14
G 10
H 8
J 6

STANDARD

Figures that are the same size and shape are **congruent**.

These triangles are congruent. A tracing of one triangle fits on the other exactly.

These squares are not congruent. A tracing of one square does **not** fit on the other.

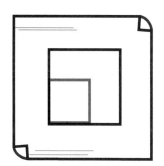

Loop the figures below that are congruent to this one:

1.

| Hint: Trace the figure and try to fit the tracing on the figures below. |

A   B   C   D

Are the figures congruent? Write *yes* or *no*.

2.

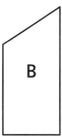 _____

 _____

 _____

Loop the shape that fits.

3.

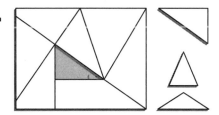

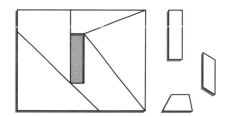

A **line of symmetry** divides a figure into **2** congruent parts.

Number of Lines of Symmetry			
0	**1**	**2**	**More than 2**

Draw as many lines of symmetry as you can for each figure.

4.

**Problem Solving
Reasoning** | Solve.

5. May uses a rubber stamp to stamp a figure. Is the figure congruent to the figure on the stamp? Why or why not?

6. Draw an isosceles triangle. How many lines of symmetry does it have. How do you know?

7. How many angles does the letter Z have? Are they right angles? How do you know?

8. Suppose you fold a rectangle in half. Are the two halves congruent? How do you know?

Test Prep ★ Mixed Review

9 Which is the correct name for this shape?

A square

B circle

C triangle

D pentagon

10 Sami found 2 dimes and a nickel under the couch. What was the total value he found?

F 3¢

G 15¢

H 20¢

J 25¢

Pictures can help you solve problems. In this lesson you will use grid maps to find places or follow directions.

Tips to Remember:

> 1. **Understand**   2. **Decide**   3. **Solve**   4. **Look back**

- Read the problem carefully. Ask yourself questions about any part that does not make sense. Reread to find the answers.
- Think about what the problem is asking you to do. What information does the problem give you? What do you need to find out?
- Use the pictures to help you solve the problem.

Solve.

1. You are at the corner of Lake St. and 2nd Ave. You walk **3** blocks north. Where are you now?

   Think: Find the corner of Lake St. and 2nd Ave. Which way should you walk to go north?

   Answer: _____

2. You are at the school. You walk **3** blocks west. Where are you now?

   Think: Find the school. Which way should you walk to go west?

   Answer: _____

Solve.

3. Write directions to the library from Angela's house.

_____

_____

_____

_____

4. Is the grocery store or Ted's house closer to Angela's house?

_____

_____

5. From the Science Center go **3** blocks east, then **2** blocks south. Identify the streets and buildings at your new location.

_____

_____

North

Oil St.
Glen St. — Science Center — Zoo
Silver St. — Planetarium — Art Museum
Gold St.
Met St. — Pet Shop
Tree St.

West **East**

Iris Ave. Rose Ave. Lilac Ave. Daisy Ave. Lily Ave. Tulip Ave. Fern Ave.

South

6. If you leave the Planetarium, in what directions do you walk to get to the zoo? How many blocks do you walk?

_____

7. Give directions to get from the Pet Shop to the Zoo.

_____

_____

8. Is the Art Museum or the Pet Shop closer to the Planetarium?

_____

_____

Extend Your Thinking

9. How is the picture like a map? How is it different?

_____

_____

_____

10. Choose one of the pictures and give directions from one location to another. See if a friend can follow your directions.

_____

Some solid objects have curved surfaces. Others have edges, corners, and flat faces.

Solid objects with curved surfaces roll.
Solid objects with no curved surfaces do not roll.

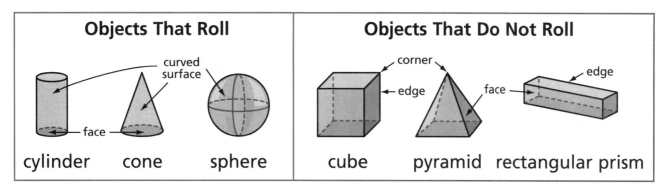

Objects That Roll	Objects That Do Not Roll
curved surface — cone — face — cylinder cone sphere	corner — edge — pyramid face — edge cube pyramid rectangular prism

Solid objects can be put together to make other objects. The object at the right is made up of a cube, rectangular prism, cylinder, pyramid, and cone.

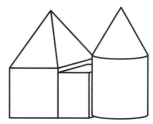

Match.

1. cylinder

2. rectangular prism

3. pyramid

4. sphere

I can roll. I am shaped like a ball.

I have **6** faces that are rectangles, and my opposite faces are congruent.

I have **5** faces, and **4** of them are triangles.

I have a curved surface with a circle at the top and bottom.

Name the solid object.

5. A and C _____

6. B _____

7. D _____

8. E and G _____

9. F and H _____

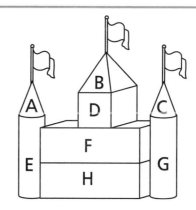

Loop what the figure looks like from the top.

10. 　　　　　

11. 　　　　　

Name the solid object used at the right.

12. Which object has **6** faces, **12** edges, and **8** corners? _____

13. Which object has **2** faces, but no corners?

_____

Problem Solving
Reasoning

Solve.

14. I am a solid figure. My bottom is a circle, my top is a point. What am I?

_____

15. Judy builds a house. The blocks are solid figures that cannot roll. They have **6** faces. What **2** solid figures could they be?

_____

✔️ **Quick Check**

How many equal sides? Write *3, 2,* or *0*.　　　　　Work Space.

1. 　**2.** 　**3.**

_____　　_____　　_____

Are the figures congruent? Write *yes* or *no*.

4. 　　**5.**

_____　　　_____

Is it a cone, cylinder, or cube?

6. 　**7.** 　**8.**

_____　　_____　　_____

Sometimes finding a pattern in pictures or numbers can help you solve problems.

Picture 1 **Picture 2** **Picture 3**

Problem

Kay is making a pattern. Each time she adds blocks to the pattern she draws a picture. If she continues, how many blocks will be in Picture 6?

❶ Understand **As you reread, ask yourself questions.**

- How are the blocks arranged in each picture?
  Each picture has two rows of blocks.
- Which row has more blocks? How many more?
  The bottom row has one more block.

❷ Decide **Choose a method for solving.**

Look at the blocks. Do you see a pattern?

- In each picture another block is added to the top row and the bottom row.
- There is always one more block in the bottom row than the top row.
- The number of blocks in the top row is the same as the number of the picture.

Draw what Picture 4 will look like.

- How many blocks?

  top row _____   bottom row _____   total _____

❸ Solve **Use the pattern to find the answer.**

- Draw the blocks in Picture 6.
- How many blocks?

  top row _____   bottom row _____   total _____

❹ Look back **Check your answer.**

- Explain how you found the answer.

  _____

  _____

Use the Find a Pattern Strategy or any other strategy you have learned.

1. The letter B is used to make a pattern. Draw the next three pairs of B's to continue it.

B B B B B B B B B B B B

Think: How do the pair of letters flip and turn?

_____

_____

_____

Answer: _____

2. Continue the pattern by drawing the next **3** circles.

Think: How does the look of the circle change form one picture to the next?

_____

_____

Answer: _____

3. Draw the next two squares to continue this pattern.

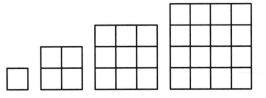

_____

4. The squares in problem 3 show multiplication facts. The first square shows $1 \times 1 = 1$. The second square shows $2 \times 2 = 4$. Make a list of all the multiplication facts pictured in each square. Describe patterns you see in the list.

_____

_____

_____

_____

5. Draw the next three figures to continue the pattern.

△ □ ⬠ ◯ △ □ ⬠ ◯ △ □ ⬠ ◯ △

_____

6. Describe a pattern that you see in problem 5.

_____

_____

Name _____   **Ordered Pairs**

You can use **ordered pairs** of numbers
to give the location of a point on a grid.

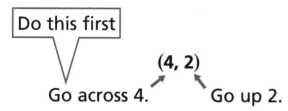

(4, 2)

Go across 4.   Go up 2.

The ordered pair (**4, 2**) locates the letter *P*.

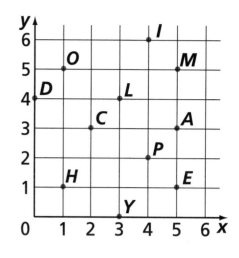

Name the letter for each ordered pair.
Find the hidden message.

1. (1, 1), (5, 3), (4, 2), (4, 2), (3, 0), (0, 4), (5, 3), (3, 0)

_____

Use the letters in the grid to write a word or phrase.

2. ordered pairs: _____

word(s): _____

3. Do the ordered pairs (**1, 5**) and (**5, 1**) locate the
same place on the grid? Explain why or why not?

_____

Mark these points on a grid. Connect the points.
What do you see?

4. (0, 6), (1, 5), (2, 4), (3, 3), (4, 2), (5, 1), and (6, 0)

_____

5. Why do you need a pair of numbers to locate
a point?

_____

Draw the figures on a grid. Write the ordered pair that names the corners.

6. square _____

7. triangle _____

8. rectangle _____

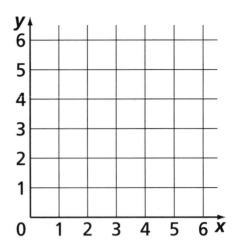

Solve.

9. Brian goes across to **5** and up to **3**. He draws a star. What ordered pair will locate the star?

_____

10. Ali finds point (**4, 4**). He changes the order of the numbers. Will the new ordered pair name the same point? Why?

_____

Test Prep ★ Mixed Review

11 **Which shape has a right angle?**

A

B

C

D

12 **Which two polygons are the same size and shape?**

F B and D

G A and D

H B and C

J A and C

Name _____

A **survey** is a way of collecting data by asking people questions. A **tally** chart helps you to organize, record, and count the data.

Favorite Sports		
Activity	**Tally**	**Number**
soccer	ЖІ	5
swimming	ЖІ II	7
baseball	ЖІ ЖІ I	11

The tally chart at the right is about Favorite Sports. What is the most popular activity? How many people took part in this survey?

A tally chart can also help you to record **possible outcomes** and results of experiments. The chart at the right shows the results of a coin toss. You can see that the possible outcomes were heads and tails.

	Tally	**Number**
heads	ЖІ ЖІ III	13
tails	ЖІ ЖІ ЖІ II	17

List the possible outcomes.

1. survey of favorite day of the week _____

_____

2. playing a game _____

3. survey of favorite season _____

Work with a partner. Toss a coin 30 times and record the results on the tally chart.

	Tally	**Number**
heads		
tails		

4. What were the possible outcomes? _____

5. How many Heads did you get? _____ Tails? _____

6. How did the tally chart help you organize the results?

_____

Problem Solving Reasoning

Solve.

11. Carlos asks **16** students to pick their favorite season. Each season got the same number of tally marks. How many students chose summer?

_____

12. Luis asks **50** students to vote for a favorite sport. Twenty-three students chose skiing. Show how the tally marks looked on the chart.

_____

✓ Quick Check

Name the shape that is found at the point named by these ordered pairs.

Work Space.

1. (4, 2) _____

2. (5, 1) _____

3. (2, 3) _____

4. (1, 5) _____

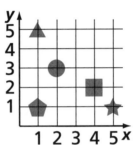

Each student used two pieces of colored paper. Complete the chart to show what they used.

5. Bob–blue and green   Lee–red and yellow

     Tanya–green and white   Liam–blue and red

     Ryan–green and blue   Ping–blue and white

     Tory–blue and yellow   Gloria–red and green

Color Used	Tally	Number
blue		
red		
green		
yellow		
white		

6. Which two colors were used the most?

_____

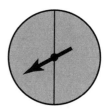

An **event** is something that takes place or happens.

An event is **certain** if it will always happen.
It is certain that you will spin red with Spinner A
shown at the right.

Spinner A

An event is **likely** if it will probably happen.
It is likely that you will spin red with Spinner B
shown at the right.

If an event will never happen, it is **impossible**.
It will be impossible to spin gray with Spinner A.

An event is **unlikely** if it will probably not happen.
The chance is unlikely that you will spin gray with
Spinner B.

Spinner B

Use the spinners at the right to solve.

1. Why is it certain that you will spin gray with
Spinner C?

_____

2. Why is it impossible that you will spin red with
Spinner C?

Spinner C

_____

3. Is it likely or unlikely that you will spin red with
Spinner D? Explain.

_____

Spinner D

Color the spinner.

4. Impossible to spin yellow	Just as likely to spin blue as green	Certain to spin red

Tell what the chances are of each.
Write _certain_, _likely_, _unlikely_, or _impossible_.

5. Feed your dog and he will say thank you. _____

6. Tomorrow is a holiday. _____

7. You will have homework tonight. _____

8. A stone dropped in a lake will sink. _____

Complete. Use the bags of cubes at the right.

Bag 1   Bag 2

9. What is the chance you will pick a blue cube

from Bag 4? _____

10. How many more blue cubes would you need to
put into Bag 3 to make the chance of picking a
blue cube just as likely as picking a red cube?

Bag 3   Bag 4

_____

11. What is the chance you will pick a blue
cube from Bag 1? _____
Bag 2? _____

Problem Solving
Reasoning
Solve.

12. Barbara adds with **2** number
cubes. Each cube shows **1, 2, 3,
4, 5,** and **6.** Name a sum that is
impossible to get.

_____

13. A bag has **5** green cubes, **5**
yellow cubes and **5** blue cubes.
What is the chance of picking a
red cube?

_____

Test Prep ★ Mixed Review

14 Which shape is a quadrilateral?

A

C

B

D

15 Kesha wants to buy a book for
$10.00. She has $5.64. How much
money does Kesha need to buy the
book?

 F $15.64

 G $11.34

 H $5.46

 J $4.36

A **line plot** is a diagram that organizes data on a number line. You can use a line plot to record data and make **predictions.** A prediction is what someone thinks may happen.

The line plot shows the daily high temperature for one town during two weeks in January.

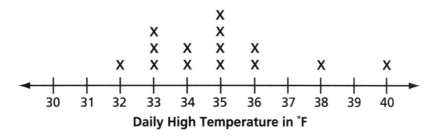

Daily High Temperature in °F

You can predict that the high temperature will probably be in the 30's the next day. It is unlikely that the next day's high temperature will be in the 70's.

You can also make a **prediction** with a spinner. The spinner at the right shows that the possible outcomes are **2, 2, 2,** and **1.**

You can predict that it is likely you will spin **2** with this spinner. It is unlikely that you will spin **1.**

Use the line plot to solve.

1. How many scores are shown on the line plot? _____

2. Which scores did most of the students get? _____

3. Which scores have no data?
_____

4. What pattern do you see?
_____
_____
_____
_____

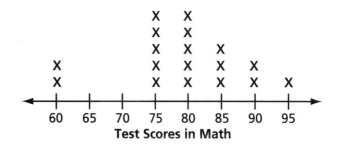

Test Scores in Math

5. If 10 more scores are included on the line plot, where do you think most of them will fall? Explain why you think so. _____
_____
_____

Use the spinner at the right.

6. Which letter do you think will occur most often? _____

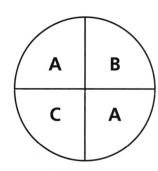

Test your prediction. Spin the spinner **50** times and record the results in a tally chart.

7.

Letter	Tally	Number
A		
B		
C		

8. Was your prediction correct? _____

✓ Quick Check

Is it certain, likely, unlikely, or impossible to get the color when you spin the spinner?

1. blue _____

2. red _____

3. green _____

4. white _____

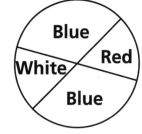

Work Space.

Solve.

5. Will the next pumpkin picked most likely weigh more or less than **15** pounds?

_____

```
                    X
                    X
        X           X
        X   X   X   X
    X   X   X   X   X
    +---+---+---+---+--->
    5  10  15  20  25
    Pounds of Pumpkins
```

Name _____

Unit 6 Review

Name the polygon.

1.

_____

2.

_____

3.

_____

4.

_____

5.

_____

6.

_____

Write whether the angle is a *right angle*, *greater than*, or *less than* a right angle.

7.

_____

8.

_____

9.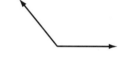

_____

Write *true* or *false*.

10. A quadrilateral is a polygon with three sides. _____

11. A rectangle has 4 right angles. _____

12. A square is a quadrilateral with no right angles. _____

13. A triangle is polygon, but not a quadrilateral _____

14. A line segment has two endpoints. _____

15. A line of symmetry divides a figure into 2 congruent parts. _____

Loop the figures that are congruent.

16.

Copyright © Houghton Mifflin Company. All rights reserved.

Unit 6 Review **167**

Write *equilateral*, *isosceles*, or *scalene triangle*.

17.

18.

19.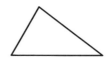

20.

_____   _____   _____   _____

Name the solid figures. Loop the ones that can roll.

21.

22.

23.

_____   _____   _____

Write whether the event is *certain*, *likely*, *unlikely*, or *impossible*.

24. A week will have six days.   _____

25. It will rain in the next two months.   _____

26. A stone dropped from a cliff will fall. _____

Use the tally chart.

27. Complete the class tally chart. Who will win the school election?

_____

Election Survey		
Student	**Tally**	**Number**
Frank	JHT II	
Eleanor	III	
Joe	JHT JHT JHT I	

28. The line plot shows the sizes of the shoes sold this week. Which two sizes will they probably sell more of next week?

_____

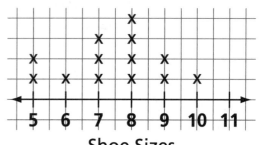

Shoe Sizes

1 The Murphy Family traveled 3,728 miles during the summer. What is the number rounded to the nearest hundred?

A 3,000   C 3,700

B 3,800   D 4,000

2 What number goes in the box and makes this number sentence true?

$4 \times 7 = \boxed{} \times 4$

F 3   H 7

G 11   J 28

3 Which number sentence belongs to the same family of facts as

$\boxed{3 \times 6 = 18}$?

A $3 + 6 = 9$

B $18 \div 6 = 3$

C $18 - 6 = 12$

D $6 - 3 = 3$

4 What is the shape of this sign?

F rectangle

G octagon

H hexagon

J pentagon

5 Which shape has 4 sides and all the sides are the same length?

A hexagon   C square

B triangle   D pentagon

6 What is the possibility of spinning the number 6?

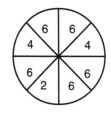

F certain

G likely

H unlikely

J impossible

7

Favorite Snacks	
Type	**Tally**
popcorn	卌 ‖
pretzels	卌 卌	
fruit	卌
muffins	?

Eight people voted for muffins. Which tally belongs in the chart to show 8?

A ‖‖

B 卌 ‖|

C 卌 卌 ‖|

D 卌|

8

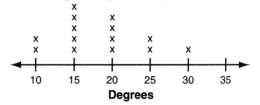

Average Temperature for 2 Weeks

Degrees

The line plot shows the average temperature for **14 days in a row.** What do you think would be the temperature on the 15th day?

F 35°

G 25°

H 15°

J 10°

9 Meadow Farms has two ponies. The Shetland pony weighs 379 pounds and the Appaloosa pony weighs 978 pounds. How many more pounds does the Appaloosa weigh?

A 599

B 699

C 1,247

D 1,357

E NH

10 Maj bought 5 posters for $20. Each poster cost the same amount. What did 1 poster cost?

F $1

G $3

H $5

J $10

K NH

11 A celery stalk has 5 calories. How many calories are in 6 celery stalks?

A 10

B 15

C 30

D 35

E NH

12 The band had 3 rows of trumpet players in the parade. There were 10 people in each row. How many trumpet players did the band have in the parade?

F 7

G 13

H 20

J 30

K NH

13 There are 15 members in the boat club. They shared 5 canoes evenly. How many members went in each canoe?

A 5

B 10

C 15

D 20

E NH

UNIT 7 • TABLE OF CONTENTS

Fractions

CALIFORNIA STANDARDS	Lesson		Page
	1	Writing Fractions	173–174
NS 3.1	2	Algebra • Comparing and Ordering Fractions	175–176
NS 3.1	3	Equivalent Fractions	177–178
NS 3.1	4	Fraction of a Number	179–180
NS 3.1	5	Fractions and Division	181–182
MR 2.2	6	Algebra • Problem Solving Strategy: Use a Simpler Problem	183–184
NS 3.1, 3.2	7	Adding and Subtracting Fractions	185–186
NS 3.1	8	Mixed Numbers	187–188
MR 1.1, 2.3, 3.2, 3.3	9	Problem Solving Application: Not Enough Information	189–190
	•	Unit 7 Review	191–192
	•	Cumulative Review ★ Test Prep	193–194

Dear Family,

During the next few weeks, our math class will be learning about fractions. Topics will include writing fractions, comparing and ordering fractions, and estimating with fractions.

You can expect to see homework that provides practice with comparing and ordering fractions. Here is a sample you may want to keep handy to give help if needed.

Comparing and Ordering Fractions

To compare $\frac{1}{2}$ and $\frac{1}{3}$, first draw and divide two bars of equal size, one into halves and one into thirds. Shade one part of each. Compare the shaded parts.

$\frac{1}{2}$ is greater than $\frac{1}{3}$.

$\frac{1}{2} > \frac{1}{3}$

To order $\frac{1}{2}$, $\frac{1}{3}$, and $\frac{1}{6}$ from

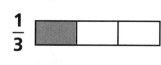

least to greatest, draw a third bar of equal size and divide it into sixths. Shade one part and compare with the other bars.

In order from least to greatest: $\frac{1}{6}$, $\frac{1}{3}$, $\frac{1}{2}$

During this unit, students will need to practice working with fractions.

Sincerely,

A **fraction** names part of a whole.

number of shaded parts → [1] ← numerator

number of equal parts → [2] ← denominator

Write fractions for the shaded parts.

1.  [ ] / [ ]    [ ] / [ ]   [ ] / [ ]

---

2. Circle the rectangle that is divided into **4** equal parts.

   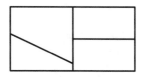   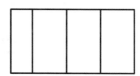

A **fraction** names part of a set.

number of shaded parts → [3] ← numerator

number in the set → [4] ← denominator

Write a fraction for the shaded part of each set.

3. 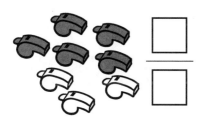 [ ] / [ ]    [ ] / [ ]   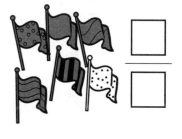 [ ] / [ ]

---

4. 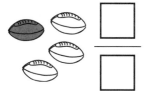 [ ] / [ ]   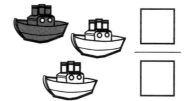 [ ] / [ ]   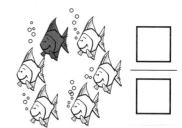 [ ] / [ ]

A group of **12** objects is **1 dozen,** so **6** objects is $\frac{1}{2}$ **dozen.**
A short way to write dozen is **doz.**

Loop the pictures that show a dozen.

5.

Loop $\frac{1}{2}$ dozen in each set.

6.

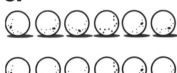  

Problem Solving Reasoning | Solve.

7. Brenda made a quilt with **8** equal-sized squares of material. If **5** squares are blue and **3** squares are white, what fraction of the quilt is blue?

_____

8. Marco has **2** dozen marbles, $\frac{1}{2}$ are red. Allysa has $\frac{1}{2}$ dozen red marbles. Who has more red marbles? How many more?

_____

Test Prep ★ Mixed Review

9 The farm sold 158 large pumpkins and 471 small pumpkins. How many pumpkins did the farm sell in all?

A 629

B 622

C 529

D 313

10 The fence company used 2,765 feet of fencing to enclose the playground. What is that number rounded to the nearest thousand?

F 4,000

G 3,000

H 2,800

J 2,700

Carlos ate $\frac{2}{8}$ of a pizza. Suzy ate $\frac{3}{8}$ of the pizza. Who ate more?

Carlos   Suzy

$\frac{3}{8}$ is greater than $\frac{2}{8}$

$$\frac{3}{8} > \frac{2}{8}$$

Suzy ate more pizza.

You can use models to **compare** and **order** the fractions.

$\frac{3}{8}$
$\frac{2}{8}$
$\frac{5}{8}$

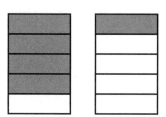

$$\frac{3}{8} > \frac{2}{8} \quad \frac{3}{8} < \frac{5}{8}$$

The order from greatest to least is:

$$\frac{5}{8} \quad \frac{3}{8} \quad \frac{2}{8}$$

Compare. Use >, <, or =.

1.

          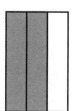

$\frac{4}{5} \bigcirc \frac{1}{5}$ $\frac{7}{8} \bigcirc \frac{4}{8}$ $\frac{2}{3} \bigcirc \frac{2}{3}$

2. $\frac{1}{3} \bigcirc \frac{3}{3}$ $\frac{5}{6} \bigcirc \frac{2}{6}$ $\frac{4}{4} \bigcirc \frac{4}{4}$ $\frac{4}{7} \bigcirc \frac{1}{7}$

3. $\frac{3}{4} \bigcirc \frac{1}{4}$ $\frac{4}{6} \bigcirc \frac{6}{6}$ $\frac{2}{8} \bigcirc \frac{5}{8}$ $\frac{2}{5} \bigcirc \frac{3}{5}$

Write the fractions in order from greatest to least.

4. $\frac{4}{6}, \frac{5}{6}, \frac{2}{6}$ _____ $\frac{7}{7}, \frac{1}{7}, \frac{4}{7}$ _____ $\frac{7}{9}, \frac{3}{9}, \frac{5}{9}$ _____

These are **unit fractions**:

$$\frac{1}{2} \quad \frac{1}{3} \quad \frac{1}{4} \quad \frac{1}{5} \quad \frac{1}{6}$$

> A **unit fraction** has a numerator of 1, which means 1 part of the whole.

You can use models to compare and order unit fractions.

$\frac{1}{6}$ is less than $\frac{1}{3}$

$\frac{1}{6} < \frac{1}{3}$

$\frac{1}{6}$ ▨☐☐☐☐☐

$\frac{1}{3}$ ▨☐☐

Compare. Use >, <, or =.

5.

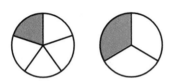

$\frac{1}{5} \bigcirc \frac{1}{3}$

$\frac{1}{2} \bigcirc \frac{1}{4}$

$\frac{1}{3} \bigcirc \frac{1}{4}$

Write the fractions in order from least to greatest.

6. $\frac{1}{4} \quad \frac{1}{3} \quad \frac{1}{6}$ _____

$\frac{1}{2} \quad \frac{1}{5} \quad \frac{1}{3}$ _____

$\frac{1}{8} \quad \frac{1}{2} \quad \frac{1}{10}$ _____

7. $\frac{1}{2} \quad \frac{1}{4} \quad \frac{1}{5}$ _____

$\frac{1}{4} \quad \frac{1}{6} \quad \frac{1}{2}$ _____

$\frac{1}{1} \quad \frac{1}{10} \quad \frac{1}{3}$ _____

Test Prep ★ Mixed Review

8 The new football stadium seats 75,430 people. What is the value of 5 in 75,430?

A 5 tens

B 5 hundreds

C 5 thousands

D 5 ones

9 The island's ferry can hold 800 people. On Monday 563 people got on board. How many more people could have fit on the ferry?

F 347

G 337

H 247

J 237

Equivalent Fractions

You can use models to find **equivalent fractions.** Equivalent fractions show the same amounts.

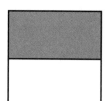 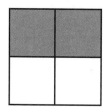

$\frac{1}{2}$ $\frac{2}{4}$

Look at the squares.

$\frac{1}{2}$ and $\frac{2}{4}$ show the same amount.

$$\frac{1}{2} = \frac{2}{4}$$

Write the equivalent fraction.

1.
$\frac{1}{3}$
$\frac{2}{6}$

$\frac{1}{3} = \frac{2}{\boxed{6}}$

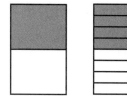
$\frac{2}{4}$
$\frac{4}{8}$

$\frac{2}{4} = \dfrac{\boxed{}}{\boxed{}}$

2.

$\frac{1}{2} = \dfrac{\boxed{}}{8}$

$\frac{1}{4} = \dfrac{\boxed{}}{8}$

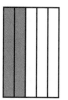

$\frac{2}{5} = \dfrac{\boxed{}}{10}$

3.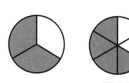

$\frac{2}{3} = \dfrac{\boxed{}}{6}$

 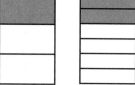

$\frac{1}{3} = \dfrac{2}{\boxed{}}$

$\frac{1}{2} = \dfrac{4}{\boxed{}}$

Shade to show equivalent fractions.

4.

$\frac{1}{2} = \frac{3}{6}$

$\frac{3}{4} = \frac{6}{8}$

$\frac{2}{5} = \frac{4}{10}$

Is the fraction equivalent to 1? Write *yes* or *no*.

5. $\dfrac{4}{4}$ _____ $\dfrac{7}{6}$ _____ $\dfrac{8}{8}$ _____ $\dfrac{2}{2}$ _____ $\dfrac{4}{3}$ _____

Problem Solving Reasoning   Solve.

6. Wanda wants to make a snack. She needs $\dfrac{1}{3}$ cup of milk. She has $\dfrac{2}{6}$ cup of milk. Does she have enough milk?

_____

7. Jason paints $\dfrac{4}{8}$ of the wall. Alexandra paints $\dfrac{2}{4}$. Who paints more of the wall?

_____

✓ **Quick Check**

Write the fraction for the shaded part.   **Work Space.**

1.   _____

2.   _____

Compare. Use <, >, or =.

3.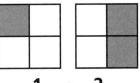

$\dfrac{1}{4}$ ◯ $\dfrac{2}{4}$

4.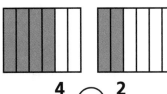

$\dfrac{4}{6}$ ◯ $\dfrac{2}{6}$

Complete to write the equivalent fractions.

5.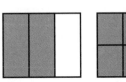

$\dfrac{2}{3} = \dfrac{\boxed{}}{6}$

6.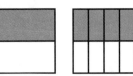

$\dfrac{1}{2} = \dfrac{\boxed{}}{10}$

Fraction of a Number

Use what you know about fractions to find a fraction of a number.

6 balls

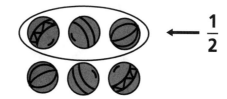

$\frac{1}{2}$ of **6** balls = **3** balls

Draw a loop to show the fraction. Write the number.

1.
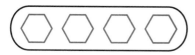

$\frac{1}{2}$ of **8** = _____

$\frac{1}{2}$ of **10** = _____

$\frac{1}{2}$ of **4** = _____

2.

$\frac{1}{3}$ of **6** = _____

$\frac{1}{3}$ of **9** = _____

$\frac{1}{3}$ of **12** = _____

3.

$\frac{1}{4}$ of **8** = _____

$\frac{1}{4}$ of **12** = _____

$\frac{1}{4}$ of **16** = _____

Use the information in the problem to complete the table.

4. Matthew has a dozen books on his shelf.
How many books is that? _____

$\frac{1}{2}$ of them are red.

$\frac{1}{12}$ of them are blue.

$\frac{1}{6}$ of them are green.

$\frac{1}{4}$ of them are yellow.

		Red Books	Blue Books	Green Books	Yellow Books
5.	Fraction of books	$\frac{1}{2}$			
6.	Number of books	6			

Problem Solving Reasoning | Solve.

7. Arwin has **6** balloons. $\frac{1}{6}$ of the balloons are red. $\frac{3}{6}$ of the balloons are striped. The rest are yellow. What fraction of the balloons are yellow?

_____

8. Maxine sold **16** books. She sold $\frac{1}{2}$ to her grandmother and $\frac{1}{4}$ to a neighbor. Her father bought the rest. How many did he buy?

_____

Test Prep ★ Mixed Review

9 Roberto scored **24** points, **17** points, and **19** points in the first three games of the season. How many points did he score in all **3** games?

A 51

B 56

C 60

D 64

10 Which is the name for a polygon that has 3 sides?

F square

G triangle

H rectangle

J pentagon

You can divide with fractions.

$\frac{1}{2}$ of the checkers are red.

$\frac{1}{2}$ of **8** = **4**   **8 ÷ 2 = 4**

Finding $\frac{1}{2}$ of a number is the same as dividing the number by **2**.

Draw loops to show the fraction. Then complete.

1.

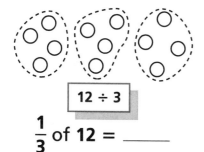

12 ÷ 3

$\frac{1}{3}$ of **12** = _____

$\frac{1}{5}$ of **10** = _____

$\frac{1}{2}$ of **18** = _____

2.

$\frac{1}{3}$ of _____ = _____

$\frac{1}{5}$ of _____ = _____

$\frac{1}{4}$ of _____ = _____

3.

$\frac{1}{2}$ of _____ = _____

$\frac{1}{4}$ of _____ = _____

$\frac{1}{5}$ of _____ = _____

Complete. $\boxed{18 \div 2}$

4. $\frac{1}{2}$ of 18 = ___9___ $\frac{1}{4}$ of 28 = _____ $\frac{1}{4}$ of 16 = _____

5. $\frac{1}{3}$ of 18 = _____ $\frac{1}{4}$ of 32 = _____ $\frac{1}{3}$ of 27 = _____

6. $\frac{1}{5}$ of 35 = _____ $\frac{1}{3}$ of 21 = _____ $\frac{1}{5}$ of 25 = _____

Problem Solving Reasoning | **Solve. Use the picture.**

7. You have **18** marbles. You give $\frac{1}{3}$ of them to a friend. How many did your friend get?

_____

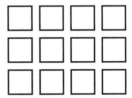

8. You have **12** crackers. You share $\frac{1}{2}$ of them with a friend. How many do you have now?

_____

 Quick Check

Draw a loop to show the fraction. Fill in the blank. | **Work Space.**

1. · · · ·
     · · · ·
     · · · ·

$\frac{1}{3}$ of 12 = _____

2. 🍎🍎🍎🍎
     🍎🍎🍎🍎

$\frac{3}{4}$ of 8 = _____

Complete.

3.

$\frac{1}{4}$ of 24	24 ÷ 4	☐
$\frac{1}{3}$ of 18	18 ÷ ☐	☐
$\frac{1}{2}$ of 12	☐ ÷ ☐	☐

Name _____

Using numbers that are easy to work with, helps you choose a plan for solving.

Problem

Chan gives his puppy food for the day. The puppy eats half in the afternoon. He eats the other **18** ounces of food in the evening. How many ounces of food does the puppy eat each day?

Morning Food	Afternoon Food
half of his food	18 ounces

1 Understand   As you reread, ask yourself questions.

- How much food does the puppy eat in the morning and in the afternoon?

  He eats half or 18 ounces in the morning and 18 ounces in the afternoon.

- What do you need to find? _____

2 Decide   Choose a method for solving.

- What numbers can you use in place of **18 + 18** that are easier to add? _____

3 Solve   First solve the problem with simpler numbers.

18 + 18 = ?

10 + 10 + 8 + 8 = 36 ounces

The puppy eats **36** ounces of dog food each day.

4 Look back   Check your answer.

- How did using simpler numbers help you?

  _____

Use the Solve a Simpler Problem strategy or any other strategy you have learned.

1. A pack of flavor strips and bones for dogs costs **$3.98** for **2** packs. What is the price for one pack?

Think: What can you use in place of **$3.98** to make the problem easier to solve?

_____

Answer: _____

_____

2. Dog food costs **39¢** a can. How much do **4** cans cost?

Think: What number is close to **$.39** and would be easier to work with mentally?

_____

Answer: _____

_____

_____

3. James works at a pet store **16** hours a week. Half of the hours he works are on the weekend. How many hours does James work on the weekend?

_____

4. Jane bought some dog biscuits for **$7.99**, a dog toy for **$3.99** and a bag of dog food for **$8.49**. How much money did Jane spend?

_____

5. Mr. Chen spent **$21.80** at the pet store. He gave the clerk **$30**. How much change should he receive?

_____

6. The book store is open from **10** A.M. to **8** P.M. Monday through Saturday, and noon to **6** P.M. on Sunday. How many hours a week is the book store open?

_____

Extend Your Thinking

7. Look back at the opening problem for this lesson. Could you add **18 + 18** another way? If so, explain how.

_____

_____

8. Four friends buy presents for each other. Each friend buys a present for each of the other **3** friends. How many presents are bought? What strategy did you use?

_____

Name _____

You can use fraction models to add fractions with the same denominator.

$\dfrac{1}{4} + \dfrac{2}{4} = \dfrac{3}{4}$

$\dfrac{1}{4}$ of the model is shaded red. $\dfrac{2}{4}$ is shaded gray.

How much of the fraction model is shaded?

$\dfrac{3}{4}$ of the fraction model is shaded.

---

1. Shade the model below to show $\dfrac{1}{8} + \dfrac{3}{8}$.
Name the sum using two different fractions.
Hint: Think about equivalent fractions.

_____

Write an addition sentence. Use the picture to help.

2. Camela painted sticks for a model fence. She
painted $\dfrac{1}{5}$ of the sticks yesterday.
She painted $\dfrac{3}{5}$ of them today. What
fraction of the sticks is painted? _____

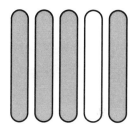

---

3. A set of counters is $\dfrac{3}{8}$ gray and $\dfrac{2}{8}$ red.
What fraction of the set is gray and red?

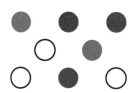

_____

Use fraction models to add. Write the sum.

4. $\dfrac{4}{6} + \dfrac{1}{6} =$ _____ $\dfrac{2}{3} + \dfrac{1}{3} =$ _____ $\dfrac{1}{10} + \dfrac{5}{10} =$ _____

5. $\dfrac{1}{4} + \dfrac{2}{4} =$ _____ $\dfrac{1}{5} + \dfrac{2}{5} =$ _____ $\dfrac{2}{4} + \dfrac{2}{4} =$ _____

You can subtract fractions with the same denominator.

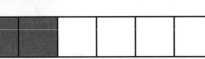

$\frac{5}{6}$ is shaded red.

$\frac{2}{6}$ is shaded grey.

How much more is shaded red?

$$\frac{5}{6} - \frac{2}{6} = \frac{3}{6}$$

$\frac{3}{6}$ more is red.

Write the difference.

6. $\frac{2}{3} - \frac{1}{3} =$ _____ $\frac{5}{6} - \frac{1}{6} =$ _____ $\frac{9}{9} - \frac{2}{9} =$ _____ $\frac{6}{8} - \frac{2}{8} =$ _____

7. $\frac{3}{4} - \frac{1}{4} =$ _____ $\frac{3}{3} - \frac{2}{3} =$ _____ $\frac{4}{5} - \frac{2}{5} =$ _____ $\frac{9}{10} - \frac{5}{10} =$ _____

| Problem Solving |
| Reasoning |

Solve.

8. Marciel used $\frac{1}{4}$ cup of sugar to make bread and $\frac{3}{4}$ cup of sugar to make muffins. How much sugar did he use in all?

_____

9. Ellen made tuna, egg, and ham sandwiches. If $\frac{5}{8}$ are tuna sandwiches, and $\frac{2}{8}$ are egg, how many are ham sandwiches?

_____

Test Prep ★ Mixed Review

10 There are 18 players to make 3 equal teams. How many people will be on each team?

A 15   C 7
B 9   D 6

11 Mosi bought a notebook for $3.65, a pen for $1.37, and some paper for $2.81. About how much did Mosi spend?

F $5   H $8
G $8   J $9

A **mixed number** has a whole number part and a fraction part.

How many apples were eaten on Tuesday?

 = **3** whole apples

= $\frac{1}{2}$ an apple

$3\frac{1}{2}$ apples were eaten.

Apples Eaten Each Day			
Monday			
Tuesday			
Wednesday			
Thursday			
Key	= 1 apple		$=\frac{1}{2}$ apple

Write a mixed number for the shaded parts.

1.   ___   ___   ___

2.   ___   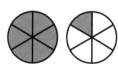 ___   ___

Write the mixed number.

3. two and two thirds _____   one and one fourth _____

4. three and two eights _____   one and one sixth _____

Shade the mixed number.

5.
$1\frac{1}{3}$

three and three fourths

You can estimate with fractions. Is $\frac{5}{6}$ closer to **0**, $\frac{1}{2}$, or **1**?

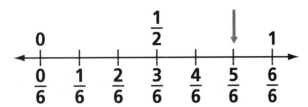

$\frac{5}{6}$ is closer to **1**

Write whether the fraction is closer to 0, $\frac{1}{2}$, or 1.

6. $\frac{2}{6}$ _____ $\frac{4}{6}$ _____ $\frac{1}{6}$ _____ $\frac{6}{6}$ _____

Estimate how much of the garden is planted. Write 0, $\frac{1}{2}$, or 1.

7. 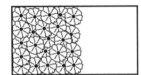 _____   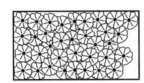 _____   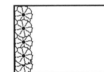 _____

Problem Solving
Reasoning   Solve.

8. Five friends each ate $\frac{1}{2}$ of a banana. How many whole bananas did they buy? Why?

_____

9. Raul painted $9\frac{7}{8}$ flower pots. His sister painted $9\frac{1}{8}$ pots. Who painted about **9** pots?

_____

 Quick Check

Use fraction models to add or subtract.

1. $\frac{1}{4} + \frac{2}{4}$ _____   **2.** $\frac{5}{6} - \frac{2}{6}$ _____   **3.** $\frac{1}{3} + \frac{1}{3}$ _____

Write a mixed number for the shaded part.

Is the fraction closer to 0, $\frac{1}{2}$, or 1?

4.  _____

5. $\frac{5}{6}$ _____   **6.** $\frac{1}{9}$ _____

Work Space.

Problem Solving Application: Not Enough Information

Sometimes there is not enough information to solve a problem. In this lesson you will decide which problems can and cannot be solved.

Tips to Remember:

1. Understand	2. Decide	3. Solve	4. Look back

- Read the problem carefully. What information does the problem give you?
- What do you need to find out?
- Write down the facts in the problem. Is any information missing?
- Change the problem into a number sentence. Ask yourself: What numbers should I use? What operations should I use?

If there is enough information, then solve the problem. If there is not enough information, write what you need to know.

1. Angelita worked very hard to make a vest in **3** days. She finished the vest Sunday evening. What day did she begin making the vest?

Think: What information is given? Is there enough information to answer the question?

_____

_____

Answer: _____

2. The cost of the ribbon for the vest was **$5.50**. Angela paid for the ribbon with a **$10** bill. How many coins did she receive in change?

Think: What information do you need to answer this question? Is the information available to you?

_____

_____

Answer: _____

If there is enough information, then solve the problem. If there is not enough information, write what you need to know.

3. Angelita is making two more vests. She uses the same amount of ribbon on each vest. How much ribbon will she need?

_____

4. To make Andy's cookies you need $\frac{1}{4}$ cup of brown sugar, $\frac{3}{4}$ cup of white sugar, $\frac{1}{2}$ cup butter, **1** teaspoon of vanilla extract, $\frac{1}{2}$ of a **12** ounce bag of raisins, and other ingredients.

How many ounces of raisins are needed in Andy's recipe?

Andy's Cookies
1/4 cup brown sugar
3/4 cup white sugar
1/2 cup butter
1 teaspoon vanilla
1/2 bag (12 ounces) raisins

_____

5. How much flour is needed to make the cookies?

_____

_____

6. How much sugar is in Andy's Cookies recipe?

_____

7. It takes **4** minutes for the oven to heat to **375** degrees. How long will the oven be on?

_____

Extend Your Thinking

8. Add information to Problem **2** so that you could solve the problem.

_____

_____

9. List the amount of each ingredient you would need if you doubled Andy's Cookies recipe.

_____

_____

Loop the correct fraction.

1.

$\dfrac{1}{3}$ $\dfrac{1}{4}$ $\dfrac{2}{7}$

2.

$\dfrac{1}{6}$ $\dfrac{1}{8}$ $\dfrac{1}{7}$

3.

$\dfrac{1}{3}$ $\dfrac{1}{4}$ $\dfrac{1}{5}$

4.

$\dfrac{2}{5}$ $\dfrac{2}{4}$ $\dfrac{2}{3}$

What part of the figure or set is shaded? Write the fraction.

5.

_____

6.

_____

7.

_____

8.

_____

Compare. Use >, < or =.

9.

$\dfrac{5}{6}$ ◯ $\dfrac{3}{6}$

10.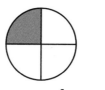

$\dfrac{1}{4}$ ◯ $\dfrac{1}{4}$

11.

$\dfrac{4}{8}$ ◯ $\dfrac{5}{8}$

Order from greatest to least.

12. $\dfrac{4}{8}$, $\dfrac{1}{8}$, $\dfrac{6}{8}$ _____

13. $\dfrac{2}{5}$, $\dfrac{5}{5}$, $\dfrac{1}{5}$ _____

Write the equivalent fraction.

14.

$\dfrac{1}{3} = \dfrac{\boxed{}}{6}$

15.

$\dfrac{2}{4} = \dfrac{4}{\boxed{}}$

16.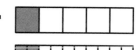

$\dfrac{1}{5} = \dfrac{\boxed{}}{10}$

Write the number.

17.

$\frac{1}{4}$ of 8 = _____

18.

$\frac{1}{2}$ of 10 = _____

19.

$\frac{1}{3}$ of 9 = _____

Write whether the shaded part is closer to 0, $\frac{1}{2}$, or 1.

20.  _____

21. 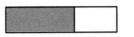 _____

Write the mixed number.

22. ___

23. 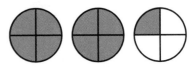 ___

Solve.

24. Carmen buys a coat and a hat. The coat costs **$75,** the hat costs **$24.** How much change does she get?

_____

25. Al has $\frac{1}{4}$ cup of raisins and $\frac{2}{4}$ cup of pears.

How many cups of fruit does Al have in all? _____

26. In a box of hats $\frac{4}{6}$ are white and $\frac{2}{6}$ are red. What fraction tells how many more white hats there are than red? What operation did you use? Why?

_____

27. On a shelf $\frac{4}{9}$ of the books are history books, $\frac{2}{9}$ are cook books, and $\frac{3}{9}$ are math books. How many books are history and math books?

_____

Name _____

1 **Which lists the type of pet sold the most to the type of pet sold the least?**

Pets Sold in a Year	
Type	**Number Sold**
dog	238
fish	806
cat	352
bird	497

A dog, cat, bird, fish

B bird, cat, fish, dog

C bird, cat, dog, fish

D fish, bird, cat, dog

2 **Which shape best describes the front of this house?**

F square

G pentagon

H triangle

J rectangle

3 **Which number goes in the box and makes this number sentence true?**

17 × 1 = ☐

A 1

B 7

C 17

D 18

4 **Which piece in this puzzle is the shape of a right triangle?**

F A

G B

H C

J E

5 **Which is a list of possible outcomes when you spin this spinner 5 times?**

A 2, 4, 6, 8, 10

B 1, 3, 5, 7, 9

C 7, 4, 1, 8, 5

D 0, 2, 7, 4, 1

6 **The tally chart shows the results when a cube is drawn from a bag and then put back.**

Color	Tally
red	|||
green	||||
blue	⊪|||
white	||

If another cube is drawn from the bag, what color will it most likely be?

F red

G blue

H green

J white

7 Tasha collected feathers around a chicken coop. She measured and recorded their lengths.

Length of Feathers

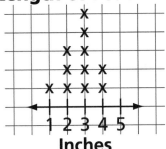

Inches

Tasha needs to use a lot of feathers of the same length for a project. Which size feather should she use?

A 2 inch

B 3 inch

C 4 inch

D 5 inch

8 What fraction of the model is shaded?

F $\frac{1}{2}$ **G** $\frac{3}{4}$ **H** $\frac{1}{3}$ **J** $\frac{3}{3}$

9 Yuki painted 3 rabbit statues in 24 minutes. At this rate, how many minutes did it take Yuki to paint 1 statue?

A 21

B 12

C 8

D 6

E NH

10 The supermarket is selling 5 cans of soup for $10.

How much does 1 can of soup cost?

F $1   **H** $5   **K** NH

G $15   **J** $10

11 Which best describes the fractions?

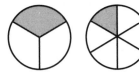

A $\frac{1}{3} > \frac{1}{6}$ **B** $\frac{1}{3} < \frac{1}{6}$

C $\frac{1}{3} = \frac{1}{6}$ **D** $\frac{1}{3} > \frac{1}{3}$

12 Kim ate $\frac{1}{4}$ of a cheese pizza and $\frac{1}{4}$ of a mushroom pizza. Which fraction tells what part of all the pizza Kim ate?

F $\frac{1}{8}$ **G** $\frac{2}{8}$ **H** $\frac{3}{8}$ **J** $\frac{3}{4}$

194 Unit 7 Cumulative Review

Multiplication and Division to 9

CALIFORNIA STANDARDS	Lesson	Page
NS 2.2, 2.3	**1** Algebra • **Related Facts:** **Multiplying and Dividing by 6**	197–198
NS 2.2, 2.3	**2** Algebra • **Related Facts:** **Multiplying and Dividing by 7**	199–200
MR 1.1	**3** Problem Solving Application: **Too Much Information**	201–202
NS 2.2, 2.3; A/F 1.3	**4** Algebra • **Related Facts:** **Multiplying and Dividing by 8**	203–204
NS 2.2, 2.3	**5** Algebra • **Related Facts:** **Multiplying and Dividing by 9**	205–206
	6 **Factors**	207–208
A/F 1.1, 1.2	**7** Algebra • **Problem Solving Strategy:** **Write a Number Sentence**	209–210
	8 **Division with Remainders**	211–214
NS 2.3, 2.8	**9** Algebra • **Checking Division**	215–216
MR 3.1	**10** **Interpreting Remainders**	217–218
	• **Unit 8 Review**	219
	• **Cumulative Review ★ Test Prep**	220

Dear Family,

During the next few weeks, our math class will be learning and practicing multiplication and division of whole numbers.

The homework you might expect to see provides practice in dividing by 1-digit numbers up to 9. Here is a sample you may want to keep handy to give help if needed.

Dividing With Remainders

Find **34 ÷ 5.** Note **5** is the divisor.

(1) Think: How many **5**'s are in **34**?

$$5 \times 7 = 35 \text{ too big}$$

$$5 \times 6 = 30$$

$$5 \times 5 = 25 \text{ too small}$$

$$\begin{array}{r} 6 \\ 5\overline{)34} \end{array}$$

So, the quotient is **6.**

(2) Multiply the divisor by the quotient.

$$5 \times 6 = 30$$

$$\begin{array}{r} 6\ \text{R4} \\ 5\overline{)34} \\ -\ 30 \\ \hline 4 \end{array}$$

(3) Subtract.

If the answer is more than **0**, you have a remainder. The remainder is **4.**

(4) Write the remainder with the quotient.

In this unit, students will need to practice their multiplication and division facts.

Sincerely,

There are **6** rows of buttons with **7** buttons in each row. Multiply to find how many buttons in all.

$$6 \times 7 = 42$$

A related multiplication fact is **7 × 6 = 42**.

If **42** buttons are divided into **6** groups, there are **7** buttons in each group.

$$42 \div 6 = 7$$

A related division fact is **42 ÷ 7 = 6**.

Here are the related facts for this array:

$$6 \times 3 = 18 \qquad 3 \times 6 = 18$$

$$18 \div 6 = 3 \qquad 18 \div 3 = 6$$

Complete.

1. $6 \times 8 =$ _____, so _____ $\div 8 = 6$ and _____ $\div 6 = 8$.

2. $6 \times 7 =$ _____, so _____ $\div 6 = 7$ and _____ $\div 7 = 6$.

3. $6 \times 9 =$ _____, so _____ $\div 9 = 6$ and _____ $\div 6 = 9$.

4. $6 \times 5 =$ _____, so _____ $\div 6 = 5$ and _____ $\div 5 = 6$.

Find the product.

5. $7 \times 6 =$ _____ $6 \times 2 =$ _____ $5 \times 6 =$ _____ $8 \times 6 =$ _____

6. $9 \times 6 =$ _____ $6 \times 6 =$ _____ $4 \times 6 =$ _____ $6 \times 0 =$ _____

Count by 6's.

7. 6, _____, _____, _____, _____, _____, _____, _____, _____

Find each product or quotient.

8.

0	2	6	5	6	6
× 6	× 6	× 2	× 6	× 5	× 8

9.

6	6	9	7	6	3
× 9	× 7	× 6	× 6	× 6	× 6

10.

$6\overline{)18}$ $2\overline{)12}$ $6\overline{)54}$ $6\overline{)36}$ $1\overline{)6}$

11.

$7\overline{)42}$ $5\overline{)30}$ $6\overline{)48}$ $6\overline{)24}$ $9\overline{)54}$

12.

$6\overline{)12}$ $4\overline{)24}$ $9\overline{)45}$ $4\overline{)36}$ $5\overline{)30}$

**Problem Solving
Reasoning**

Solve.

13. Roy is saving for a gift. After the first week he has **$4**. After the second week he has **$8**. After the third week he has **$12**. If Roy continues saving in this pattern, how much will he have after **7** weeks?

_____

14. Start with **30**. Subtract **6** again and again until you reach **0**. How many times did you subtract?

_____

Test Prep ★ Mixed Review

15 Mrs. Robinson bought a package with an even number of pencils. Which size package did she buy?

 A 25 pencils

 B 39 pencils

 C 41 pencils

 D 52 pencils

16 Six fish are in an aquarium. $\frac{1}{6}$ of the fish are goldfish. How many are goldfish?

 F 6

 G 5

 H 3

 J 1

There are **7** groups of stars. Each group has **8** stars. You can count all the stars or you can multiply to find **7 × 8.**

Complete. Use the stars above.

1. There are _____ groups of _____ stars.

How many stars are there in all? _____   **7 × 8 =** _____

Write a related multiplication fact.   _____ **× 7 =** _____

2. If **56** stars are divided into **7** groups,

there will be _____ stars in each group.   **56 ÷ 7 =** _____

Write a related division fact.   _____ **÷** _____ **=** _____

3. If **56 ÷ 7 = 8**, then $\frac{1}{7}$ of **56 =** _____.

If **56 ÷ 8 = 7**, then $\frac{1}{8}$ of **56 =** _____.

Write the related facts.

4.   **7 × 4 =** _____   **7 × 6 =** _____   **5 × 7 =** _____

_____ **×** _____ **=** _____   _____ **×** _____ **=** _____   _____ **×** _____ **=** _____

_____ **÷** _____ **=** _____   _____ **÷** _____ **=** _____   _____ **÷** _____ **=** _____

_____ **÷** _____ **=** _____   _____ **÷** _____ **=** _____   _____ **÷** _____ **=** _____

5.   **7 × 9 =** _____   **7 × 8 =** _____   **7 × 7 =** _____

_____ **×** _____ **=** _____   _____ **×** _____ **=** _____   _____ **÷** _____ **=** _____

_____ **÷** _____ **=** _____   _____ **÷** _____ **=** _____

_____ **÷** _____ **=** _____   _____ **÷** _____ **=** _____

Count by 7's.

6. 7, _____, _____, _____, _____, _____, _____, _____, _____

Find each product or quotient.

7. $7 \times 3 =$ _____ $0 \times 7 =$ _____ $4 \times 7 =$ _____ $1 \times 7 =$ _____

$5 \times 7 =$ _____ $7 \times 6 =$ _____ $7 \times 7 =$ _____ $8 \times 7 =$ _____

8.
$$7\overline{)28} \qquad 3\overline{)21} \qquad 7\overline{)49} \qquad 7\overline{)35} \qquad 9\overline{)63}$$

9. $\frac{1}{7}$ of 14 = _____ $\frac{1}{7}$ of 7 = _____ $\frac{1}{7}$ of 21 = _____ $\frac{1}{7}$ of 42 = _____

| Problem Solving |
| Reasoning |

Solve.

10. Tonya saves **7¢** on Monday, **14¢** on Tuesday, and **21¢** on Wednesday. If the pattern continues, how much will she save on Friday?

_____

11. There are **7** friends. Each friend gives one sticker to each other friend. How many stickers are given out in all? Draw a diagram.

_____

Test Prep ★ Mixed Review

12 Soto ate $\frac{2}{8}$ of the pizza. Inez ate $\frac{3}{8}$ of the pizza. How much of the pizza did they eat in all?

A $\frac{1}{8}$

B $\frac{1}{4}$

C $\frac{5}{16}$

D $\frac{5}{8}$

13 The quilt is $\frac{4}{6}$ dotted, $\frac{1}{6}$ striped, and the rest is a solid color. How much more of the quilt is dotted than striped?

F $\frac{5}{6}$

G $\frac{5}{12}$

H $\frac{3}{6}$

J $\frac{3}{12}$

Problem Solving Application: Too Much Information

Sometimes there is more information in a problem than you need. Decide which facts are needed and which are not before you solve a problem.

Tips to Remember:

> 1. Understand   2. Decide   3. Solve   4. Look back

- Read each problem carefully and underline the question asked.
- Think about each fact in the problem. Ask yourself: Is this a fact I need to solve the problem? Is this an extra fact?
- Circle important words and numbers. Cross out the words and numbers you do not need.

Solve.

1. Beth baked muffins in the oven at **350** degrees for **25** minutes. She put the muffins in the oven at **12:25**. When were the muffins finished?

Think: What question do you need to answer? What information in the problem is needed to answer the question?

_____

_____

_____

Answer: _____

_____

2. Betty is making 24 muffins. She needs $\frac{3}{4}$ cup of sugar. She uses $\frac{1}{4}$ cup of sugar to mix in the batter and the rest of the sugar she used for the icing. How much sugar was used for the icing?

Think: What information is not necessary to solve the problem?

_____

_____

Answer: _____

Solve. Cross out the information you do not need.

3. Beth arranged **24** muffins on a plate that was **9** inches long. Then she put **4** muffins in each row. How many rows of muffins were there?

_____

4. The table is set for **12** people. Beth spent **$2.49** for a package of **12** paper plates which came in **3** different colors. The plates are set around the table in a red, yellow, blue pattern. How many yellow plates are used? What is the color of the last plate put on the table?

_____

5. The party starts at **2:00**. Beth wants to be ready one-half hour before the party. The party ends $3\frac{1}{2}$ hours after it starts. What time does the party end?

_____

6. Beth is buying **2** containers of ice cream for **$13.78**. Each container costs **$6.89**. If she gives the clerk **$15.00**, how much change will she get?

_____

7. A group of **12** friends want to go to a movie. The movie begins at **3:00** and lasts for **90** minutes. Four children can ride in each car. How many cars are needed to take everyone?

_____

8. A ticket for the afternoon show costs **$3** for children and **$4** for adults. The three adults who are driving cars are going to the movie. What is the total cost of the adult tickets?

_____

Extend Your Thinking

9. Create a question for Problem 5 that would require you to use all the information to answer the question.

_____

_____

_____

10. Go back to Problem **8** and change the question so that you use different information to solve the problem.

_____

_____

_____

There are **8** rows of triangles with **9** triangles in each row. Multiply to find how many triangles in all.   **8 × 9 = 72**

A related multiplication fact is **9 × 8 = 72**.

If **72** buttons are divided into **8** groups, there are **9** buttons in each group. **72 ÷ 8 = 9**. A related division fact is **72 ÷ 9 = 8**.

You can use what you know about multiplying with **4** to help you multiply by **8**.

To find **8 × 8**................... Think **4 × 8 = 32**.
                                    Double the product of **4 × 8**.   **32 + 32 = 64**
                                    So, **8 × 8 = 64**.

Write the related facts.

1.   3 × 8 = _____   5 × 8 = _____   8 × 7 = _____

_____ × _____ = _____   _____ × _____ = _____   _____ × _____ = _____

_____ ÷ _____ = _____   _____ ÷ _____ = _____   _____ ÷ _____ = _____

_____ ÷ _____ = _____   _____ ÷ _____ = _____   _____ ÷ _____ = _____

Write each product.

2. 4 × 4 = _____   4 × 6 = _____   4 × 9 = _____

     8 × 4 = _____   8 × 6 = _____   8 × 9 = _____

Count by 8's.

3. 8, _____, _____, _____, _____, _____, _____, _____, _____

Write the answer.

7. $\frac{1}{8}$ of 64 = _____ $\frac{1}{8}$ of 72 = _____ $\frac{1}{8}$ of 16 = _____ $\frac{1}{8}$ of 32 = _____

8. $\frac{1}{7}$ of 56 = _____ $\frac{1}{8}$ of 40 = _____ $\frac{1}{6}$ of 48 = _____ $\frac{1}{8}$ of 8 = _____

Use × or ÷ to make the sentence true.

9. 8 △ 3 = 24   8 △ 8 = 64   8 △ 8 = 1   40 △ 5 = 8

10. 72 △ 9 = 8   8 △ 0 = 0   32 △ 4 = 8   16 △ 2 = 8

Problem Solving
Reasoning

Solve.

11. Nina runs **8** miles every day. How many days will it take her to run **64** miles? How do you know?

_____

12. Start with **8**. Add **8** again and again until you get **40**. How many times did you add **8**? Why is your answer correct?

_____

✓ **Quick Check**

Multiply.

Work Space.

1. 6 × 4 _____   **2.** 5 × 6 _____

3. 7 × 7 _____   **4.** 4 × 7 _____

5. 7   **6.** 8   **7.** 3   **8.** 6
   × 3   × 8   × 8   × 3

Divide.

9. 48 ÷ 6 _____   **10.** 54 ÷ 6 _____

11. 36 ÷ 6 _____   **12.** 72 ÷ 8 _____

13. 8)‾5‾6‾   **14.** 8)‾4‾0‾   **15.** 7)‾6‾3‾   **16.** 7)‾4‾2‾

Related Facts: Multiplying and Dividing by 9

There are **9** groups of baseballs with **10** baseballs in each row. Multiply to find how many in all.

$$9 \times 10 = 90$$

There are **90** baseballs. They are divided into **10** groups. How many are in each group?

$$90 \div 10 = 9$$

Helpful Hints for multiplying with 9

Use the commutative property to change the fact with **9** into one you already know.

To find **9 × 6** think
6 × 9 = 54, so **9 × 6 = 54**

Use multiplying with **10** and subtraction to find products with **9**.

To find **9 × 5**	To find **9 × 8**	To find **9 × 7**
10 × 5 = 50	**10 × 8 = 80**	**10 × 7 = 70**
50 − 5 = 45	**80 − 8 = 72**	**70 − 7 = 63**
so **9 × 5 = 45**	so **9 × 8 = 72**	so **9 × 7 = 63**

Complete the chart of related facts.

1.

9 × 1 =	1 × 9 =	9 ÷ 9 =	9 ÷ 1 =
9 × 2 =	2 × 9 =		18 ÷ 2 =
9 × 3 =		27 ÷ 9 =	
	4 × 9 =		
9 × 5 =			45 ÷ 5 =
		54 ÷ 9 =	
9 × 7 =	7 × 9 =		
9 × 8 =			72 ÷ 8 =
9 × 10 =	10 × 9 =	90 ÷ 9 =	

Count by 9's.

2. 9, _____, _____, _____, _____, _____, _____, _____, _____

Find each quotient.

3. 9$\overline{)36}$ 9$\overline{)45}$ 3$\overline{)27}$ 9$\overline{)18}$ 6$\overline{)54}$

4. 7$\overline{)63}$ 9$\overline{)72}$ 4$\overline{)36}$ 9$\overline{)81}$ 8$\overline{)24}$

Find each product.

5.   7   9   0   5   9
     $\times 9$ $\times 4$ $\times 9$ $\times 9$ $\times 9$

Problem Solving Reasoning **Solve.**

6. Shana can make **9** paper snowflakes in **1** hour, **18** in **2** hours, **27** in **3** hours, and so on. At this rate, how many paper snowflakes can she make in **7** hours?

_____

7. Look at Problem **6.** Shana wants to make **54** snowflakes for party decorations. How many hours will it take her to make them?

_____

8. Earlene wrote **72 ÷ 9 = 8.** What two multiplication sentences can she use to check?

_____

9. A box holds one layer of **45** baseballs. How can the baseballs be arranged?

_____

Test Prep ★ Mixed Review

10 What is another way to write
    6 + 6 + 6 + 6?

A 6 + 4
B 12 + 6
C 6 × 6 × 6 × 6
D 4 × 6

11 What number goes in the box to make the number sentence true?

    4 × 3 = ☐ × 4

F 3   H 7
G 4   J 12

Name _____

Factors are the numbers that you multiply in a multiplication problem.

The factors of **6** are **1, 2, 3,** and **6** because

$1 \times 6 = 6$ $6 \times 1 = 6$ $2 \times 3 = 6$ $3 \times 2 = 6$

The factors of **16** are **1, 2, 4, 8,** and **16** because

$1 \times 16 = 16$ $16 \times 1 = 16$ $2 \times 8 = 16$ $8 \times 2 = 16$ $4 \times 4 = 16$

Write all the multiplication sentences for the number. Then name the factors.

1.

14	9	15

Factors of **14:**
_____

Factors of **9:**
_____

Factors of **15:**
_____

2.

10	12	20

Factors of **10:**
_____

Factors of **12:**
_____

Factors of **20:**
_____

Write *true* or *false*.

3. _____ **4** is a factor of **8**.   _____ **5** is a factor of **9**.

4. _____ **4** and **6** are factors of **12**.   _____ **7** is a factor of **14**.

5. _____ **2** and **3** are factors of **16**.   _____ **18** is a factor of **18**.

6. _____ **15** has **4** factors.   _____ **17** has only **2** factors.

7. _____ **3** has no factors   _____ **6** is a factor of **25**.

8. _____ **9** is a factor of **27**.   _____ **2** is a factor of **19**.

Numbers can be factored in another way.
Complete.

9. $18 = 3 \times 6$ $20 = 5 \times \rule{1cm}{0.4pt}$ $12 = 2 \times \rule{1cm}{0.4pt}$

   $= 3 \times 2 \times \rule{1cm}{0.4pt}$ $= 5 \times \rule{1cm}{0.4pt} \times \rule{1cm}{0.4pt}$ $= 2 \times \rule{1cm}{0.4pt} \times \rule{1cm}{0.4pt}$
   $\qquad\quad \uparrow \qquad \uparrow$

   Think: $6 = 2 \times 3$

| Problem Solving |
| Reasoning |

Solve.

10. Kizzie says **13** has only two factors. Do you agree or disagree? Why?

_____

_____

11. One factor is **9**. The other factor is a **1**–digit number. What is the greatest product you can get?

_____

Test Prep ★ Mixed Review

12 Diego's Market sells 3 pizzas for $21. What is the cost for 1 pizza?

   A $24

   B $18

   C $9

   D $7

13 Celia bought a magazine for $3.95. She paid with a ten dollar bill. About how much change should she receive?

   F $2

   G $4

   H $6

   J $8

208   Unit 8 Lesson 6

Problem Solving Strategy: Write a Number Sentence

Sometimes writing a number sentence can help you solve a problem.

Problem

Emily collects stamps. She has **8** new stamps to add to her collection. Then she will have **30** stamps. How many stamps did Emily have in her collection before adding the new stamps?

1 Understand As you reread, ask yourself questions.

- What do you know about Emily's stamps?

   Emily will have 30 stamps after adding 8 stamps.

- What do you need to find out?

   How many stamps Emily had before she added 8.

2 Decide Choose a method for solving.

- Write a number sentence to solve the problem.

- Think: She has **30** stamps now. Before the **8** new stamps, how many did she have? What operation will you use?

   _____

- How would you write this as a number sentence?

   _____

3 Solve Complete the subtraction sentence.

   30 − 8 = _____

4 Look back Check your answer.

   Use your answer to write an addition sentence.

   Answer: _____

   How did writing a number sentence help you?

   _____

Use the Write a Number Sentence Strategy or any other strategy you have learned.

1. Tim is **6** years old. Emily is twice Tim's age. How old is Emily?

Think: What does the word "twice" make you think about in math?

_____

Answer: _____

_____

2. Emily has **30** stamps to put in a book. One book holds **5** stamps on each page. Another book holds **6** stamps on a page. Which book should Emily buy if she wants to fill the fewest number of pages?

Think: Should she put more stamps or less stamps on a page?

_____

Answer: _____

_____

_____

3. Tim has **12** stamps. Michael has half as many stamps as Tim. How many stamps does Michael have?

_____

4. One-third of Tim's **12** stamps are **5¢** stamps. The rest are **33¢** stamps. How many **33¢** stamps does Tim have?

_____

5. Tara bought two stamps for **$3.28.** She received **$1.72** change. How much money did Tara give the clerk?

_____

6. Tara received the **$1.72** change as **11** coins. What value were the coins, and how many of each did she receive?

_____

7. Rosa had **30** stamps. If she put her stamps in a book, how many pages of stamps would she fill?

_____

8. In Problem **3**, what if Michael had twice as many stamps as Tim? How would this change the problem?

_____

Name _____

There are **13** dots. Make as many groups of **3** dots as you can.

How many groups of **3** could you make? _____

How many dots do you have left over? _____

Complete.

1. Divide **16** blocks into groups of **5**.

▢ ▢ ▢ ▢ ▢ ▢ ▢ ▢
▢ ▢ ▢ ▢ ▢ ▢ ▢ ▢

☐ groups of **5**

☐ left over

2. Divide **14** stars into groups of **4**.

☐ groups of **4**

☐ left over

3. Divide **9** dots into groups of **2**.

● ● ● ● ●
● ● ● ●

☐ groups of **2**

☐ left over

4. Divide **12** hats into groups of **5**.

☐ groups of **5**

☐ left over

---

5. Divide **40** dots into groups of **9**.

☐ groups of **9**

☐ left over

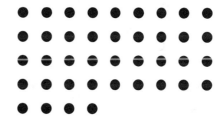

This picture shows that **13** marbles can be divided into **4** groups with **3** marbles in each group and **1** marble left over.

We can write: **(4 × 3) + 1 = 13**

4 groups of 3   1 left over

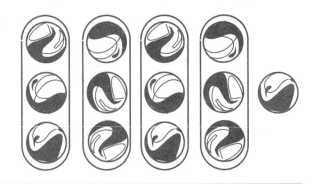

Write a number sentence for each.

6. 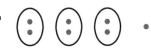 .

(**3 × 2**) + _____ = _____

_____

7.  .

_____

_____

8. 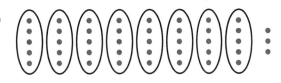 :

_____

_____

Multiply first. Then add.

9. (3 × 5) + 3 = _____   (4 × 3) + 2 = _____   (6 × 3) + 1 = _____

10. (7 × 0) + 4 = _____   (5 × 3) + 4 = _____   (7 × 3) + 1 = _____

11. (9 × 3) + 2 = _____   (8 × 3) + 0 = _____   (1 × 1) + 1 = _____

Problem Solving Reasoning   **Solve.**

12. Ling has some cards. She puts them in **4** groups of **4**. There are **2** left over. How many cards does she have?

_____

13. Max has **26** muffins. He puts **5** muffins in each package and has **1** muffin left. How many packages did he make?

_____

Name _____

Here is another way to show left overs in division.

$9 \div 2$

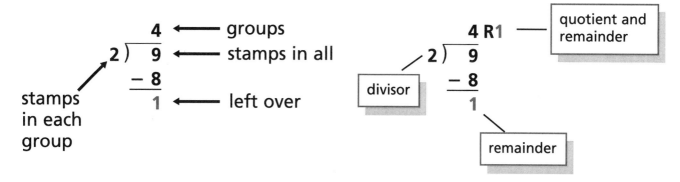

There is **1** stamp left over. It is called the **remainder.**

$$\begin{array}{r} 4 \\ 2\overline{)9} \\ -8 \\ \hline 1 \end{array}$$ ← groups
← stamps in all
← left over

stamps in each group

$$\begin{array}{r} 4\ R1 \\ 2\overline{)9} \\ -8 \\ \hline 1 \end{array}$$

quotient and remainder

divisor

remainder

The answer is written **4 R 1.**

The remainder is always less than the divisor.

Complete. Write the quotient and remainder.

14.

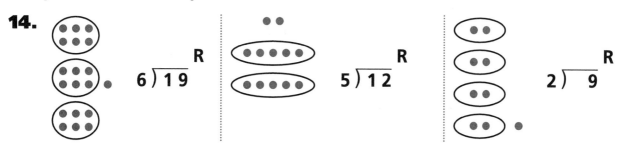

$6\overline{)19}$ R ___

$5\overline{)12}$ R ___

$2\overline{)9}$ R ___

Use the models. Find each quotient and remainder.

15.

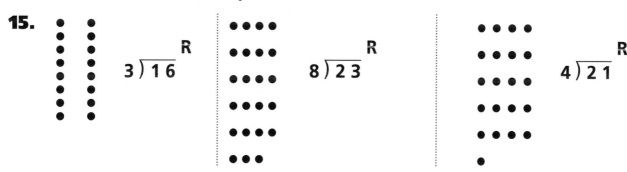

$3\overline{)16}$ R ___

$8\overline{)23}$ R ___

$4\overline{)21}$ R ___

Use the models. Find each quotient and remainder.

16. ● ● ● ● ● ● ● ●

$$3\overline{)8}^{R}$$

● ● ● ● ● ● ● ● ● ●
● ● ● ● ● ● ● ● ● ●

$$6\overline{)2\,0}^{R}$$

● ● ● ● ● ● ● ● ● ●
● ● ● ● ● ● ● ● ● ●
● ● ● ● ●

$$3\overline{)2\,5}^{R}$$

Complete.

17.

$$
\begin{array}{r}
5\,R \\
2\overline{)1\,1} \\
-\,\boxed{} \\
\hline
1
\end{array}
$$

18.

$$
\begin{array}{r}
\boxed{}\boxed{} \\
4\overline{)3\,9}\,R \\
-\,3\,6 \\
\hline
\boxed{}
\end{array}
$$

19.

$$
\begin{array}{r}
3\,R\ \boxed{} \\
6\overline{)} \\
\boxed{} \\
-\,\boxed{} \\
\hline
1
\end{array}
$$

✓ Quick Check

Multiply or divide.

1. $9 \times 5 = $ _____   **2.** $9 \times 7 = $ _____

3. $81 \div 9 = $ _____   **4.** $54 \div 9 = $ _____

Write as many different pairs of factors as you can for each product.

5.

8
1 × 8

6.

12
1 × 12

7.

18
1 × 18

Divide.

8. $5\overline{)2\,6}$ **9.** $7\overline{)4\,6}$ **10.** $6\overline{)5\,7}$

Work Space.

Checking Division

Multiplication and division are inverse operations.

We can always check division by multiplication.

$$\begin{array}{r} 8 \\ 5\overline{)40} \end{array} \qquad 8 \times 5 = 40$$

$$\begin{array}{r} 8\ R2 \\ 5\overline{)\ 42} \\ -40 \\ \hline 2 \end{array} \qquad \begin{array}{l} (8 \times 5) + 2 = \\ \\ 40 \quad + 2 = 42 \end{array}$$

Complete.

1.
$$\begin{array}{r} 5\ R\ 2 \\ 3\overline{)\ 17} \\ -15 \\ \hline 2 \end{array}$$

(_____ × _____) + _____ =

_____ + _____ = _____

2.
$$\begin{array}{r} 9\ R\ 1 \\ 2\overline{)\ 19} \\ -18 \\ \hline 1 \end{array}$$

(_____ × _____) + _____ =

_____ + _____ = _____

3.
$$\begin{array}{r} 6\ R\ 3 \\ 4\overline{)\ 27} \\ -24 \\ \hline 3 \end{array}$$

(_____ × _____) + _____ =

_____ + _____ = _____

Find the quotient and remainder. Check by writing a multiplication and addition sentence.

4.
$$\begin{array}{r} R \\ 6\overline{)\ 21} \end{array}$$

(_____ × 6) + _____ = 21

5.
$$\begin{array}{r} R \\ 4\overline{)\ 9} \end{array}$$

(_____ × 4) + _____ = 9

6.
$$\begin{array}{r} R \\ 9\overline{)\ 24} \end{array}$$

(_____ × _____) + _____ = 24

7.
$$\begin{array}{r} R \\ 3\overline{)\ 26} \end{array}$$

(_____ × _____) + _____ = 26

Divide.

8.

R	R	R	R	R
4$\overline{)15}$	3$\overline{)13}$	4$\overline{)34}$	6$\overline{)29}$	5$\overline{)49}$

9.

3$\overline{)7}$	5$\overline{)12}$	3$\overline{)8}$	4$\overline{)18}$	2$\overline{)7}$

10.

5$\overline{)31}$	4$\overline{)29}$	5$\overline{)18}$	3$\overline{)10}$	4$\overline{)21}$

11.

5$\overline{)27}$	4$\overline{)35}$	2$\overline{)9}$	3$\overline{)20}$	5$\overline{)29}$

Problem Solving Reasoning **Solve.**

12. Mrs. Rox has **28** apples. She puts **5** apples in each bag. How many apples are left over? How do you know?

_____

_____

13. Raul places **7** roses in each vase. There are **8** vases. He has **5** roses left over. How many roses does Raul have in all?

_____

Test Prep ★ Mixed Review

14 Each child needs 3 bottles of water for the hike. There are 9 children going hiking. How many bottles of water will they need in all?

A 6

B 12

C 21

D 27

15 What is the possibility that the children will see a bird while hiking?

F impossible

G unlikely

H likely

J certain

Sometimes you get a remainder when you divide. Here are **3** ways to decide what to do with the remainder.

1. Plato has **20** baseball cards. He gives an equal number to each of **6** friends. He gives the left over cards to Roger. How many cards will Roger get?

Divide: **20 ÷ 6**

$$6 \overline{)\ 2\ 0}$$

Use the remainder.

Roger gets _____ cards.

2. Letisha needs **8** tent pegs to set up each tent. She has **77** pegs. How many tents can she set up?

Divide: **77 ÷ 8**

$$8 \overline{)\ 7\ 7}$$

Drop the remainder.

She can set up _____ tents.

3. A group of **9** girls and **5** boys are planning a canoe trip. Each canoe holds **3** people. How many canoes does the group need?

Divide: **14 ÷ 3**

$$3 \overline{)\ 1\ 4}$$

Include the remainder in the answer.

Write the next whole number.

The group needs _____ canoes.

4. Each canoe needs **2** paddles. There are **17** paddles in the boathouse. How many canoes can the campers use at one time?

_____

5. A group of **29** campers and **3** counselors go on a fishing trip. Can each counselor be in charge of the same number of campers? Explain.

_____

Solve.

6. At a campfire, **9** campers share **48** marshmallows. Each camper gets the same number. What is the least number of marshmallows that can be left over?

_____

7. Yoko is buying **1** frozen yogurt bar for each of the **35** campers. The bars come in packages of **8**. How many packages should she buy?

_____

8. Winonah shares **24** shells equally among her **3** sisters. Were any shells leftover? How do you know?

_____

_____

9. Heroshi runs **9** miles each week. How many miles does he run in **4** weeks? What operation did you choose?

_____

_____

 Quick Check

Complete.

1. 8 × 7 = 56 because 56 ÷ ☐ = ☐

2. 6 × 9 = ☐ because ☐ ÷ ☐ = ☐

Solve.

3. There are **42** people taking vans to the zoo. Each van holds **8** people. What is the fewest number of vans needed to take the people to the zoo? _____

4. The chef is making pie crusts. Each crust uses **3** eggs. How many pie crusts can the chef make with **14** eggs? _____

Work Space.

Name _____

Find the answer.

1. $4 \times 8 =$ _____

2. $0 \times 8 =$ _____

3. $6 \times 6 =$ _____

4. $9 \times 8 =$ _____

5. $7 \times 9 =$ _____

6. $9 \times 4 =$ _____

7. $\begin{array}{r} 8 \\ \times\,6 \\ \hline \end{array}$

8. $\begin{array}{r} 6 \\ \times\,7 \\ \hline \end{array}$

9. $\begin{array}{r} 9 \\ \times\,3 \\ \hline \end{array}$

10. $21 \div 7 =$ _____

11. $72 \div 8 =$ _____

12. $64 \div 8 =$ _____

13. $\frac{1}{9}$ of 45 = _____

14. $\frac{1}{6}$ of 54 = _____

15. $\frac{1}{7}$ of 49 = _____

16. $7\overline{)56}$

17. $8\overline{)32}$

18. $5\overline{)40}$

Find the quotient and remainder.

19. _____ R _____
$6\overline{)55}$

20. _____ R _____
$9\overline{)77}$

21. _____ R _____
$8\overline{)50}$

Complete.

22. $43 \div 8 = 5$ R3 because (_____ $\times$ _____) + _____ = _____.

 Solve.

23. Troy read **8** pages each day for **7** days. What number sentence shows the total pages he read?

_____

24. Mr. Lei builds chairs. Each chair needs **4** legs. How many chairs can he make with **30** legs?

_____

1 What is the possibility of spinning the number 3?

A certain   **C** unlikely

B likely   **D** impossible

2 Juanita collected 12 shells at the beach. Which tally shows the correct way to record this amount?

F 𝍸𝍸 𝍸𝍸 ‖   **H** 𝍸𝍸 𝍸𝍸

G 𝍸𝍸 𝍸𝍸 ‖   **J** 𝍸𝍸 𝍸𝍸 𝍸𝍸

3 Luis gave $\frac{1}{3}$ of a cracker to his bird in the morning and $\frac{1}{3}$ of a cracker to his bird at night. How much of a cracker did the bird eat that day?

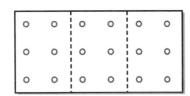

A $\frac{1}{3}$ **C** $\frac{2}{3}$

B $\frac{1}{2}$ **D** 1

4 Diego is building 8 birdhouses. He needs 6 pieces of wood for each birdhouse. How many pieces of wood will he need for all the birdhouses?

F 14   **H** 48   **K** NH

G 24   **J** 54

5 The baker needs to pack 59 muffins into boxes. Each box can hold 8 muffins. How many muffins will be left after he completely fills as many boxes as he can?

A 3   **C** 31   **E** NH

B 7   **D** 51

6 Which number sentence is in the same fact family as $9 \times 7 = 63$?

F $9 - 7 = 2$ **H** $9 + 7 = 16$

G $63 \div 7 = 9$ **J** $9 \div 3 = 3$

7 David made a flag for his club. What fraction of David's flag is dotted?

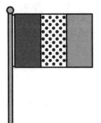

A $\frac{1}{2}$ **C** $\frac{1}{4}$

B $\frac{1}{3}$ **D** $\frac{2}{3}$

UNIT 9 • TABLE OF CONTENTS

Multiplying and Dividing by 1-Digit Numbers

CALIFORNIA STANDARDS		Lesson	Page
NS 2.4	1	Multiplication without Regrouping	223–224
NS 2.4	2	Multiplication with Regrouping	225–226
NS 2.4	3	Multiplying 3-Digit Numbers	227–228
NS 2.4	4	Regrouping Ones	229–230
NS 2.4	5	Regrouping Tens	231–232
NS 2.4	6	Regrouping More than Once	233–234
NS 2.4, 2.6	7	Multiplication with Zeros	235–236
MR 2.3, A/F 2.2	8	Algebra • Problem Solving Strategy: Make a Table	237–238
NS 2.4	9	Multiplying 4-Digit Numbers	239–240
NS 2.5	10	2-Digit Quotients	241–242
NS 2.5	11	3-Digit Quotients	243–244
NS 2.8; MR 1.1, 1.2, 2.3, 3.2	12	Problem Solving Application: Multistep Problems	245–246
	•	Unit 9 Review	247
	•	Cumulative Review ★ Test Prep	248

Dear Family,

During the next few weeks, our math class will be learning about multiplying and dividing with 1-digit numbers. Topics will include multiplication with regrouping.

You can expect to see homework that provides practice with multiplication. Here is a sample you may want to keep handy.

Multiplication: Regrouping More than Once

To multiply **5** by **387**, first write the problem:

$$\begin{array}{r} 3\ 8\ 7 \\ \times\quad 5 \\ \hline \end{array}$$

Then multiply the ones and regroup.

$$\begin{array}{r} {}^{3} \\ 3\ 8\ 7 \\ \times\quad 5 \\ \hline 5 \end{array}$$

Multiply: **5 × 7** ones = **35** ones

Regroup: **35** ones = **3** tens and **5** ones.

Next, multiply the tens. Then add and regroup.

$$\begin{array}{r} {}^{4\ 3} \\ 3\ 8\ 7 \\ \times\quad 5 \\ \hline 3\ 5 \end{array}$$

Multiply: **5 × 8** tens = **40** tens

Add: **40** tens + **3** tens = **43** tens

Regroup: **43** tens = **4** hundreds and **3** tens

Then multiply the hundreds and add.

$$\begin{array}{r} {}^{4\ 3} \\ 3\ 8\ 7 \\ \times\quad 5 \\ \hline 1,9\ 3\ 5 \end{array}$$

Multiply: **5 × 3** hundreds = **15** hundreds

Add: **15** hundreds + **4** hundreds = **19** hundreds

Regroup: **19** hundreds = **1** thousand and **9** hundreds

5 × 387 = 1,935.

During this unit, students will need to continue practicing multiplication and division facts.

Sincerely,

Multiplication without Regrouping

To find the total number of blocks, you can multiply **2 × 34.**

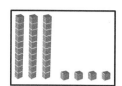 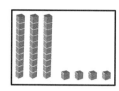

T	O	
3	4	← blocks in each group
×	2	← groups
		← blocks in all

1. Multiply the ones.

T	O
3	4
×	2
	8	← 2 × 4 ones = 8 ones

2. Multiply the tens.

T	O
3	4
×	2
6	8	2 × 3 tens = 6 tens

The product is **68.**

Multiply.

1.

T	O
2	3
×	3

T	O
1	4
×	2

T	O
3	3
×	3

T	O
2	1
×	4

T	O
3	2
×	2

You can multiply without using a table.

1. Multiply the ones.

```
  5 3
×   2
─────
    6
```

2. Multiply the tens.

```
  5 3
×   2
─────
1 0 6
```

Multiply with money.

```
 $. 6 3
 ×    3
───────
 $1. 8 9
```

Find the products.

2.

```
  5 4        4 3        6 3      $. 3 1       8 4        6 0      $. 6 1
× 2        × 3        × 2      ×   5        × 2        × 8      ×   9
```

3.

```
  6 3      $. 7 2       5 0        7 0        8 0      $. 9 0       3 4
× 3        ×   4        × 6        × 2        × 6      ×   7        × 2
```

You can multiply with **10** mentally. Find the pattern.

12 tens = **120**	**25** tens = **250**	**50** tens = **500**
12 × 10 = 120	**25 × 10 = 250**	**50 × 10 = 500**
10 × 12 = 120	**10 × 25 = 250**	**10 × 50 = 500**

Complete. Use the pattern.

4. **16 × 10 =** _____ **12 × 10 =** _____ **10 × 37 =** _____

5. **29 × 10 =** _____ **10 × 25 =** _____ **10 × 13 =** _____

6. **10 × 40 =** _____ **11 × 10 =** _____ **62 × 10 =** _____

Problem Solving
Reasoning

Solve.

7. How much does it cost to buy **4** boxes of noodles and **1** bag of napkins?

_____

8. How much change will there be from **$5.00** if you buy **5** dozen eggs?

_____

GROCERIES

Item	Cost
eggs	$.91 a dozen
noodles	$.60 a box
napkins	$.78 a bag

Test Prep ★ Mixed Review

9 **Which comes next in the pattern?**

A

B

C

D

10 The art club is making necklaces. They need 8 beads for each necklace. There are 50 beads. How many necklaces can the art club make?

 F 8

 G 7

 H 6

 J 577

Name _____

Multiplication with Regrouping

STANDARD

Sometimes when you multiply you have to regroup.

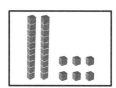 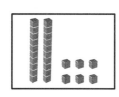

T	O
2	6	← blocks in each group
×	2	← groups
		← blocks in all

1. Multiply the ones. Regroup.

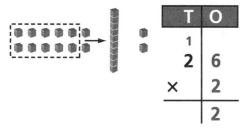

	T	O
	¹	
	2	6
×		2
		2

2 × 6 ones = 12 ones
12 ones = 1 ten and 2 ones

2. Multiply the tens. Then add.

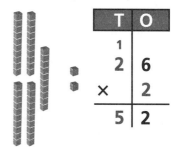

	T	O
	¹	
	2	6
×		2
	5	2

There are **52** blocks in all.

Multiply.

1.

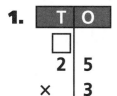

T	O
□	
2	5
×	3

T	O
□	
3	7
×	2

T	O
□	
1	3
×	4

T	O
□	
2	7
×	3

2.

T	O
□	
3	8
×	2

T	O
□	
1	4
×	8

T	O
□	
1	2
×	7

T	O
□	
3	5
×	2

3. □ □ □ □ □

```
  8 5      6 9      7 8      5 7      3 6
× 3      × 3      × 6      × 5      × 3
```

4.
```
  9 9      4 6      6 7      6 6      9 6
× 3      × 8      × 3      × 4      × 3
```

Sometimes when you multiply with money you have to regroup.

$$
\begin{array}{r}
\overset{2}{} \\
\$.5\,8 \\
\times 3 \\
\hline
\$1.7\,4
\end{array}
$$

3×8 ones = **24** ones

24 ones = **2** tens and **4** ones

Multiply.

5.
$$
\begin{array}{r}
\square \\
\$.2\,8 \\
\times2 \\
\hline
\end{array}
\qquad
\begin{array}{r}
\square \\
\$.2\,5 \\
\times6 \\
\hline
\end{array}
\qquad
\begin{array}{r}
\square \\
\$.3\,7 \\
\times3 \\
\hline
\end{array}
\qquad
\begin{array}{r}
\square \\
\$.4\,8 \\
\times3 \\
\hline
\end{array}
\qquad
\begin{array}{r}
\square \\
\$.3\,6 \\
\times2 \\
\hline
\end{array}
\qquad
\begin{array}{r}
\square \\
\$.1\,5 \\
\times5 \\
\hline
\end{array}
$$

6.
$$
\begin{array}{r}
\$.2\,7 \\
\times4 \\
\hline
\end{array}
\qquad
\begin{array}{r}
\$.4\,9 \\
\times2 \\
\hline
\end{array}
\qquad
\begin{array}{r}
\$.1\,6 \\
\times5 \\
\hline
\end{array}
\qquad
\begin{array}{r}
\$.2\,9 \\
\times6 \\
\hline
\end{array}
\qquad
\begin{array}{r}
\$.4\,7 \\
\times3 \\
\hline
\end{array}
\qquad
\begin{array}{r}
\$.1\,8 \\
\times7 \\
\hline
\end{array}
$$

**Problem Solving
Reasoning**

Solve.

7. Henri sells shirts. He has **7** boxes with **24** shirts in each box. How many shirts does he have in all?

_____

8. Alicia has **$5.00**. She wants to buy a bag of beads for each of **6** friends. Each bag of beads costs **$.86**. Does she have enough money? Explain.

_____

Test Prep ★ Mixed Review

9 Marco has to pack 18 books into boxes. Each box will hold 3 books. How many boxes will Marco need to use?

A 21
B 15
C 6
D 5

10 The town built a new wall along the beach using 3,045 cement blocks. The old wall that was torn down contained 2,468 blocks. How many more blocks were used in the new wall?

F 6,413
G 5,513
H 5,405
J 577

Multiply to find the total number of blocks.

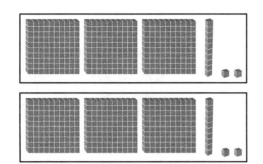

H	T	O	
3	1	2	← blocks in each group
×		2	← group
			← blocks in all

1. Multiply the ones.

H	T	O
3	1	2
×		2
		4

2×2 ones = 4 ones

2. Multiply the tens.

H	T	O
3	1	2
×		2
	2	4

2×1 ten = 2 tens

3. Multiply the hundreds.

H	T	O
3	1	2
×		2
6	2	4

2×3 hundreds = 6 hundreds
The product is **624.**

Multiply.

1.

H	T	O
2	3	1
×		3

H	T	O
4	0	3
×		3

H	T	O
1	1	1
×		4

H	T	O
1	2	1
×		3

H	T	O
1	3	3
×		2

2.   141   322   230   414   420   330
        × 2   × 4   × 3   × 2   × 4   × 3

3.   124   513   102   713   320   343
        × 2   × 3   × 4   × 3   × 4   × 2

4.   131   821   903   500   831   401
        × 2   × 3   × 3   × 8   × 3   × 5

You can multiply with money the same way.

$$
\begin{array}{r}
\$1.23 \\
\times\ \ \ \ 2 \\
\hline
\$2.46
\end{array}
\qquad
\begin{array}{r}
\$4.12 \\
\times\ \ \ \ 3 \\
\hline
\$12.36
\end{array}
$$

Remember to write $ and . in the product.

Multiply.

5.
$$
\begin{array}{r}
\$.81 \\
\times\ \ 2 \\
\hline
\end{array}
\quad
\begin{array}{r}
\$9.20 \\
\times\ \ \ 4 \\
\hline
\end{array}
\quad
\begin{array}{r}
\$8.01 \\
\times\ \ \ 5 \\
\hline
\end{array}
\quad
\begin{array}{r}
\$.43 \\
\times\ \ 3 \\
\hline
\end{array}
\quad
\begin{array}{r}
\$7.43 \\
\times\ \ \ 2 \\
\hline
\end{array}
\quad
\begin{array}{r}
\$6.22 \\
\times\ \ \ 3 \\
\hline
\end{array}
$$

6.
$$
\begin{array}{r}
\$1.21 \\
\times\ \ \ \ 4 \\
\hline
\end{array}
\quad
\begin{array}{r}
\$1.13 \\
\times\ \ \ 3 \\
\hline
\end{array}
\quad
\begin{array}{r}
\$3.12 \\
\times\ \ \ 2 \\
\hline
\end{array}
\quad
\begin{array}{r}
\$3.11 \\
\times\ \ \ 5 \\
\hline
\end{array}
\quad
\begin{array}{r}
\$8.11 \\
\times\ \ \ 7 \\
\hline
\end{array}
\quad
\begin{array}{r}
\$4.10 \\
\times\ \ \ 6 \\
\hline
\end{array}
$$

Problem Solving Reasoning Solve.

7. Matthew bought **3** loaves of bread. Each loaf cost **$1.31**. How much did Matthew spend?

_____

8. Elsie's dog eats **5** pounds of food in a week. If each pound costs **$.64,** how much does dog food cost for a week?

_____

 Quick Check

Multiply.

Work Space.

1.
$$
\begin{array}{r}
23 \\
\times\ 2 \\
\hline
\end{array}
$$
2.
$$
\begin{array}{r}
41 \\
\times\ 3 \\
\hline
\end{array}
$$
3.
$$
\begin{array}{r}
62 \\
\times\ 4 \\
\hline
\end{array}
$$
4.
$$
\begin{array}{r}
33 \\
\times\ 3 \\
\hline
\end{array}
$$

5.
$$
\begin{array}{r}
37 \\
\times\ 4 \\
\hline
\end{array}
$$
6.
$$
\begin{array}{r}
53 \\
\times\ 5 \\
\hline
\end{array}
$$
7.
$$
\begin{array}{r}
46 \\
\times\ 7 \\
\hline
\end{array}
$$
8.
$$
\begin{array}{r}
89 \\
\times\ 2 \\
\hline
\end{array}
$$

9.
$$
\begin{array}{r}
214 \\
\times\ \ 2 \\
\hline
\end{array}
$$
10.
$$
\begin{array}{r}
312 \\
\times\ \ 3 \\
\hline
\end{array}
$$
11.
$$
\begin{array}{r}
943 \\
\times\ \ 2 \\
\hline
\end{array}
$$
12.
$$
\begin{array}{r}
712 \\
\times\ \ 4 \\
\hline
\end{array}
$$

To find the product you need to regroup ones.

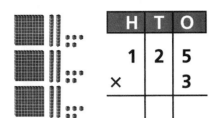

H	T	O
1	2	5
×		3

1. Multiply the ones. Regroup.

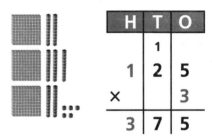

H	T	O
	¹	
1	2	5
×		3
		5

15 ones = 1 ten and 5 ones

2. Multiply the tens. Then add.

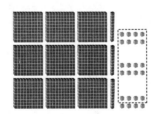

H	T	O
	¹	
1	2	5
×		3
	7	5

3. Multiply the hundreds.

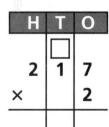

H	T	O
	¹	
1	2	5
×		3
3	7	5

The product is 375.

Multiply. Remember, always start with the ones!

1.

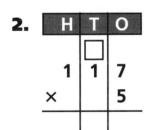

H	T	O
	☐	
3	1	8
×		3

H	T	O
	☐	
1	2	3
×		4

H	T	O
	☐	
2	1	7
×		2

2.

H	T	O
	☐	
1	1	7
×		5

H	T	O
	☐	
2	1	7
×		3

H	T	O
	☐	
2	1	5
×		3

H	T	O
	☐	
4	2	6
×		3

3.

☐
119
× 5

☐
616
× 2

☐
113
× 4

☐
119
× 3

Multiply.

4.
$$219 \times 2$$
$$\$1.15 \times 2$$
$$318 \times 3$$
$$114 \times 7$$
$$324 \times 4$$

5.
$$624 \times 3$$
$$\$2.39 \times 2$$
$$712 \times 5$$
$$915 \times 6$$
$$285 \times 3$$

6.
$$613 \times 7$$
$$518 \times 5$$
$$319 \times 5$$
$$229 \times 2$$
$$312 \times 8$$

7.
$$519 \times 2$$
$$413 \times 7$$
$$725 \times 3$$
$$\$1.36 \times 2$$
$$818 \times 3$$

Problem Solving Reasoning	Solve.

8. Jane bought **4** pairs of socks that cost **$2.19** a pair. She paid with **$10**. How much change did she receive?

_____

9. Mrs. Sanchez bought **6** books for her classroom. Each costs **$5.15**. How much did she spend?

_____

Test Prep ★ Mixed Review

10 Mrs. Ling has 22 eggs. She needs 4 eggs for each cake. How many cakes can she make?

A 18
B 6
C 5
D 4

11 The class hangs 7 posters in each hallway to advertise the winter fair. There are 9 hallways in the building. How many posters did the class hang?

F 72
G 68
H 63
J 54

Unit 9 Lesson 4

Copyright © Houghton Mifflin Company. All rights reserved.

Sometimes when you multiply, you must regroup tens to hundreds.

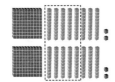

H	T	O
1	8	2
×		2

1. Multiply the ones.

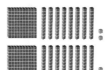

H	T	O
1	8	2
×		2
		4

2 × 2 ones = 4 ones

---

2. Multiply the tens. Regroup.

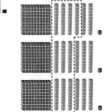

H	T	O
	1	
1	8	2
×		2
	6	4

2 × 8 tens = 16 tens
16 tens = 1 hundred, 6 tens

3. Multiply the hundreds. Then add.

H	T	O
	1	
1	8	2
×		2
3	6	4

2 × 1 hundred = 2 hundreds
The product is **364**.

Multiply. Remember to regroup and add.

1.
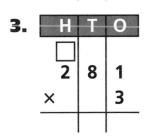

H	T	O
□		
1	6	1
×		3

H	T	O
□		
3	8	1
×		2

H	T	O
□		
1	4	2
×		4

2.

H	T	O
□		
1	4	1
×		5

H	T	O
□		
4	8	1
×		2

H	T	O
□		
2	7	2
×		3

H	T	O
□		
1	5	1
×		5

3.

H	T	O
□		
2	8	1
×		3

H	T	O
□		
1	7	2
×		3

H	T	O
□		
1	4	1
×		7

H	T	O
□		
2	9	1
×		3

Multiply.

4.
□	□	□	□	□	□
480	691	250	381	471	870
× 5	× 4	× 3	× 5	× 7	× 8

5.
553	881	771	591	671	712
× 2	× 4	× 3	× 5	× 6	× 8

6.
561	983	651	861	673	851
× 9	× 2	× 8	× 7	× 3	× 5

7.
491	394	721	880	642	572
× 8	× 2	× 6	× 8	× 4	× 3

Problem Solving Reasoning **Solve.**

8. Mei Ling visited her cousins **2** times last year. The trip is **281** miles each way. How many miles did she drive in all?

_____

9. Kyle bought **3** bags of treats for his gerbil. Each treat bag cost **$1.61**. How much did Kyle spend?

_____

Test Prep ★ Mixed Review

10 There is a bag of 10 marbles. Seven of the marbles are blue, two are red, and one is green. Which best describes the possibility of picking a blue marble from the bag without looking?

A certain

B likely

C unlikely

D impossible

11 Lilla is making a tally chart to show things she discovered in the woods. She found 17 acorns. Which is the correct way to record this using tally marks?

F ЖЖ II

G ЖЖЖ II

H ЖЖЖ

J Ж IIIIIIIII

Regrouping More than Once

Sometimes you need to regroup more than once.

Example.
```
  2 6 5
×     5
```

1. Multiply the ones. Regroup.	2. Multiply the tens. Then add and regroup.	3. Multiply the hundreds. Then add.
$\begin{array}{r} {\scriptstyle 2} \\ 2\,6\,5 \\ \times \quad 5 \\ \hline 5 \end{array}$	$\begin{array}{r} {\scriptstyle 3\ 2} \\ 2\,6\,5 \\ \times \quad 5 \\ \hline 2\,5 \end{array}$	$\begin{array}{r} {\scriptstyle 3\ 2} \\ 2\,6\,5 \\ \times \quad 5 \\ \hline 1,3\,2\,5 \end{array}$
		The product is **1,325**.

Find the product.

1.

$\square\square$	$\square\square$	$\square\square$	$\square\square$	$\square\square$
1 6 5	4 4 4	1 9 2	2 3 3	1 8 6
× 4	× 3	× 5	× 4	× 2

2.

$\square\square$	$\square\square$	$\square\square$	$\square\square$	$\square$
6 4 8	2 7 5	4 9 6	2 5 8	4 7 6
× 4	× 9	× 5	× 2	× 2

3.

8 9 6	4 6 3	9 3 6	4 2 8	5 3 6
× 9	× 6	× 8	× 9	× 7

4.

$7.29	$1.32	$7.53	$2.99	$3.83
× 4	× 5	× 4	× 2	× 4

5.

8 1 9	6 4 8	3 6 9	$8.43	5 7 9
× 9	× 8	× 7	× 9	× 2

Find the product.

6.
464	896	328	$2.69	586
× 3	× 4	× 8	× 2	× 6

7.
295	387	$4.69	697	259
× 4	× 2	× 3	× 4	× 7

8.
355	$1.23	273	$3.29	224
× 6	× 5	× 8	× 4	× 7

Problem Solving Reasoning **Solve.**

9. Mrs. Barns buys each of her **6** children a pair of slippers. A pair costs **$7.85**. She has **$40.00**. Does she have enough money?

10. If **1** box of mints costs **$1.88** and **1** pack of gum costs **$.57**. Which costs more **4** boxes of mints or **8** packs of gum?

11. If a cap costs **$.89**, what is the cost of **7** caps?

12. Spiro bought **3** pencils for **$.39**. How much do **6** pencils cost?

✔ Quick Check

Multiply.

1. 236	**2.** 118	**3.** 327	**4.** 216
× 2	× 6	× 4	× 9

5. 172	**6.** 463	**7.** 382	**8.** 891
× 4	× 2	× 3	× 5

9. 654	**10.** 386	**11.** 475	**12.** 793
× 7	× 5	× 8	× 6

Work Space.

When you multiply zero by a number the product is zero.
Example.

$$\begin{array}{r} 3\ 0\ 7 \\ \times\quad 4 \\ \hline \end{array}$$

1. Multiply the ones. Regroup.

$$\begin{array}{r} \overset{2}{3}\ 0\ 7 \\ \times\quad\ \ 4 \\ \hline 8 \end{array}$$

28 ones = 2 tens, 8 ones

2. Multiply the tens. Then add and regroup.

$$\begin{array}{r} \overset{2}{3}\ 0\ 7 \\ \times\quad\ \ 4 \\ \hline 2\ 8 \end{array}$$

4 × 0 tens = 0 tens
0 tens + 2 tens = 2 tens

3. Multiply the hundreds.

$$\begin{array}{r} \overset{2}{3}\ 0\ 7 \\ \times\quad\ \ 4 \\ \hline 1,\ 2\ 2\ 8 \end{array}$$

The product is **1,228**.

Multiply.

1.

$$\begin{array}{r} 5\ 0\ 6 \\ \times\quad 7 \\ \hline \end{array}$$
$$\begin{array}{r} 3\ 4\ 0 \\ \times\quad 5 \\ \hline \end{array}$$
$$\begin{array}{r} 4\ 0\ 9 \\ \times\quad 2 \\ \hline \end{array}$$
$$\begin{array}{r} \$4.5\ 0 \\ \times\quad\ \ 7 \\ \hline \end{array}$$
$$\begin{array}{r} 3\ 0\ 8 \\ \times\quad 9 \\ \hline \end{array}$$

2.

$$\begin{array}{r} 5\ 0\ 8 \\ \times\quad 3 \\ \hline \end{array}$$
$$\begin{array}{r} 7\ 0\ 0 \\ \times\quad 8 \\ \hline \end{array}$$
$$\begin{array}{r} \$8.0\ 6 \\ \times\quad\ \ 5 \\ \hline \end{array}$$
$$\begin{array}{r} 3\ 9\ 0 \\ \times\quad 2 \\ \hline \end{array}$$
$$\begin{array}{r} 2\ 0\ 4 \\ \times\quad 8 \\ \hline \end{array}$$

3.

$$\begin{array}{r} 9\ 0\ 6 \\ \times\quad 3 \\ \hline \end{array}$$
$$\begin{array}{r} 6\ 0\ 3 \\ \times\quad 8 \\ \hline \end{array}$$
$$\begin{array}{r} 8\ 9\ 0 \\ \times\quad 9 \\ \hline \end{array}$$
$$\begin{array}{r} \$3.7\ 0 \\ \times\quad\ \ 6 \\ \hline \end{array}$$
$$\begin{array}{r} 4\ 0\ 0 \\ \times\quad 4 \\ \hline \end{array}$$

4.

$$\begin{array}{r} \$5.9\ 0 \\ \times\quad\ \ 7 \\ \hline \end{array}$$
$$\begin{array}{r} 4\ 0\ 2 \\ \times\quad 2 \\ \hline \end{array}$$
$$\begin{array}{r} \$3.4\ 0 \\ \times\quad\ \ 8 \\ \hline \end{array}$$
$$\begin{array}{r} 2\ 0\ 9 \\ \times\quad 5 \\ \hline \end{array}$$
$$\begin{array}{r} 6\ 7\ 0 \\ \times\quad 8 \\ \hline \end{array}$$

5.

$$\begin{array}{r} 4\ 0\ 8 \\ \times\quad 3 \\ \hline \end{array}$$
$$\begin{array}{r} \$7.2\ 0 \\ \times\quad\ \ 7 \\ \hline \end{array}$$
$$\begin{array}{r} 9\ 0\ 4 \\ \times\quad 9 \\ \hline \end{array}$$
$$\begin{array}{r} 7\ 6\ 0 \\ \times\quad 6 \\ \hline \end{array}$$
$$\begin{array}{r} \$8.0\ 0 \\ \times\quad\ \ 8 \\ \hline \end{array}$$

6.

$7.08	605	830	807	201
× 6	× 5	× 9	× 4	× 2

7.

900	807	340	$2.05	506
× 8	× 7	× 3	× 8	× 4

Use mental math to multiply.

8. $5 \times 700 =$ _____ $3 \times 600 =$ _____ $5 \times 400 =$ _____

9. $9 \times 900 =$ _____ $7 \times 200 =$ _____ $4 \times 300 =$ _____

Problem Solving Reasoning **Solve.**

10. Arthuro bought **9** painting kits as party favors. They each cost **$5.50**. How much did he spend?

_____

11. Li packed **8** boxes with **204** items in each. Then he packed **3** boxes with **400** items in each. How many items did he pack in all?

_____

Test Prep ★ Mixed Review

12 The school needs 24 orange cones to mark off each path for the hike. There are 7 paths to mark. How many cones are needed?

A 168

B 148

C 98

D 31

13 Tala practices her violin for 75 minutes every day. She has already practiced for 45 minutes. Which number sentence could you use to find how many more minutes Tala has to practice?

F $75 \times 45 =$ ☐

G $75 + 45 =$ ☐

H $75 - 45 =$ ☐

J $75 \div 45 =$ ☐

Making a table can help you organize and use patterns so you can solve a problem.

Problem

Ashley goes to basketball practice. She practices **15** minutes the first day and adds **15** minutes to her practice each day for a week. How long will Ashley's practice time be on the last day of the week?

❶ Understand   As you reread, ask yourself questions.

- How long does Ashley practice the first day?

    She practices 15 minutes.

- How long does she practice each day?

    15 minutes more than the day before.

- For how many days does Ashley add to her practice time?

    For a week, or 7 days.

❷ Decide   Choose a method for solving.

- A table can show Ashley's practice time.

- What information is in the top row of the table?

    the day

Day	1	2	3
Minutes of Practice	15	30	

- What information is in the bottom row of the table?

    the minutes of practice

❸ Solve   Complete the table to solve the problem.

-

Day	1	2	3	4	5	6	7
Minutes of Practice	15	30	45	60			

❹ Look back   Check your answer. Write the answer as a full sentence.

- Answer _____

Use the Make a Table Strategy or any other strategy you have learned.

1. During practice time the coach makes sure each player gets $1\frac{1}{2}$ oranges. There are **14** people on the team. How many oranges do they need at each practice?

   Think: You can make a table to show the number of players and the total number of oranges.

   _____

   Answer: _____

2. Ashley is saving her money to buy a basketball that costs **$36**. In Week **1** she has **$8**. She will save **$7** more each week until she has **$36**. In what week will Ashley have enough money? Complete the table to help you solve the problem.

   Think: How could you make a table of the money Ashley has saved and the number of weeks she has been saving?

Week	Money
1	$8
2	$15
3	
4	
5	
6	

   _____

   Answer: _____

3. There are a dozen basketballs. The balls are in **2** bins. At the end of practice **8** basketballs were in one bin and **4** in the other. How many basketballs need to be moved so there are the same number in each bin?

   _____

   _____

4. There are always **3** bottles of water for every two people on the basketball team. If there are **12** people at practice, how many water bottles do they need?

   _____

   _____

5. The basketball team plays **4** quarters that last **7** minutes each. Ashley plays in **2** quarters. How many minutes does she play?

   _____

6. The basketball tickets costs **$2.00** for adults and **$1.00** for children. The entire Johnson family went to the game. How much money did they spend?

   _____

Use what you know about regrouping to multiply.

1. Multiply the ones. Regroup.

T	H	T	O
		²	
1	2	7	8
×			3
			4

24 ones = **2** tens and **4** ones.

2. Multiply the tens. Then add and regroup.

T	H	T	O
	²	²	
1	2	7	8
×			3
		3	4

23 tens = **2** hundreds and **3** tens.

3. Multiply the hundreds. Add.

T	H	T	O
	²	²	
1	2	7	8
×			3
	8	3	4

4. Multiply the thousands.

T	H	T	O
	²	²	
1	2	7	8
×			3
3,	8	3	4

The product is **3,834.**

Multiply.

1.

T	H	T	O
	¹	²	
2	1	5	7
×			3
6,	4	7	1

T	H	T	O
	□	□	
5	1	4	9
×			6

T	H	T	O
	□	□	
6	2	4	5
×			4

T	H	T	O
	□	□	
3	4	5	7
×			2

2.

```
  7,358          $61.78          9,276          7,116
×     2         ×      5         ×    3         ×    8
```

3.

```
  4,237          2,239          $84.78          6,155
×     4         ×     3         ×     2         ×     3
```

Sometimes we have to regroup to the thousands place.

1. Multiply ones and regroup.

T	H	T	O
		4	
4	5	2	7
×			6
			2

2. Multiply tens. Add and regroup.

T	H	T	O
	1	4	
4	5	2	7
×			6
		6	2

3. Multiply hundreds. Add and regroup.

T	H	T	O
3	1	4	
4	5	2	7
×			6
	1	6	2

4. Multiply thousands and add.

T	H	T	O
3	1	4	
4	5	2	7
×			6
27,	1	6	2

Multiply.

4.

```
  1 2 3
 5,4 6 8
×      4
```

```
□□□
 7,3 4 9
×      3
```

```
□□□
 2,5 9 8
×      7
```

```
□□
 4,0 6 4
×      9
```

Problem Solving
Reasoning

Solve.

5. Mulberry Concert Hall has **4,134** seats. A play ran for **4** nights. It was sold out every night. How many people saw the show?

_____

6. Ed bought **2** sweaters that cost **$29.99** each. He paid with **3** twenty-dollar bills. How much change did Ed get?

_____

 Quick Check

Find the product.

1.
```
  8 0 5
×     7
```

2.
```
  6 7 0
×     4
```

3.
```
  4 0 3
×     9
```

4.
```
  9 5 0
×     6
```

5.
```
 2,4 0 7
×      3
```

6.
```
 5,0 6 4
×      5
```

7.
```
 3,0 8 1
×      9
```

Work Space.

Name _____

You can use models to divide.

Divide **64** by **4**.

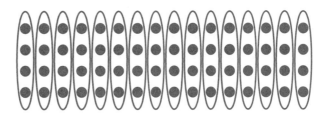

You can divide without models.

64 ÷ 4 = 16

16 ← quotient

divisor ⟶ 4)6 4 ← dividend

---

1. Divide tens.	2. Multiply and subtract.	3. Regroup, bring down next digit.	4. Divide ones, multiply and subtract.
Think: ? tens 4)6 tens		Think: 2 tens and 4 ones = 24 ones	Think: ? ones 4)2 4 ones
$\begin{array}{r} 1 \\ 4\overline{)6\ 4} \end{array}$	$\begin{array}{r} 1 \\ 4\overline{)6\ 4} \\ -\ 4 \\ \hline 2 \end{array}$ ← 10 × 4	$\begin{array}{r} 1 \\ 4\overline{)6\ 4} \\ -\ 4\ \downarrow \\ \hline 2\ 4 \end{array}$ ↑ 24 ones	$\begin{array}{r} 1\ 6 \\ 4\overline{)6\ 4} \\ -\ 4 \\ \hline 2\ 4 \\ -\ 2\ 4 \\ \hline 0 \end{array}$

Divide first. Loop the dots to check the quotient.

1. 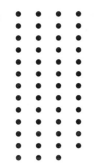 3)5 1

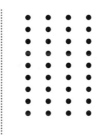 2)3 6

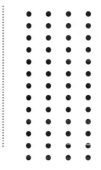 4)5 2

Sometimes when you divide there is a remainder.

Complete.

2.
$$\begin{array}{r} 14\text{ R1} \\ 6\overline{)85} \\ -6 \\ \hline 25 \\ -24 \\ \hline 1 \end{array}$$
remainder

$$\begin{array}{r} 12 \\ 7\overline{)89} \\ -7\downarrow \\ \hline 19 \\ -14 \end{array}$$

$$\begin{array}{r} 1 \\ 4\overline{)58} \\ -4\downarrow \\ \hline 18 \end{array}$$

$$3\overline{)74}$$

Divide.

3. $5\overline{)66}$ $7\overline{)98}$ $2\overline{)43}$ $8\overline{)96}$ $6\overline{)85}$

Problem Solving Reasoning | **Solve.**

4. Tivon has **46** crayons he wants to share. How many will he and his **3** friends each get if he divides them equally. How many will be leftover?

5. Chika picks **86** strawberries. If **7** people share the strawberries equally, how many does each person get?

Test Prep ★ Mixed Review

1 You have 40¢ in your pocket. What could the coins in your pocket be?

A 2 dimes, 2 nickels

B 1 quarter, 1 dime, 5 pennies

C 1 quarter, 1 nickel, 5 pennies

D 2 dimes, 2 nickels, 5 pennies

2 Ana traveled 387 miles by train to visit her aunt. After her visit, Ana took the train home. How many miles did Ana travel in all?

F 387

G 774

H 764

J 787

Name _____

Dividing with hundreds is like dividing with tens.

Example 1. Divide 246 by 2 the short way.

246 ÷ 2	Divide the hundreds.	Divide the tens.	Divide the ones.
	Think: **200 ÷ 2** ↓	Think: **40 ÷ 2** ↓	Think: **6 ÷ 2** ↓
	1 $2\overline{)246}$	12 $2\overline{)246}$	123 $2\overline{)246}$
			The quotient is **123**.

Example 2. Divide 936 by 4 the long way.

936 ÷ 4

```
    2              23               234
4)936          4)936            4)936
 -8             -8               -8
  1             13               13
               -12              -12
                 1               16
                                -16
                                  0
```

The quotient is **234**.

Divide the short way.

1. $3\overline{)936}$ $2\overline{)282}$ $4\overline{)484}$ $2\overline{)642}$

Divide the long way.

2. $5\overline{)820}$ $4\overline{)992}$ $6\overline{)918}$ $5\overline{)615}$

Here are some ways to divide with money.

$$4\overline{)48¢} = 12¢$$

$$3\overline{)81¢} = 27¢$$
$$-6$$
$$\overline{21}$$
$$-21$$
$$\overline{0}$$

$$3\overline{)\$6.39} = \$2.13$$

Divide.

3. $3\overline{)96¢}$ $6\overline{)78¢}$ $4\overline{)\$9.36}$ $7\overline{)\$8.61}$

Problem Solving / Reasoning   Solve.

4. Takashi bought a pack of **7** computer disks for **$9.52**. How much did each disk cost?

_____

5. Red apples are **2** for **90¢** or **5** for **$2.05**. Which is a better buy? Explain.

_____

 Quick Check

Divide.   **Work Space**

1. $6\overline{)66}$ **2.** $3\overline{)96}$ **3.** $2\overline{)68}$ **4.** $4\overline{)848}$

6. $3\overline{)543}$ **7.** $4\overline{)532}$

Unit 9 Lesson 11   **243**

Sometimes it takes more than one step to solve a problem. In this lesson you will use information from the chart to solve multiple step problems.

TODAY'S MENU					
Sandwiches		**Side Orders**		**Drinks**	
Cheese	$2.55	Apple	$.79	Milk	$1.25
Tuna	$2.79	Banana	$.79	Juice	$1.30
Chicken	$3.00	Yogurt	$1.00	Bottle	$1.10
Turkey	$3.00	Bran Muffin	$1.00	of Water	
		Bagel	$.75		

Tips to Remember:

1. Understand	2. Decide	3. Solve	4. Look back

- Read the problem carefully. Ask yourself questions about any part that does not make sense. Reread to find answers.
- Think about the action in the problem. Is there more than one action?
- Which operation best represents each action— addition, subtraction, multiplication or division?

Solve.

1. A family of **4** ordered **2** chicken sandwiches, **2** cheese sandwiches, **2** bottles of milk, and **2** bottles of water. What did lunch for this family cost?

Think: What information do you need from the chart? What operations will you use to solve this problem?

_____

_____

_____

Answer: _____

2. Jamal and his friend decided to share a lunch. They bought a tuna sandwich, one bottle of juice, and a banana. If they each paid half the cost, how much did each person pay?

Think: What operation comes to mind when you share something between two people, or split it in half?

_____

Answer: _____

_____

Solve.

3. Charo bought a turkey sandwich, a bottle of milk and a yogurt. She gave the clerk **$10**. How much change should she receive?

_____

_____

_____

4. Which lunch costs less and how much less? First lunch: cheese sandwich with an apple and juice; Second lunch: a chicken sandwich with a bottle of water and a banana.

_____

_____

_____

_____

5. The chart shows that the sandwich shop gives **2** free cookies for every **$10** a customer spends. Complete the chart. How many free cookies would you get if you spent **$50?**

_____

Money Spent	Number of free cookies
$10	2
$20	4
$30	6
$40	_____
$50	_____

Extend Your Thinking

6. Which problem do you think was easiest to solve and why?

_____

_____

_____

_____

7. Use the chart to write your own multistep problem. Give your problem to a friend to solve.

_____

_____

_____

_____

Name _____

Multiply.

1. 44
   × 2

2. 31
   × 3

3. 11
   × 8

4. 503
   × 2

5. 66
   × 9

6. 77
   × 6

7. 44
   × 8

8. 403
   × 6

9. 82
   × 9

10. 94
   × 5

11. 46
   × 4

12. 1,826
   × 2

13. 145
   × 4

14. 298
   × 8

15. 378
   × 4

16. 893
   × 9

17. $1.97
   × 4

18. $2.26
   × 9

19. $1.36
   × 6

20. $10.98
   × 8

Divide.

21.

$6\overline{)79}$

22.

$4\overline{)748}$

Solve.

23. Dolores wants to buy a coat for $67. She earns $4.00 a day walking dogs. How many days will it take to have enough money?

_____

24. Suppose you have **28** marbles, $\frac{1}{2}$ are red and **6** are blue. The rest are pink. How many pink marbles do you have?

_____

1 The Parker Family rented a cabin for a 2 week vacation. What other information do you need to figure out how much they paid to rent the cabin?

A Where the cabin was located

B How much it cost to rent the cabin

C How many days are in a week

D In what season of the year did they travel

2 Which part in this figure is a triangle?

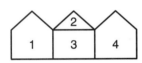

F 1   **G** 2   **H** 3   **J** 4

3 Which shape is a right triangle?

A a   **B** b   **C** c   **D** d

4 Ruth has 26 pieces of wood. She needs 3 pieces of wood to make a shelf. What is the most number of shelves Ruth can make? How many pieces of wood will be left over?

F 9 shelves, 0 extra pieces

G 7 shelves, 5 extra pieces

H 8 shelves, 2 extra pieces

J 6 shelves, 1 extra piece

5 What number sentence is in the same family of facts as

$$8 \times 9 = 72$$

A $72 \div 8 = 9$ **C** $9 - 8 = 1$

B $8 + 9 = 17$ **D** $9 \div 3 = 3$

6 Kiesha bought 3 notebooks for $1.38 each. How much did she spend in all?

F $4.94   **H** $.14   **K** NH

G $3.14   **J** $3.94

7 Dov has 846 baseball cards. He put the same number of cards in each of 6 books. How many cards are in each book?

A 30   **C** 140   **E** NH

B 36   **D** 141

8 Around the baseball field are 8 tall posts. There are 6 spot lights on each post. How many spotlights are there in all?

F 14

G 24

H 42

J 48

K NH

UNIT 10 • TABLE OF CONTENTS

Measurement

CALIFORNIA STANDARDS	Lesson	Page
M/G 1.1, 1.4; A/F 1.4	**1** Algebra • **Customary Units of Length**	251–252
M/G 1.1, 1.4; A/F 1.4	**2 Customary Units of Capacity and Weight**	253–254
M/G 1.1, SDP 1.4	**3 Temperature: Fahrenheit**	255–256
MR 3.1	**4** Problem Solving Application: **Is the Answer Reasonable?**	257–258
M/G 1.1, 1.4	**5 Metric Units of Length**	259–260
M/G 1.1	**6 Metric Units of Mass and Capacity**	261–262
M/G 1.1	**7** Algebra • **Temperature: Celsius**	263–264
M/G 1.3; A/F 1.1	**8** Algebra • **Perimeter**	265–266
M/G 1.2; A/F 1.1	**9** Algebra • **Area**	267–268
MR 2.3; M/G 1.3; NS 2.8	**10** Problem Solving Strategy: **Make a List**	269–270
M/G 1.2	**11** Volume	271–272
	• Unit 10 Review	273–274
	• Cumulative Review ★ Test Prep	275–276

Dear Family,

During the next few weeks, our math class will be learning about perimeter, area, and volume of geometric figures.

You can expect to see homework that provides practice with finding the area of rectangles. Here is a sample you may want to keep handy to give help if needed.

Finding the Area of a Rectangle

Look at the rectangle to the right.

To find the area of a rectangle, write the rule:

Area = length × width

Next, find the length of the rectangle.

The length is **7** cm.

Then, find the width of the rectangle.

The width is **3** cm.

Multiply the length and width to follow the rule.

Area = 7 cm × 3 cm or 21 sq cm

The area of the rectangle is **21** square centimeters.

During this unit, students will need to continue practicing addition and multiplication facts.

Sincerely,

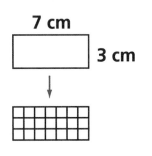

7 cm

3 cm

Customary Units of Length

One customary unit of length is the **inch (in.)**

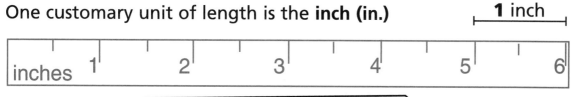

The comb is about $4\frac{1}{2}$ inches long.

Measure to the nearest inch.

1.

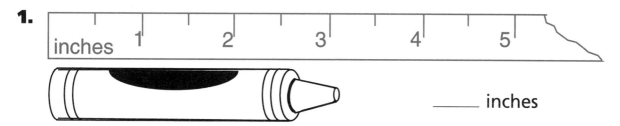

_____ inches

2.

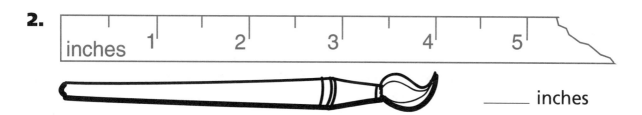

_____ inches

Measure to the nearest half inch.

3.

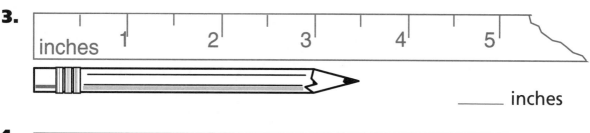

_____ inches

4.

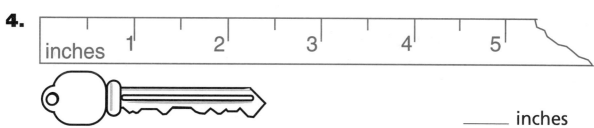

_____ inches

Use a ruler. Measure each item to the nearest inch or half inch.

5. length of your foot _____ in.

6. width of your desk _____ in.

7. length of a finger _____ in.

8. width of the crayon above _____ in.

1 foot (ft) = 12 inches (in.)	1 mile (mi) = 5,280 feet
1 yard (yd) = 3 feet	1 mile = 1,760 yards
1 yard (yd) = 36 inches	

9. How many inches are in **4** feet?　　　How many feet are in **7** yards?

Multiply by **12** because there are **12** in. in **1** foot.

Multiply by **3** because there are **3** ft in **1** yd.

4 ft × 12 = _____ in.　　　　7 yd × 3 = _____ ft

Write a number sentence. Change each length to inches, feet, or yards.

10. 6 ft × _____ = _____ in.　　　5 yd × _____ = _____ ft

11. 3 yd × _____ = _____ in.　　9 yd × _____ = _____ ft

12. 2 mi × _____ = _____ ft　　　2 mi × _____ = _____ yd

Problem Solving Reasoning　Solve.

13. A tree is **5** ft tall. It grows **5** in. How many inches high is the tree now?

_____

14. A board is **2** yd long. Tim cuts **20** in. off. How many inches are left?

_____

Test Prep ★ Mixed Review

15 The garden club needs to pack 37 plants of different sizes into boxes. Four large plants can fit in a box or 6 small plants can fit. Which is the most reasonable estimate of how many boxes they will need to pack the plants?

　A 4

　B 6

　C 8

　D 12

16 An elevator can hold 1,000 pounds. There are people on the elevator weighing a total of 643 pounds. Which number sentence shows how many more pounds are allowed on the elevator?

　F 1,000 + 643 = ☐

　G 643 + 643 = ☐

　H 1,000 + 1,000 = ☐

　J 1,000 − 643 = ☐

Name _____

Capacity is the amount of liquid a container can hold. In the customary system, liquids are measured in **cups, pints, quarts,** and **gallons.**

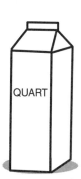

CUP

QUART

PINT

GALLON

2 cups (c) = 1 pint (pt)

2 pints = 1 quart (qt)

4 quarts = 1 gallon (gal)

Loop the better estimate.

1. a sink   a wading pool   a juice glass

    8 c or **8** qt   **20** c or **20** gal   **1** c or **1** gal

2. a bathtub   a bucket of paint   a dog's bowl

    35 qt or **35** gal   **1** gal or **1** c   **2** pt or **2** gal

---

Loop the greater amount.

3. **4** qt or **4** pt   **2** gal or **2** qt   **5** c or **5** pt

4. **7** qt or **2** gal   **4** pt or **7** c   **6** qt or **1** gal

---

Write a number sentence. Change each measure to cups, pints, or quarts.

5. 2 qt × _____ = _____ pt   1 gal × _____ = _____ qt

6. 3 pt × _____ = _____ c   3 gal × _____ = _____ qt

Write *true* or *false*.

7. _____ A gallon of milk will fill **4** quart bottles.

8. _____ Only **2** pints of juice will fit in a gallon container.

9. _____ A quart of water is as much as a quart of paint.

10. _____ Three pints of juice will fill a quart bottle with no juice left over.

11. _____ There are **4** cups of lemonade in a quart.

12. _____ A gallon container will not hold **3** quarts of water.

Weight is measured in ounces and pounds.

| 16 ounces (oz) = 1 pound (lb) |

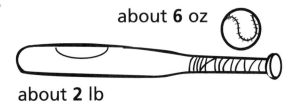

about **6** oz

about **2** lb

Loop the items that weigh more than 1 pound.

13. crackers **2** oz   book **29** oz   cereal **18** oz

ruler **7** oz   peanuts **14** oz   rice **10** oz

| Problem Solving |
| Reasoning |

Solve.

14. Jim has **2** pounds of grapes. He eats **7** ounces. How many ounces are left?

_____

15. There is $\frac{1}{2}$ gallon of juice. Ed drinks **1** pint. How many pints are left?

_____

16. You drink **2** quarts of milk from a full gallon container. How much milk is left? How do you know?

_____

_____

17. A jar of popcorn weighs 1 lb 14 oz. How many ounces is that? How did you find out?

_____

_____

Test Prep ★ Mixed Review

18 The parking garage is 4 floors high. Each floor can fit 145 cars. How many cars can fit in the entire parking garage?

A 420

B 460

C 520

D 580

19 There are 6 classes that equally share 210 boxes of chalk. How many boxes does each class receive?

F 25

G 30

H 35

J 40

STANDARD

In the customary system, temperature is measured in **degrees Fahrenheit** (°F).

Water boils at **212°F.**

Use the thermometer. Write the temperature.

1. Normal body temperature: _____

2. Room temperature: _____

3. Water freezes: _____

4. A cool fall day: _____

5. A hot summer day: _____

Write the temperature.

6.

_____   _____   _____

7. Use arrows to mark these temperatures on the thermometer at the right.

0°   124°   88°   45°   212°   76°   141°

This line graph shows the change in temperature during a week in January.

What was the temperature on Friday?

Look across to Friday. Look up to find the point. Find the temperature by looking at the number on the same line as the point. The temperature on Friday was **6°F.**

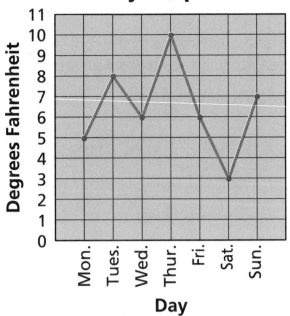

January Temperatures

Problem Solving Reasoning

Solve. Use the graph.

8. How much colder was Saturday than Thursday?

_____

9. On which **2** days was the temperature the same?

_____

☑ Quick Check

1. **Measure to the nearest inch.**

_____ inches

Complete.

2. 24 in. = _____ ft   **3.** 12 ft = _____ yd

4. 3 ft = _____ in.   **5.** 2 yd = _____ in.

Loop the better estimate.

6. a kitchen sink
   10 gal   10 c

7. a book
   3 oz   3 lb

8. a soup bowl
   2 c   2 gal

9. a summer day
   85°F   **45°F**

Work Space.

Problem Solving Application: Is the Answer Reasonable?

It is important for you to check that your answer to a problem is reasonable.

> **Tips to Remember:**
>
> | 1. Understand | 2. Decide | 3. Solve | 4. Look back |
>
> - Read each statement after each problem carefully. Does the statement answer the question?
> - Read each measurement carefully. Is it the correct unit for what is being measured?
> - Should the answer be exact or an estimate?
> - Does the answer use the remainder correctly?

Decide if the answer is reasonable or not.
If it is not reasonable, explain why not.

1. Marty went hiking one day. It was so hot that Marty drank water every **2** hours. He hiked **6** hours. How many times did he drink water? Answer: **3** times

Think: How many times did he drink water in **2** hours? In **4** hours? Does **3** times in **6** hours make sense?

_____

_____

Answer: _____

_____

_____

2. Marty and his Dad hiked **12** miles the first day, **15** miles the second day, and **18** miles the third day. About how many miles did he hike? Answer: About **100** miles

Think: Is **100** a good estimate for **12 + 15 + 18**?

_____

_____

_____

Answer: _____

_____

_____

Decide if the answer is reasonable or not. If it is not reasonable, explain why not.

3. Marty brought **3** rolls of film. There were **24** pictures on each roll. How many pictures can he take? Answer: **27** pictures

_____

_____

_____

4. He took a **15** minute break after every hour of hiking. How many minutes did he rest on a **5** hour hike? Answer: **75** minutes or **1** hour **15** minutes.

_____

_____

5. Marty asked his dad how high the tent was. His dad stood on his tiptoes to touch the top of the tent. He said, "It's about **7** inches high!" Is his answer reasonable?

_____

6. Marty got up at **6** A.M. and started hiking at **8** A.M. He hiked until **4** p.m. How many hours did he hike? Answer: **4** hours

_____

_____

7. The water jugs each held about a gallon of water. About how many cups were in each gallon jug? Answer: about **16** cups.

_____

8. Marty wanted to put the **72** pictures in a photo album. Each page of the album holds **5** pictures. How many pictures will be on the last page? Answer: **6** pictures

_____

_____

_____

Extend Your Thinking

9. Go back to problem **2**. Change the miles he hiked each of the **3** days so that **100** miles would be a good estimate of the distance they had hiked.

_____

10. Create your own situation with a reasonable or unreasonable answer. Let a friend solve it.

_____

Metric Units of Length

A metric unit of length is the **centimeter (cm):** |—| 1 cm

This is a centimeter ruler.

| centimeters |
| 1 2 3 4 5 6 7 8 9 10 11 12 |

Measure to the nearest centimeter.

1.

_____ cm

2.
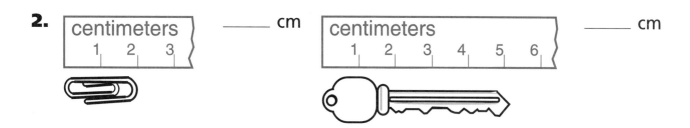
_____ cm   _____ cm

3.
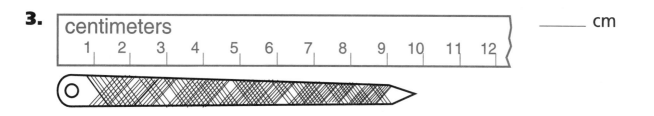
_____ cm

Use a centimeter ruler. Measure to the nearest centimeter.

4. length of your pencil _____ cm

5. length of your thumb _____ cm

6. width of your shoe _____ cm

7. length of the lesson title _____ cm

8. length of the Name line above _____ cm

9. width of a finger _____ cm

The **meter** is used to measure rooms or buildings.

The **kilometer** is used to measure long distances.

1 meter (m) = 100 centimeters	1 kilometer (km) = 1,000 meters

Which unit would you use to measure each?
Write *cm*, *m*, or *km*.

10. the length of a pin _____

11. width of the school _____

12. the distance between two cities _____

13. the length of a pen _____

14. the width of a street _____

15. the length of a grasshopper _____

Complete.

16. 2 m = _____ cm   300 cm = _____ m

17. 3,000 m = _____ km   2 km = _____ m

Problem Solving
Reasoning   **Solve.**

18. Estimate the length of your desk in centimeters. Then measure it.

Estimate _____ Actual _____

19. Each day Rumi walks **500** m to school and back. How many kilometers does he walk in **10** days?

_____

Test Prep ★ Mixed Review

20 Which number sentence is in the same fact family as **7 × 8 = 56**?

  A 7 + 8 = 15

  B 8 − 7 = 1

  C 7 × 7 = 49

  D 56 ÷ 7 = 8

21 Tomas was supposed to be at home by 3:15. He missed the bus and was 25 minutes late. What time did he get home?

  E 3:30

  F 3:35

  G 3:40

  H 4:05

Name _____

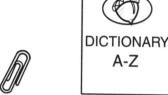

The **gram** measures the **mass,** or heaviness, of small objects. For larger objects use **kilograms.**

| 1 kilogram (kg) = **1,000** grams (g) |

1 gram   **1 kilogram**

Loop the better estimate.

1. paper cup   new pencil   peach

   2 g   or   **12** g   **50** g   or   **5** g   **80** g   or   **800** g

2. penny   eraser   drinking glass

   3 g   or   **30** g   **15** g   or   **800** g   **30** g   or   **300** g

3. television   baseball   can of soup

   19 g   or   **19** kg   **1** kg   or   **200** g   **5** g   or   **305** g

4. hammer   cake   tennis shoes

   1 kg   or   **10** g   **10** kg   or   **1** kg   **10** g   or   **800** g

---

Compare. Write >, <, or =.

5. **300** kg ◯ **300** g   **6,000** g ◯ **3** kg

6. **9,000** g ◯ **9** kg   **4** kg ◯ **3,000** g

Which unit would you use to measure these items? Write *g* or *kg*.

7. your pen _____   a horse _____

8. a paper clip _____   a bag of peanuts _____

9. a slice of cheese _____   a spoonful of sugar _____

10. yourself _____   a car _____

11. a bag of apples _____   a bookbag _____

In the metric system, liquids are measured in **liters (L)** and **milliliters (mL)**. An eyedropper holds about 1 milliliter.

| 1 liter (L) = **1,000** milliliters (mL) |

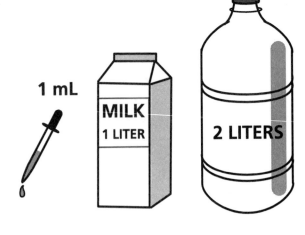

1 mL

MILK
1 LITER

2 LITERS

Loop the more reasonable measure.

12. fish tank

    15 L   or   **15** mL

bathtub

    400 L   or   **40** mL

teaspoon

    50 L   or   **5** mL

13. cup

    400 mL   or   **4,000** mL

pitcher of water

    4 L   or   **400** L

sink

    20 L   or   **20** mL

14. teapot

    1 L   or   **10** mL

glass of milk

    30 L   or   **300** mL

jug

    4 L   or   **40** L

Problem Solving
Reasoning

Solve.

15. The kitten weighed **500** g. The puppy weighed **2** kg. Which weighed more? How much more?

16. A baby gets **1** mL of vitamins each day. About how many weeks will a **50** mL bottle last?

Test Prep ★ Mixed Review

17 What number goes in the box and makes this number sentence true?

    38 × 1 = ☐

    A 40
    B 38
    C 37
    D 1

18 The clerk in the grocery store weighed a sack of potatoes. What unit would be used to measure the weight of the potatoes?

    F pounds
    G quarts
    H yards
    J inches

In the metric system, temperature is measured in **degrees Celsius** (°C). Water boils at **100°C.**

Use the thermometer. Write the temperature.

1. Normal body temperature: _____

2. Room temperature: _____

3. Water freezes: _____

4. A cool fall day: _____

5. A hot summer day: _____

Write the temperature.

6.

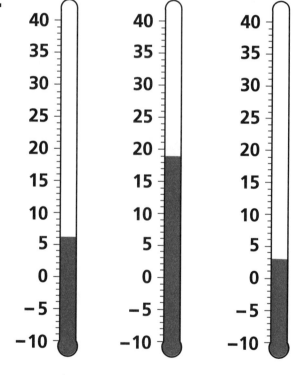

_____ °C   _____ °C   _____ °C

Loop the colder temperature in each pair.

7. 86° or 68°   0° or −10°   5° or −5°   95° or 85°

Average Monthly Temperatures

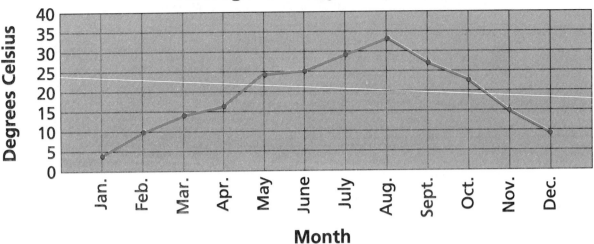

Solve. Use the graph.

8. Which month was the hottest?

How hot? _____

Which month was the coldest?

How cold? _____

9. What does the shape of the line tell you about the temperatures? Explain.

_____

_____

 Quick Check

Measure to nearest centimeter.

Work Space.

1. ⊱≋≋≋≋≋≋≋≋≋≋≋≋≋≋≋≋⊰

_____ centimeters

Complete.

2. 300 cm = _____ m   **3.** 5 m = _____ cm

4. 800 cm = _____ m   **5.** 7 m = _____ cm

Loop the better estimate.

6. a table

30 g   30 kg

7. a watering can

2 L   2 mL

8. an orange

25 kg   25 g

9. a winter day

2°C   25°C

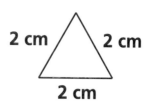

The distance around a figure is called the **perimeter.** To find the perimeter, add the measures of the sides.

The perimeter is **2 + 2 + 2**, or **6** cm.

2 cm   2 cm

2 cm

Use a centimeter ruler to measure each side. Find the perimeter.

1.

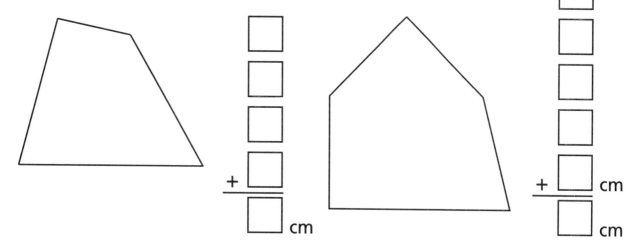

Find the perimeter.

2.

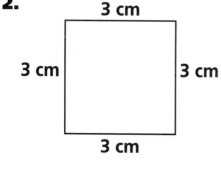

3 cm
3 cm   3 cm
3 cm

_____ cm

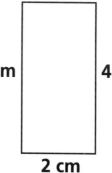

2 cm
4 cm   4 cm
2 cm

_____ cm

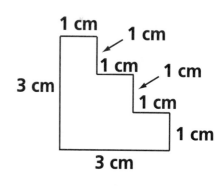

1 cm   1 cm
1 cm   1 cm
3 cm   1 cm
        1 cm
3 cm

_____ cm

Solve.

3. If you doubled the length of the sides of the square in Exercise **2,** would the length of the perimeter double also?

_____

4. A rectangle has a length of **7** centimeters and a width of **4** centimeters. What is the perimeter?

_____

To find the perimeter of a triangle, follow this rule:

perimeter = side 1 + side 2 + side 3

perimeter = 30 + 30 + 20, or 80 cm

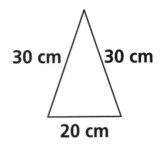

30 cm   30 cm

20 cm

Use the rule to find the perimeter.

5. triangle with sides **13** cm, **20** cm, and **25** cm perimeter = _____ cm

6. triangle with two sides **27** cm and one side **14** cm perimeter = _____ cm

7. triangle with all sides **80** cm perimeter _____ cm

| **Problem Solving** |
| **Reasoning** |

Solve.

8. One side of a square measures **45** cm. What is the perimeter?

_____

9. A square has a perimeter of **36** cm. What is the length of one side?

_____

10. Each side of an octagon measures **4** m. What is the perimeter? How did you find out?

_____

11. An equilateral triangle has a perimeter of **27** m. If the length of one side is **9** m, what are the lengths of the other **2** sides?

_____

Test Prep ★ Mixed Review

12 The Dairy Farm ordered 300 pounds more grain this month than last month. If 4,530 pounds were ordered last month, how many pounds were ordered this month?

A 4,230

B 4,560

C 4,830

D 7,530

13 Use your centimeter ruler.

| |
| Park |

On this map what is the perimeter of the park?

F 4 centimeters

G 6 centimeters

H 8 centimeters

J 12 centimeters

Area is the number of square units needed to cover a figure. To find the area, count the square units.

The area is **6** square units.

Find the area.

1.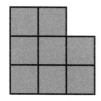

_____ square units

_____ square units

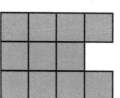

_____ square units

2.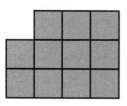

_____ square units

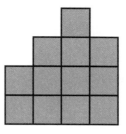

_____ square units

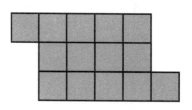

_____ square units

3.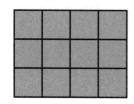

_____ square units

_____ square units

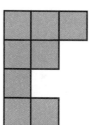

_____ square units

4.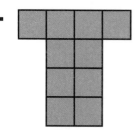

_____ square units

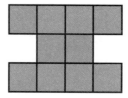

_____ square units

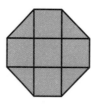

_____ square units

STANDARD

To find the area of a rectangle, follow this rule: **area = length × width**

Area = **4 × 3**, or **12** square centimeters

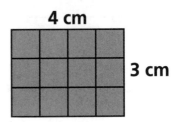

4 cm

3 cm

Find the area.

5. rectangle with length **7** cm and width **5** cm   Area =_____ sq cm

6. rectangle with length **9** cm and width **3** cm   Area =_____ sq cm

7. rectangle with length **8** cm and width **6** cm   Area =_____ sq cm

---

Problem Solving Reasoning   Solve.

8. Two different rectangles both have an area of **24** sq cm. Give the length and width of each rectangle.

_____

_____

9. Cara plans to carpet her room. Will she use the area or perimeter of the room? Explain your answer.

_____

_____

10. The length of a rectangular garden is **12** meters and the width is **7** meters. What is the area? How did you find it?

_____

11. A deck covers an area of **20** square meters. If the width is **4** meters, what is the length of the deck?

_____

Test Prep ★ Mixed Review

12 Which number will complete the pattern in the chart?

square erasers	3	6		12
round erasers	1	2	3	4

A 7

B 8

C 9

D 11

13 Use your inch ruler. About how long is the arrow?

F 1 inch

G 3 inches

H 5 inches

J 7 inches

Problem Solving Strategy: Make a List

Making a list can help you organize your information so you can solve a problem.

Problem

Alex is painting his room and adding a wallpaper border. He can use blue or green paint. He can use a wallpaper border with stripes or circles. How many different choices does Alex have to choose from?

1 Understand   As you reread, ask yourself questions.

- How many paint choices does Alex have?

  Alex has two paint choices.

- How many border choices does Alex have?

  Alex has two border choices.

- What must Alex decide?

  The paint color and border design he wants.

2 Decide   Choose a method for solving.

- Make a list of Alex's choices.
- What will your list show?

  paint and border combinations

3 Solve   Look at the list to solve the problem.

blue paint and _____ border

blue paint and _____ border

green paint and striped border

green paint and _____ border

How many choices does Alex have? _____

4 Look back   Check your answer.

- Write your answer in a full sentence.

_____

Use the Make a List Strategy or any other strategy you have learned.

1. Alex wants green paint and a circle border. He needs **2** gallons of paint and **8** yards of border. How much money will these materials cost?

Think: How can you find the cost? _____

Answer: _____

_____

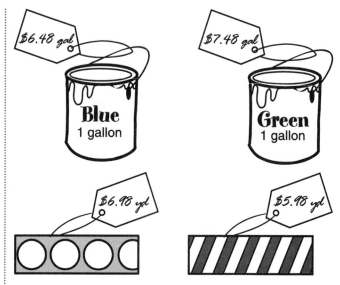

Blue
1 gallon

$6.48 gal

Green
1 gallon

$7.48 gal

$6.98 yd

$5.98 yd

2. Alex pays for the items with a **$100** bill. He gets **$19.80** in change. How may different combinations of bills could he have gotten as change?

Think: How can you list the combinations? _____

_____

Answer: _____

_____

_____

3. If Alex had chosen blue paint and the striped border, how much money would he have saved? Explain how you found the answer.

_____

_____

_____

_____

4. Soo-Ling wants to make a rectangular dog pen. She buys a fence **24** ft long. Then she draws all the rectangles she can with a perimeter of **24** ft. List the length and width of each rectangle she drew. Hint: Draw them first.

_____

5. The cost of **24** ft of fence is **$2.99** a foot and **$4.64** tax. Soo-Ling pays for the fence with four **$20** bills. How much change does she receive?

_____

_____

Volume is the measure of the space inside a container or a solid. It is measured in cubic units.

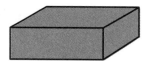

This is one cubic unit.

To find the volume of a figure, count the number of cubic units needed to fill it.

The volume of this figure is **6** cubic units.

In some figures, you cannot see all the cubic units. To find the volume, think about how the figure is made.

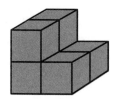

Find the volume.

1.

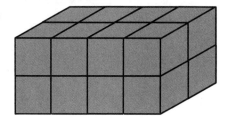

_____ cubic units

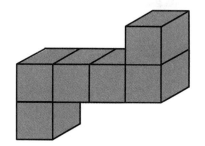

_____ cubic units

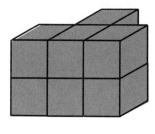

_____ cubic units

2.

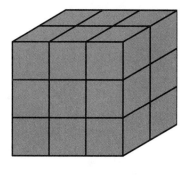

_____ cubic units

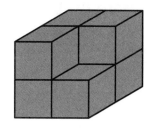

_____ cubic units

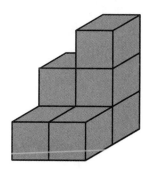

_____ cubic units

3.

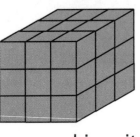   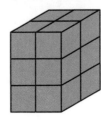   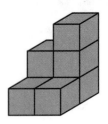

_____ cubic units   _____ cubic units   _____ cubic units

**Problem Solving
Reasoning**   Solve.

4. Two boxes have different shapes. Can they have the same volume? Explain your answer.

_____

_____

5. Blanca is comparing the sizes of 2 fish tanks. Should she find the perimeter or volume of each tank? Explain.

_____

6. Which solid do you think has the greater volume? Explain. _____

_____

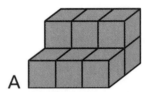   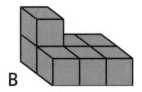

A   B

 Quick Check

Find the perimeter.   **Work Space.**

1.
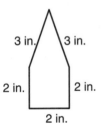

3 in.   3 in.

2 in.   2 in.

2 in.

_____ inches

2.
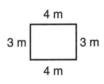

4 m

3 m   3 m

4 m

_____ meters

Find the area. = 1 square unit

3.
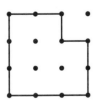

_____ square units

4.
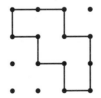

_____ square units

5. Find the volume: 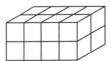   _____ cubic units

272   Unit 10 Lesson 11

Name _____

Measure each segment in centimeters.

1.  _____ cm   **2.** _____ cm

3. _____ cm

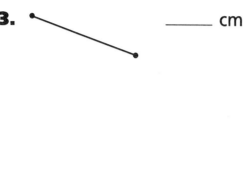

Loop the better estimate.

4. weight of a letter   **5.** length of a room   **6.** mass of a child

    2 oz   or   **1** lb   **13** ft   or   **13** mi   **200** g   or   **20** kg

7. temperature of classroom   **8.** temperature on a cold day

    70°C   or   **19°C**   **12°F**   or   **80°F**

Measure each segment in inches.

9. _____ in.

10. _____ in.

Complete.

11. 1 pt = _____ c   **12.** 1 gal = _____ qt

13. 1 yd = _____ ft   **14.** 1 ft = _____ in.

15. 1 lb = _____ oz   **16.** 1 yd = _____ in.

Find the perimeter.

17.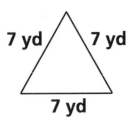

7 yd / 7 yd

7 yd

_____ yd

18.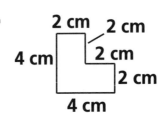

2 cm 2 cm

4 cm 2 cm

2 cm

4 cm

_____ cm

19.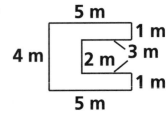

5 m 1 m

4 m 2 m 3 m

1 m

5 m

_____ m

Find the area.

20.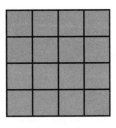

_____ sq units

21.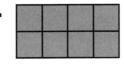

_____ sq units

22.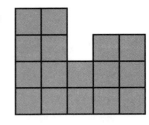

_____ sq units

Find the volume.

23.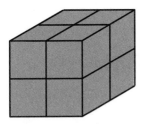

_____ sq units

24.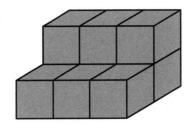

_____ sq units

25.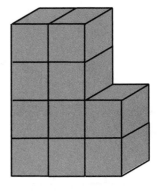

_____ sq units

Solve.

26. The temperature was **30°F** at **8** A.M. It rose **3°** each hour. What was the temperature at **2** P.M.? _____

27. Ben is getting dressed for a dance. He can wear a white, blue, or yellow shirt. He can wear a dotted or striped tie. How many different combinations of shirts and ties can Ben wear? _____

Name _____

1 The line plot shows the amount of snowfall on the first day of winter over the last ten years.

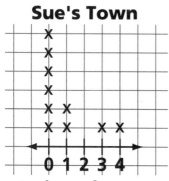

Sue's Town

Inches of snow

What are the chances there will be snow next year on the first day of winter?

A certain

B likely

C unlikely

D impossible

2 The students mixed 3 types of liquid to make a special drink.

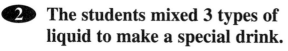

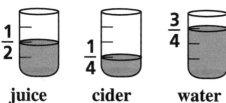

juice   cider   water

Which shows the amount of liquid from greatest to least?

F juice, cider, water

G water, cider, juice

H juice, water, cider

J NH

3 Which fraction of the model is shaded?

A $\dfrac{1}{5}$ **C** $\dfrac{3}{5}$

B $\dfrac{2}{5}$ **D** $\dfrac{5}{5}$

4 Which number goes in the box and makes this number sentence true?

$$53 \times 1 = \boxed{} \times 53$$

F 54

G 52

H 2

J 1

5 Odessa needs 4 feet of ribbon to complete her sewing project. Which number sentence shows how to find the number of inches of ribbon Odessa needs?

A $4 \times 3 = \boxed{}$

B $4 \times 12 = \boxed{}$

C $12 \div 4 = \boxed{}$

D $12 \div 2 = \boxed{}$

6 Use this as a unit.

How many units will fit in the figure below?

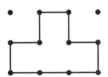

F 2   **H** 4

G 3   **J** 5

7 The store manager wants Alek to stack the soup cans in pyramids using 6 cans for each pyramid. How many pyramids can Alek make with 48 cans?

A 288

B 54

C 9

D 8

E NH

8 The club is sharing its collection of marbles equally among its 5 members. There are 49 marbles. How many marbles will each member get? How many will be left over?

F 10 marbles; 0 left over

G 9 marbles; 4 left over

H 8 marbles; 8 left over

J 7 marbles; 2 left over

K NH

9 Which is the sum?

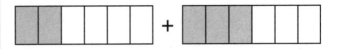

A $\dfrac{6}{6}$

B $\dfrac{5}{12}$

C $\dfrac{5}{6}$

D $\dfrac{1}{6}$

E NH

10 Each passenger car of the train holds 65 people. There are 8 passenger cars. How many people can ride the train in all?

F 57

G 73

H 130

J 520

K NH

11 Cleo is helping at the library. She puts 57 books on 3 shelves. Each shelf has the same number of books. How many books are on each shelf?

A 16

B 19

C 54

D 57

E NH

UNIT 11 • TABLE OF CONTENTS

Decimals

CALIFORNIA STANDARDS	Lesson	Page
NS 3.4	**1** Tenths	279–280
NS 3.4	**2** Decimals Greater than 1	281–282
NS 3.4	**3** Hundredths	283–284
A/F 1.1	**4** Algebra • Compare and Order Decimals	285–286
NS 3.3; MR 3.2	**5** Problem Solving Strategy: Conjecture and Verify	287–288
NS 3.3	**6** Addition and Subtraction of Decimals	289–290
NS 2.2, 3.3; A/F 2.1	**7** Algebra • Multiplication and Division with Money	291–292
NS 3.4	**8** Decimals, Fractions, and Money	293–294
NS 2.8, MR 1.1, 1.2, 1.3	**9** Problem Solving Application: Multistep Problems	295–296
	• Unit 11 Review	297
	• Cumulative Review ★ Test Prep	298

Dear Family,

During the next few weeks, our math class will be learning and practicing addition, subtraction, multiplication, and division involving decimals and money.

You can expect to see homework that provides practice with adding and subtracting decimals. Here is a sample you may want to keep handy to give help if needed.

Subtracting Decimals

To find **37.4 − 16.9**, first write the problem vertically. Be sure to line up the decimal points.

Begin at the right. To subtract tenths, you need to regroup 1 one as 10 tenths.

Then subtract the ones.

Then subtract the tens.

The difference is **20.5**.

$$\begin{array}{r} \overset{6\ \ 14}{3\cancel{7}.\cancel{4}} \\ -\ 1\ 6.9 \\ \hline 2\ 0.5 \end{array}$$

During this unit, students will need to continue practicing addition, subtraction, multiplication, and division facts.

Sincerely,

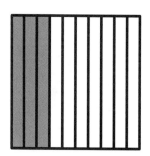
This model shows the fraction $\frac{3}{10}$.

It can be written as the **decimal 0.3.**

We read **0.3** as *three tenths*.

$\frac{3}{10}$ or **0.3** or **3 tenths**

↑
decimal point

> A **tenth** is **1** of **10** equal parts of a whole.
>
> The **decimal point** separates the whole number from tenths.

Write the decimal.

1.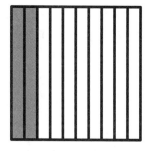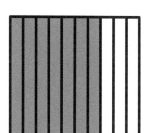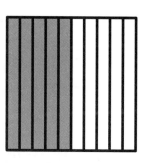

_____   _____   _____

2.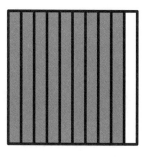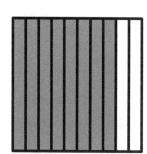

_____   _____

3. **9** tenths   **1 tenth**   **4 tenths**   **5 tenths**

_____   _____   _____   _____

4. $\frac{2}{10}$ $\frac{8}{10}$ $\frac{6}{10}$ $\frac{9}{10}$ $\frac{4}{10}$

_____   _____   _____   _____   _____

Write the tenths. Use the word name.

5. $\frac{3}{10}$ $\frac{7}{10}$ $\frac{1}{10}$ $\frac{5}{10}$

_____   _____   _____   _____

Write the fraction.

6. 0.2   0.5   0.9   0.4   0.1

_____   _____   _____   _____   _____

7. Count by tenths. Write the decimals from **1** tenth to **9** tenths.

_____ _____ _____ _____ _____ _____ _____ _____ _____

Problem Solving Reasoning   Solve.

8. Three tenths of the flowers are red and six tenths are yellow. Write the number of red flowers as a decimal.

_____

9. Nine tenths of the students like art class. Write the number as a decimal and a fraction.

_____

10. Mrs. Diaz told the class to write six tenths. Jill wrote $\frac{6}{10}$, Bill wrote **0.6**. Who is correct?

_____

11. Loop the number that shows **3** tenths.

310   0.3   3.0

Test Prep ★ Mixed Review

12 The Holt family went skiing in the mountains during winter vacation. Which was the most likely temperature that day in the mountains?

  A 25°F

  B 41°F

  C 53°F

  D 74°F

13 The carpet salesman measured the length of a hallway for a customer. What units would be used to measure the length of the hallway?

  F miles

  G pounds

  H feet

  J gallons

$2\frac{4}{10}$ squares are shaded.

2      $\frac{4}{10}$

The mixed number can be written as the decimal **2.4**. We read **2.4** as *two and four tenths*.

$2\frac{4}{10}$ or **2.4** or two and four tenths.

↑
decimal point

Ones	Tenths
2 .	4

2.4

Write the decimal.

1.      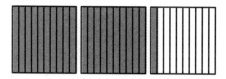

_____   _____   _____

2.

Ones	Tenths
3 .	7

Ones	Tenths
9 .	2

Ones	Tenths
7 .	3

_____   _____   _____

3. $\frac{5}{10}$ $1\frac{7}{10}$ $4\frac{4}{10}$ $7\frac{1}{10}$

_____   _____   _____   _____

4. nine and two tenths   eleven and one tenth

_____   _____

5. twenty and zero tenths   six and nine tenths

_____   _____

6. **13** and **6** tenths   **34** and **8** tenths

_____   _____

7. **4** and **2** tenths   **56** and **5** tenths

_____   _____

Loop the matching decimal.

8.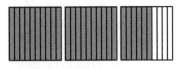

Ones	Tenths
3 .	2

Ones	Tenths
6 .	2

Ones	Tenths
2 .	6

9.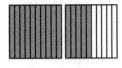

Ones	Tenths
5 .	1

Ones	Tenths
1 .	5

Ones	Tenths
2 .	6

10.

Ones	Tenths
2 .	7

Ones	Tenths
3 .	7

Ones	Tenths
7 .	2

Write a mixed number and a decimal for each.

11. two and seven tenths

_____

12. one and nine tenths

_____

Problem Solving
Reasoning

Solve.

13. Lamont bought one and six tenths pounds of ham. Is that more or less than a pound? How do you know?

_____

_____

14. Andre bought **2.5** pounds of ham. Maria bought $2\frac{5}{10}$ pounds of ham. Who bought more ham?

_____

Test Prep ★ Mixed Review

15 The school bought a fence for the front of the school that was 24 yards long. Which number sentence shows how to find how many feet long the fence is?

A $24 \times 3 = \boxed{}$

B $24 + 3 = \boxed{}$

C $24 \div 3 = \boxed{}$

D $24 - 3 = \boxed{}$

16 Sal wants to make a frame for his painting. How many inches of material will he need to make the frame?

F 34

G 54

H 68

J 80

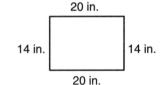

20 in.

14 in.   14 in.

20 in.

Name _____

The quilt has **100** squares.

$\frac{20}{100}$ of the quilt is white.

You can write $\frac{20}{100}$ as **0.20**.

Read **0.20** as *twenty hundredths*.

$\frac{5}{100}$ of the quilt is striped.

You can write $\frac{5}{100}$ as **0.05**.

Read **0.05** as *five hundredths*.

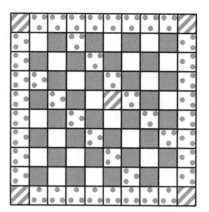

A **hundredth** is **1** of **100** equal parts of a whole.

Write the decimal.

1.

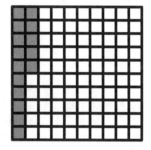   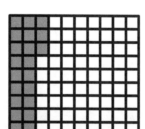   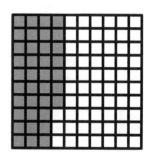

_____   _____   _____

2.

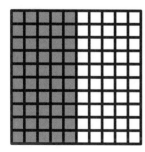   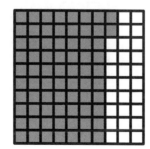   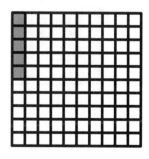

_____   _____   _____

3. $\frac{78}{100}$ $\frac{92}{100}$ $\frac{51}{100}$ $\frac{4}{100}$ $\frac{60}{100}$

_____   _____   _____   _____   _____

Write the decimal.

4.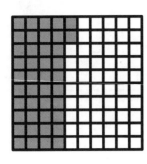

———   ———   ———

5. **24** hundredths   **7** hundredths   **93** hundredths

———   ———   ———

Solve.

6. A quilt has **100** squares. There are **53** red squares, **13** blue squares, and **34** green squares. What decimal stands for the red part of the quilt?

———

7. There are **100** students in the Ski Club. Sixty are boys, forty are girls. Write a decimal and a fraction that stand for the boys in the club.

———

 Quick Check

Write the decimal.

Work Space.

1.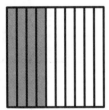

———

2.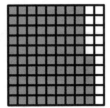

———

3. **5** and **8** tenths

———

4. six and two tenths

———

5. $\dfrac{7}{10}$

———

6. $\dfrac{1}{10}$

———

7. $\dfrac{23}{100}$

———

8. $\dfrac{49}{100}$

———

Compare and Order Decimals

Kate walks **0.3** miles to school. Seth walks **0.7** miles to school. Who has the longer walk? Use models to compare.

Kate   Seth

 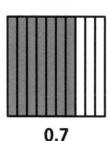

0.3   **0.7**

0.7 is greater than **0.3**.
0.7 > 0.3

Seth has the longer walk.

You can compare hundredths.

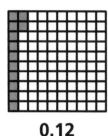 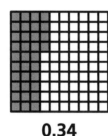

0.12   **0.34**

0.34 is greater than **0.12**.
0.34 > 0.12

Compare. Choose >, <, or = .

1. 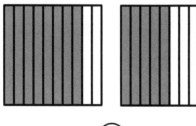   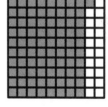

0.8 ◯ 0.5   0.52 ◯ 0.81

2. 0.4 ◯ 0.7   0.65 ◯ 0.79

3. 0.25 ◯ 0.80   0.9 ◯ 0.2

4. 60 hundredths ◯ 0.60   3 tenths ◯ 0.5

5. 31 hundredths ◯ 0.40   7 tenths ◯ 0.6

6. 1 hundredths ◯ 0.1   6 tenths ◯ 0.06

Order from least to greatest.

7. 0.5, 0.7, 0.2 _____ _____ _____

8. 0.71, 0.34, 0.58 _____ _____ _____

9. 0.63, 0.51, 0.82 _____ _____ _____

10. 0.3, 0.6, 0.5 _____ _____ _____

Write *true* or *false*.

11. 0.93 > 0.54 _____   0.7 > 0.9 _____

12. 0.74 < 0.39 _____   0.3 < 0.6 _____

13. 0.5 = 0.50 _____   0.37 < 0.36 _____

| Problem Solving Reasoning | Solve. |

14. A puppy is **0.24** m tall. A kitten is **0.20** m tall. A chick is **0.12** m tall. Which animal is tallest?

_____

15. An apple weighs **0.34** pound. A pear weighs **0.27** pound. Which weighs more?

_____

16. Josette says these decimals are in order from greatest to least. Is she correct? Why or why not?

0.4   0.04   4   44

_____

17. Mikos runs two and seven tenths kilometers each Sunday. Write the number as a decimal.

_____

Test Prep ★ Mixed Review

18 Toby's Toy Store is having a sale on toy cars. The sign says "3 cars for $21". How much would 1 car cost?

A $6

B $7

C $18

D $24

19 What is the next number in the pattern? 4, 7, 10, 13?

F 14

G 16

H 19

J 23

To solve some problems you may need to begin with a "first guess" or conjecture. Then check, or verify, your first guess to see if it is correct.

Problem
Yolanda has some dimes and pennies in her pocket. She has more than **0.3** of a dollar and less than **0.8** of a dollar. She has twice as many dimes as pennies. The sum of the digits for this amount of money is **9**. How many dimes and how many pennies does Yolanda have?

❶ Understand   As you reread, ask yourself questions.

• What do you know about the coins Yolanda has?

She has twice as many dimes as pennies.

She has more than **0.3** of a dollar and less than **0.8**.

The sum of the digits for this amount of money is **9**.

• What information do you already know?

0.3 of a dollar is **30¢** and **0.8** of a dollar is **80¢**.

❷ Decide   Choose a method for solving.

• Try the strategy conjecture and verify.

• What is the first guess? Dimes: **4**   Pennies: **2**

❸ Solve   Verify your conjecture. Try again if you need to.

	First guess	Try again
Dimes	4	
Pennies	2	
Value	42¢	
Between 30¢ and 80¢?	yes	
Numbers add to 9?	no	

❹ Look back   Check your answer.

• Write the answer as a full sentence

_____

Use the Conjecture & Verify Strategy or any other strategy you have learned.

1. Michael is thinking of a decimal number that is greater than **0.10** and less than **0.40**. The sum of the digits is **8**. What number could Michael be thinking about? Is there more than one number?

   Think: What are the key clues about Michael's number?

   _____

   _____

   Answer: _____

2. Elizabeth said that she was thinking of two numbers. The product of these two numbers is **27** and their quotient is **3**. What two numbers is Elizabeth thinking about?

   Think: What two numbers have a product of **27**?

   _____

   Answer: _____

3. Juan is thinking of a number. When you add **12** to his number you get **30**. What do you get if you subtract **8** from Juan's number?

   _____

4. There are **18** students in Shirley's class. There are **4** more boys than girls. How many boys and how many girls are in Shirley's class?

   _____

5. Monica is making a new table. The new table will be **2 ft** longer than twice the length of the old table. The old table was **2 yd** long. How long will the new table be?

   _____ ft

6. Twenty people arrange some picnic tables. Each table is a rectangle and seats **3** people on a side and **1** person at each end. If they put the tables end to end, how many picnic tables do they need?

   _____

7. For which problem did you use the Conjecture and Verify Strategy? List the other strategies you used.

   _____

   _____

8. Create your own problem for the Conjecture and Verify Strategy. Trade with a friend and solve.

   _____

   _____

How much snow fell in Dallas and Atlanta together?

Line up the decimals.

$$\begin{array}{r} 1\,.\,9 \\ +\,3\,.\,1 \\ \hline \end{array} \qquad \begin{array}{r} {\scriptstyle 1} \\ 1\,.\,9 \\ +\,3\,.\,1 \\ \hline 0 \end{array} \qquad \begin{array}{r} {\scriptstyle 1} \\ 1\,.\,9 \\ +\,3\,.\,1 \\ \hline 5\,.\,0 \end{array}$$

City	Inches of Snow
Atlanta, GA	1.9
Cleveland, OH	53.6
Dallas, TX	3.1
Seattle, WA	12.8

So, 5.0 or **5** inches of snow fell in Dallas and Atlanta together.

Add.

1.
$$\begin{array}{r} 4\,.\,5 \\ +\,2\,.\,3 \\ \hline \end{array} \qquad \begin{array}{r} 5\,.\,9 \\ +\,3\,.\,5 \\ \hline \end{array} \qquad \begin{array}{r} 2\,.\,1 \\ +\,6\,.\,2 \\ \hline \end{array} \qquad \begin{array}{r} 4\,.\,7 \\ +\,3\,.\,8 \\ \hline \end{array}$$

2.
$$\begin{array}{r} 36\,.\,7 \\ +\,18\,.\,9 \\ \hline \end{array} \qquad \begin{array}{r} 28\,.\,3 \\ +\,83\,.\,8 \\ \hline \end{array} \qquad \begin{array}{r} 21\,.\,3 \\ +\,17\,.\,9 \\ \hline \end{array} \qquad \begin{array}{r} 56\,.\,9 \\ +\,34\,.\,5 \\ \hline \end{array}$$

3.
$$\begin{array}{r} 16\,.\,4 \\ +\,29\,.\,7 \\ \hline \end{array} \qquad \begin{array}{r} 29\,.\,4 \\ +\,16\,.\,9 \\ \hline \end{array} \qquad \begin{array}{r} 54\,.\,9 \\ +\,\;\,2\,.\,9 \\ \hline \end{array} \qquad \begin{array}{r} 63\,.\,5 \\ +\,48\,.\,8 \\ \hline \end{array}$$

4.
$$\begin{array}{r} 20\,.\,4 \\ +\,12\,.\,5 \\ \hline \end{array} \qquad \begin{array}{r} 41\,.\,2 \\ +\,\;\,1\,.\,9 \\ \hline \end{array} \qquad \begin{array}{r} 16\,.\,4 \\ +\,59\,.\,1 \\ \hline \end{array} \qquad \begin{array}{r} 74\,.\,6 \\ +\,\;\,9\,.\,2 \\ \hline \end{array}$$

5.
$$\begin{array}{r} 83\,.\,2 \\ +\,\;\,9\,.\,5 \\ \hline \end{array} \qquad \begin{array}{r} 3\,.\,7 \\ +\,16\,.\,9 \\ \hline \end{array} \qquad \begin{array}{r} 44\,.\,2 \\ +\,20\,.\,8 \\ \hline \end{array} \qquad \begin{array}{r} 7\,.\,8 \\ +\,35\,.\,2 \\ \hline \end{array}$$

6. 4.5 + 3.3 = _____   57.9 + 26.4 = _____

7. 42.7 + 6.2 = _____   30.7 + 42.8 = _____

8. 8.7 + 1.3 + 2.7 = _____   9.6 + 5.8 + 1.4 = _____

9. 9.1 + 1.2 + 0.5 = _____   1.5 + 20.7 + 2.3 = _____

Cleveland, OH, had **53.6** inches of snow. Seattle, WA, had **12.8** inches of snow. How many more inches of snow fell in Cleveland than Seattle?

Line up the decimals.

$$
\begin{array}{r} 5\,3\,.\,6 \\ -\,1\,2\,.\,8 \\ \hline \end{array}
\qquad
\begin{array}{r} {}^{2}\ {}^{16} \\ 5\,\cancel{3}\,.\,\cancel{6} \\ -\,1\,2\,.\,8 \\ \hline 0\,.\,8 \end{array}
\qquad
\begin{array}{r} {}^{2}\ {}^{16} \\ 5\,\cancel{3}\,.\,\cancel{6} \\ -\,1\,2\,.\,8 \\ \hline 4\,0\,.\,8 \end{array}
$$

So, **40.8** more inches of snow fell in Cleveland than Seattle.

___

Subtract.

10.
$$\begin{array}{r} 1\,4\,.\,5 \\ -\ \ 8\,.\,1 \\ \hline \end{array} \qquad \begin{array}{r} 2\,3\,.\,7 \\ -1\,7\,.\,6 \\ \hline \end{array} \qquad \begin{array}{r} 1\,2\,.\,4 \\ -\ \ 9\,.\,8 \\ \hline \end{array} \qquad \begin{array}{r} 7\,2\,.\,1 \\ -2\,0\,.\,7 \\ \hline \end{array}$$

11.
$$\begin{array}{r} 4\,5\,.\,8 \\ -1\,9\,.\,6 \\ \hline \end{array} \qquad \begin{array}{r} 2\,3\,.\,4 \\ -1\,8\,.\,8 \\ \hline \end{array} \qquad \begin{array}{r} 5\,6\,.\,1 \\ -4\,1\,.\,9 \\ \hline \end{array} \qquad \begin{array}{r} 3\,9\,.\,3 \\ -1\,2\,.\,6 \\ \hline \end{array}$$

___

Problem Solving Reasoning Solve.

12. It rained **3.8** cm in April, **5.2** cm in May, and **1.8** cm in June. Was the total rainfall more than **10** cm? Explain your answer.

_____

13. The average temperature in May was **57.8°F.** It rose to **74.2°F.** in June. Was the difference in temperature more than **20°**? How do you know?

_____

✓ Quick Check

Compare. Choose > or <.

1. 0.7 ◯ 0.4   **2.** 0.3 ◯ 0.5   **3.** 0.81 ◯ 0.29

Work Space.

Write the decimals in order from least to greatest

4. 0.9, 0.2, 0.8 _____

5. 0.6, 0.45, 0.31 _____

Add or subtract.

6.
$$\begin{array}{r} 4\,.\,5 \\ +3\,.\,8 \\ \hline \end{array} \qquad \begin{array}{r} 9\,.\,7 \\ -2\,.\,9 \\ \hline \end{array} \qquad \begin{array}{r} 1\,7\,.\,1 \\ +\ \ 6\,.\,5 \\ \hline \end{array}$$

Multiplication and Division with Money

STANDARD

You can multiply and divide decimals just like you do whole numbers.

Find the cost of **3** boxes of cereal.

$$\begin{array}{r} \overset{2\ \ 2}{\$3.79} \\ \times \quad 3 \\ \hline \$11.37 \end{array}$$

↑ Write the dollar sign and decimal point.

Find the cost of **1** banana.

$$\begin{array}{r} \$\ .27 \\ 6)\overline{\$1.62} \\ -\ 1\ 2\ \downarrow \\ \hline 4\ 2 \\ -\ 4\ 2 \\ \hline 0 \end{array}$$

← Write the dollar sign and decimal point.

Think: **16 tens ÷ 6**

160 ÷ 6

Find the cost. Multiply or divide.

1. **5** boxes of cereal _____   1 muffin _____

2. **1** apple _____   **3** grapefruit _____

3. **3** bananas _____   **6** muffins _____

Multiply.

4.
$$\begin{array}{r} \$3.73 \\ \times \quad 4 \end{array}$$
$$\begin{array}{r} \$6.75 \\ \times \quad 2 \end{array}$$
$$\begin{array}{r} \$9.13 \\ \times \quad 7 \end{array}$$
$$\begin{array}{r} \$6.09 \\ \times \quad 5 \end{array}$$
$$\begin{array}{r} \$1.98 \\ \times \quad 9 \end{array}$$

Divide.

5. $4)\overline{\$2.68}$ $8)\overline{\$3.12}$ $7)\overline{\$5.88}$ $5)\overline{\$3.75}$

Solve. Find the cost.

6. **5** video tapes _____   **1** cassette tape _____

7. **3** compact discs _____   **2** video tapes _____

Multiply or divide.

8. $\begin{array}{r} \$15.70 \\ \times7 \\ \hline \end{array}$ $\begin{array}{r} \$2.68 \\ \times6 \\ \hline \end{array}$ $4\overline{)\$1.56}$ $3\overline{)\$4.23}$

Problem Solving Reasoning | Solve.

9. The Music Club is buying **5** music stands. A music stand costs **$29.95**. How much will the stands cost?

_____

10. Estella paid **$3.40** for **10** music folders. Tim paid **$2.97** for **9** folders. Who paid less for *each* folder?

_____

Test Prep ★ Mixed Review

11 There are 5 cubes in a bag: 2 red cubes, 1 blue cube, 1 green cube, and 1 yellow cube. Without looking you pick out 4 cubes and put them side by side to make a train. Which is a list of what your color train could look like?

A blue, blue, red, yellow

B yellow, blue, yellow, green

C green, red, green, red

D red, blue, yellow, red

12 Last year's winter carnival raised $459 for the elementary school. This year's winter carnival raised $786. About how much more money did the school raise this year?

F $100

G $200

H $300

J $1200

Name _____

$25¢ = \dfrac{1}{4}$ of a dollar $\$.50 = \dfrac{1}{2}$ of a dollar

$\$.10 = \dfrac{1}{10}$ of a dollar $30¢ = \dfrac{3}{10}$ of a dollar

---

Use the models to find each answer.

1. What decimal tells $\dfrac{9}{10}$ of a dollar? _____

How much money is it? _____

2. What decimal tells $\dfrac{2}{10}$ of a dollar? _____

How much money is it? _____

3. You have **75¢**. Name the fraction and
decimal that tells the part of a dollar. _____

4. Jan has one dollar. Name the fraction and decimal. _____

Complete the chart.

5.

50¢	$\dfrac{1}{2}$ of a dollar	$.50
10¢	$\dfrac{1}{10}$ of a dollar	$.10
75¢		
60¢		
40¢		
70¢		

Write each amount as a fraction and a decimal.

6.

_____   _____

7.

_____   _____

Loop the fraction that tells the part of a dollar.

8.

$\dfrac{1}{5}$ $\dfrac{1}{4}$ $\dfrac{1}{2}$

9.

$\dfrac{1}{6}$ $\dfrac{2}{3}$ $\dfrac{6}{10}$

Problem Solving Reasoning   Solve.

10. Kim has $\dfrac{8}{10}$ of a dollar. Her sister has **$.70**. Who has more money? How do you know?

_____

11. Ed found a half dollar and spent **$.10**. He says he now has $\dfrac{4}{10}$ of a dollar left. Do you agree? Why or why not?

_____

✓ **Quick Check**

Multiply or divide.

1. $3 . 1 4	**2.** $5 . 6 1	**3.** $1 . 8 2
$\times$ 2	$\times$ 4	$\times$ 3

4. $2.34 ÷ 3 = _____

5. $4.30 ÷ 5 = _____

Give the fraction and decimal that tells what part of a dollar.

6. 40¢ _____   _____

7. 50¢ _____   _____

Work Space.

Name _____

Problem Solving Application: Multistep Problems

Often problems involve more than one step to arrive at a solution. In this lesson, you will use two or more steps to solve problems.

Tips to Remember:

1. Understand 2. Decide 3. Solve 4. Look back

- Think about the action in the problem. Is there more than one action?
- Which operation addition, subtraction, multiplication, or division best represents each action?
- Do you need to use two operations to show what is happening? Which should you use first?
- Try to break the problem into parts before you solve.

Ice World			
Admission		**Refreshments**	
Adults	$4.00	Hot chocolate	$1.25
Children	$2.50	Hot cider	$1.25
Rentals		Popcorn	$1.30
Skates	$1.25	Hot Pretzels	$1.30
		Nachos	$2.25
Hours			
Mon.–Thurs.	Noon–7 P.M.		
Fri.–Sat.	11 A.M.–10 P.M.		
Sun.	11 A.M.–8 P.M.		

Solve. Use the information in the chart.

1. The Leahy family is going ice-skating. How much will it cost a family of **2** adults and **3** children to buy the tickets?

Think: What information do you need to solve this problem?

_____

_____

Answer: _____

2. Steven and Jennifer Leahy rented ice skates. Steven gave the clerk **$5** to pay the rental fee. How much change should he receive?

Think: What operations will you use to solve this problem?

_____

_____

Answer: _____

3. The three children each bought a hot drink and **2** bags of popcorn to share. How much money did they spend?

_____

4. How many different choices of a hot drink and a snack do they have to choose from on the refreshment list?

_____

5. How many hours each week is the ice-skating rink open?

_____

6. Three of Steven's friends were at the rink. Together they ordered one of every item on the menu. Would **$7** cover the cost of their purchases? Explain.

_____

_____

7. If the three boys from Problem **6** split the cost of their snack bill, how much would each person pay?

_____

8. Another family met the Leahys at the skating rink. The family paid **$17** for tickets. How many children's and adults tickets did the family buy?

_____

Extend Your Thinking

9. Think of one price the ice skating rink could charge for both children and adults that would result in about a $17 admission price for the Leahy family.

_____

_____

10. Look back at Problem **4.** What if there were **3** hot drinks and **3** snack choices? How many different choices of a hot drink and a snack would they have to choose from?

_____

Name _____

Write the decimal.

1.

_____

2.

_____

3.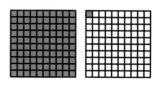

_____

4. six hundredths

_____

5. $\dfrac{74}{100}$

_____

6. six tenths

_____

Add or subtract.

7.
$$\begin{array}{r} 8.4 \\ +12.7 \\ \hline \end{array}$$

8.
$$\begin{array}{r} 9.3 \\ -3.9 \\ \hline \end{array}$$

9.
$$\begin{array}{r} 1.9 \\ +5.8 \\ \hline \end{array}$$

10.
$$\begin{array}{r} 24.7 \\ -15.6 \\ \hline \end{array}$$

Multiply or divide.

11.
$$\begin{array}{r} \$2.73 \\ \times\quad 6 \\ \hline \end{array}$$

12.
$$\begin{array}{r} \$8.19 \\ \times\quad 4 \\ \hline \end{array}$$

13. $7\overline{)\$7.63}$

14. $8\overline{)\$9.60}$

Write the part of a dollar.
Use a fraction and a decimal.

15.

_____ _____

16.

_____ _____

Solve.

17. Mario wants **3** sweaters that cost **$17.59** each. He has **$50**. Estimate to see if he has enough money.

_____

18. Lynn has **2** quarters, **5** dimes, **2** pennies, and **3** nickels. By Friday, she will have three times that amount. How much money will she have then?

_____

1 Ari has 138 acorns. He wants to put the same number of acorns in each of 6 jars. Which number sentence could you use to find out how many acorns will be in each jar?

A $138 \div 6 = \boxed{}$

B $6 \times 138 = \boxed{}$

C $138 - 6 = \boxed{}$

D $138 + 6 = \boxed{}$

2 Mr. Ling is 6 feet tall. Which number sentence will help you find out how many inches tall he is?

F $6 \times 3 = \boxed{}$

G $6 + 3 = \boxed{}$

H $6 + 12 = \boxed{}$

J $6 \times 12 = \boxed{}$

3 Use this as a square unit. How many square units will fit into the figure below?

A 2   C 3

B 4   D 5

4 Which decimal is represented by the shaded part of the model?

F 7.0   G 0.7   H 3.0   J 0.3

5 Raul lives six tenths of a mile from school. Which shows six tenths as a decimal?

A 6.0   C 0.6

B 6.10   D 0.06

6 Tia bought 3 flashlights for a camping trip. Each flashlight cost **$6.29**. How much did the flashlights cost in all?

F $19.67   H $18.67   K NH

G $18.87   J $9.29

7 Alphonse has 3.7 meters of blue rope and 2.5 meters of red rope. How many meters of rope does Alphonse have in all?

A 0.62   C 6.2   E NH

B 1.2   D 62

8 The 9 workers had to put up 405 posters around the city. Each worker received the same number of posters. How many posters did each worker receive?

A 30   C 40   E NH

B 35   D 42

9 Mrs. Rickle bought scarves for her 3 children. Each scarf cost **$12.50**. What was the total price for the scarves?

F $2500   H $37.50   K NH

G $30.25   J $41.25

Tables of Measures

Metric Measures

Length

1 kilometer (km)	=	1,000 meters (m)
1 decimeter (dm)	=	10 centimeters (cm)
1 meter (m)	=	100 centimeters (cm)

Capacity

1 liter (L)	=	1,000 milliliters (mL)

Mass

1 kilogram (kg)	=	1,000 grams (g)

Customary Measures

Length

1 foot (ft)	=	12 inches (in.)
1 yard (yd)	=	3 feet
1 yard	=	36 inches
1 mile (mi)	=	5,280 feet

Capacity

1 pint (pt)	=	2 cups
1 quart (qt)	=	2 pints
1 gallon (gal)	=	4 quarts

Weight

1 pound (lb)	=	16 ounces (oz)

Other Measures

Time

1 minute (min)	=	60 seconds (s)		1 week (wk)	=	7 days
1 hour (h)	=	60 minutes		1 year (yr)	=	12 months
1 day	=	24 hours		1 year	=	52 weeks

Symbols

=	is equal to Example: 3 + 4 = 7; 3 plus 4 equals 7
<	is less than Example: 4 < 7; 4 is less than 7
>	is greater than Example: 8 > 2; 8 is greater than 2
( )	(grouping symbols) The operation in these symbols should be done first. (5 + 4) + 1 = 9 + 1

¢	(cents sign) 4 dimes and 6 pennies = 46¢
$	(dollar sign) a five-dollar bill = $5 ($5.00)
.	(decimal point) Used to separate dollars and cents in money amounts, such as $1.50 Used to separate ones and tenths in decimals, such as 1.3

Glossary

A

addend A number that is added to another number.

$$\begin{array}{r} 9 \\ +\ 4 \\ \hline 13 \end{array}$$ addends

A.M. The time from 12:00 midnight to 12:00 noon.

angle A corner that can be of different sizes.

area The number of square units needed to cover a figure. If the unit square is 1 square centimeter, then the area of this figure is 6 square centimeters.

associative property of addition Changing the grouping of the addends does not change the sum. This is sometimes called the *grouping property of addition*.
(4 + 2) + 6 = 4 + (2 + 6)

associative property of multiplication Changing the grouping of the factors does not change the product. This is sometimes called the *grouping property of multiplication*.
(2 × 3) × 3 = 2 × (3 × 3)

B

bar graph A graph that uses bars to show data.

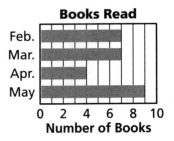

C

capacity The amount of liquid a container can hold.

centimeter (cm) A metric unit of length. 100 cm = 1 meter

circle A curved figure that is shaped like this:

commutative property of addition Changing the order of the addends does not change the sum. This is sometimes called the *order property of addition*.
6 + 4 = 4 + 6

commutative property of multiplication Changing the order of the factors does not change the product. This is sometimes called the *order property of multiplication*.
4 × 5 = 5 × 4

cone A solid that has a circular base and comes to a point.

congruent figures Figures that have the same size and shape.

cube A solid having six square faces of equal size.

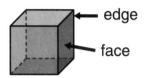

customary system The measurement system that uses foot, quart, pound, and degrees Fahrenheit.

cylinder A solid having circles of equal size at each end.

D

data Information, facts.

decimal A number with one or more digits to the right of a decimal point. Example: 0.9 and 1.08 are decimals.

degree A unit for measuring temperature.

degree Celsius (°C) The metric unit for measuring temperature.

degree Fahrenheit (°F) The customary unit for measuring temperature.

denominator The number written below the bar in a fraction.
Example: $\frac{1}{4}$ ← denominator

difference The answer in a subtraction problem.

$$9 - 4 = 5 \longleftarrow \text{difference}$$

digit Any of the symbols 0, 1, 2, 3, 4, 5, 6, 7, 8, 9.

dividend The number that is divided in a division problem.
Example: $12 \div 4 = 3$
↑
dividend

divisor The number to divide by in a division problem.

$7 \overline{)\ 28}$ $12 \div 2$
↑   ↑
divisor   divisor

E

equivalent fractions Fractions that show the same amount.
Example:

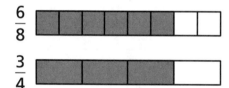

estimate A number close to an exact amount. An estimate tells about how much.

even number A whole number ending in 0, 2, 4, 6, or 8.

event Something that takes place or happens.

expanded form A way to write a number to show the value of each digit.
Example: The way to expand 3,962 is 3000 + 900 + 60 + 2.

F

factor A number that is multiplied in a multiplication problem.

$$\begin{array}{r} 5 \\ \times\ 3 \\ \hline 15 \end{array} \quad \text{factors}$$

fraction A number that names a part of a whole or part of a set. $\frac{1}{2}$, $\frac{3}{4}$, and $\frac{2}{3}$ are all fractions.

G

gram (g) A metric unit of mass or heaviness.

graph A picture that shows information by using bars, lines, or symbols.

H

hundredth One of 100 equal parts of a whole.

I

inverse The opposite. For example, subtraction is the inverse of addition. $5 - 2 = 3$ because $3 + 2 = 5$. (Division is the inverse of multiplication.)

K

kilogram (kg) A metric unit of mass. 1 kilogram equals 1,000 grams

kilometer (km) A metric unit of length. 1 kilometer equals 1,000 meters

L

line A straight path that goes on forever in two directions.

line graph A graph that uses line segments to show changes over time.

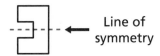

line of symmetry The line at which a figure can be folded so that the two halves match exactly.

Line of symmetry

line plot A diagram that organizes data on a number line.

line segment Part of a line having 2 endpoints.

liter (L) A metric unit of capacity. 1 liter equals 1,000 milliliters

M

mass The heaviness of an object. Often measured with grams or kilograms.

meter (m) A metric unit of length. 1 meter equals 100 centimeters

metric system The measurement system that uses units such as meter, liter, gram, and degrees Celsius.

milliliter (mL) A metric unit of capacity.

mixed numbers Numbers that have a whole number and a fraction part.

Example: $3\frac{1}{2}$

multiplication property of one If 1 is a factor, the product always equals the other factor.

Example: 6 × 1 = 6

1 × 51 = 51

N

numerator The number written above the bar in a fraction.
Example:

$$\frac{1}{4} \longleftarrow \text{numerator}$$

O

odd number A whole number ending in 1, 3, 5, 7, or 9.

ordered pair The numbers used to name a point on a grid.

ordinal numbers The numbers *first, second, third, fourth, fifth*, and so on, are ordinal numbers. They are used to show order or position.

P

parallel lines Lines that are always the same distance apart.

parallelogram A quadrilateral with opposite parallel sides.

perimeter The distance around a figure. The perimeter of the triangle below is 9 cm.

2 cm 3 cm
4 cm

pictograph A graph that shows data with pictures.

Favorite Sport	
Baseball	★ ★ ★ ★
Football	★ ★
Key Each ★ = 4 people	

place value The value of each place in a number.

Example: In 7,943, the digit 7 is in the thousands place.

Thousands	Hundreds	Tens	Ones
7	9	4	3

P.M. The time from 12:00 noon to 12:00 midnight.

polygon A flat closed figure with three or more sides.

possible outcome A possible result of an experiment in probability.

prediction What someone thinks may happen.

product The answer in a multiplication problem.

7 × 2 = 14 ◀— product

pyramid A solid having 1 base that varies in shape. The faces are triangles and meet at a point.

Q

quadrilateral A polygon with 4 line segments, or sides, and 4 angles.

quotient The answer in a division problem.

16 ÷ 4 = 4 ◀— quotient

R

rectangle A figure with four straight sides and four square corners. A square is a kind of rectangle.

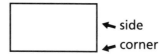

← side
← corner

303

rectangular prism A solid with 2 rectangular bases and 4 rectangular faces.

remainder The number left over when one number does not divide another equally.

$$\begin{array}{r} 5 \text{ R } 1 \\ 3\overline{)16} \\ -15 \\ \hline 1 \end{array}$$ ← remainder

right angle A square corner.

round To find the ten, hundred, or thousand nearest to an exact number. For example, 52 rounded to the nearest ten is 50.

S

sphere A solid having the shape of a ball.

square A figure with four square corners and four equal sides.

standard form The usual way of writing a number, using digits. *Example:* The standard form of twenty-seven is 27.

sum The answer in an addition problem.

$$\begin{array}{r} 4 \\ +3 \\ \hline 7 \end{array}$$ ← sum

survey A way to collect data by asking people questions.

T

tally A count made using tally marks. *Example:*

The tally is 10.

temperature The measurement of how warm or cold something is.

tenth One of ten equal parts of a whole.

thermometer An instrument that measures temperature.

triangle A figure with three sides and three corners.

U

unit cost The price for one item. *Example:* 3 mugs cost $12 so 1 mug costs $4. The unit cost is $4.

unit fraction A fraction that has a numerator of 1, which means 1 part of the whole.

V

volume The measure of the space inside a container or a solid.

Z

zero property of addition If 0 is added to a number, the sum equals that number.
Example: $4 + 0 = 4$

$0 + 26 = 26$

zero property of multiplication If 0 is a factor, the product is always 0.
Example: $8 \times 0 = 0$

$0 \times 17 = 0$